Preface

For someone whose particular interest is the history of communities with an identity and sense of independence, the history of Guernsey is a stimulating and exciting subject. Having spent some years working on other such areas, I came to Guernsey and found a community which was particularly aware of the distinctiveness of its position and its rooted-ness in the past. It was coincidental, but fortunate, that the eight-hundredth anniversary of King John's loss of Normandy brought a particular focus onto that theme of difference and distinctiveness.

Thanks are due to those who made the project possible, namely Deputy Mike Burbridge and Ken Tough (Her Majesty's Greffier); the Royal Court, the States' Heritage Committee, and the 1204 Working Party, who funded some of the research. Heather Sebire and Alan Howell of Guernsey Museums assisted in various ways, notably in the provision of high-quality images of the documents. Keith Robilliard, Senior Strong Room Clerk, was consistently welcoming and helpful in providing access to the treasure-house of documents in his care at the Greffe. Particular thanks go to Darryl Ogier of the Island Archives Service. He has always been a great supporter of work on the island's history and was a particular advocate of this project. He and his colleagues, especially Nathan Coyde, provided a splendid base for a researcher into the island's history; and Ali, Harriet, Edward and Lucy were generous in their hospitality.

Back in England, although it is invidious to mention names when so many have contributed in so many ways, it is important that the assistance of the Special Collections team in the Brotherton Library, University of Leeds, guardians of the books and manuscripts of John le Patourel, and the consistent support of my colleagues in History and more widely in the University of Huddersfield, are acknowledged. My wife, Sue Johns, and our children, Carys and Gwyn, have been, as always, a constant rock of support and encouragement.

Abbreviations

ABSJ	*Annual Bulletin of the Société Jersiaise*
APC	*Acts of the Privy Council of England*, n.s., ed. John Roche Dasent et al. (London: printed for Her Majesty's Stationery Office by Eyre & Spottiswoode, 1890-)
BIHR	*Bulletin of the Institute of Historical Research*
CCR	*Calendar of Close Rolls* (London: HMSO, 1892-)
CP	G.E.C. Cokayne, *The Complete Peerage* (13 vols. in 14; 2nd edn, London: St Catherine Press, 1910-59)
CPR	*Calendar of Patent Rolls* (London: HMSO, 1893-)
CSPD	*Calendar of State Papers, Domestic Series* (London: HMSO)
DKR	*Annual Reports of the Deputy Keeper of the Public Records* (London: HMSO, 1840-)
DNB	Leslie Stephen and S. Lee (eds), *Dictionary of National Biography* (66 vols, London: Smith, Elder, & Co., 1885-1901)
EHR	*English Historical Review*
Greffe	Greffe, Royal Court House, Guernsey
HJ	*Historical Journal*
Le Patourel *Channel Islands*	J.H. Le Patourel, *The Medieval Administration of the Channel Islands, 1199-1399* (London: Oxford University Press, 1937)
LP	*Letters and Papers, Foreign and Domestic, of the Reign of Henry VIII, Preserved in the Public Record Office, the British Museum, and Elsewhere in England*, ed. J. S. Brewer, James Gairdner, and R. H. Brodie (21 vols in 37, London: Longman, 1862-[1932])
Marr *Guernsey*	L. James Marr, *A History of the Bailiwick of Guernsey: The Islanders' Story* (Chichester: Phillimore, 1982)
n.s.	new series
o.s.	original series
Prison Board	*Jersey Prison Board Case Papers* 10 vols inc. appendices (London: Privy Council, 1894)
PRO	Kew, Public Record Office
TRHS	*Transactions of the Royal Historical Society*
TSG	*Transactions of la Société Guernesiaise*

THE CHARTERS OF GUERNSEY

Published with the support of
the Royal Court of Guernsey

THE
Charters of
Guernsey

TIM THORNTON

Woodfield

First edition
published in 2004 by
Woodfield Publishing, Bognor Regis,
West Sussex PO21 5EL England
www.woodfieldpublishing.com

ISBN 1-903953-65-0

Front cover illustration:
Charter of Elizabeth I, 1559

Contents

Introduction

Guernsey's position amongst the various territories subject to the English crown was thrown into flux by the loss of Normandy in 1204. During the previous century, Guernsey had been a small part of that larger duchy which had influenced its social and political life since the extension of Norman influence there in the tenth and eleventh centuries. The century following John's loss of Normandy saw the customs of the island tested by forces which were increasingly and dominantly English, but it saw them successfully defended. The story of the island's charters is the story of the way this defence of the island's customs and privileges played out, and of the way that further privileges were granted and won. This reflects on the power and influence of the island community, but also on the power and interests of the crown. The context for this was provided chiefly by the wider relationships and tensions between the English and the French.

This is not, however, a simple history of inevitable conflict between metropolitan centre and distant island locality, or even of the uncomplicated rivalry between English and French. The late medieval and early modern periods covered by this book were ones in which many in communities like Guernsey could see an advantage to closer ties with the centre, at least for some of the time; and also ones in which the crown itself and the English regime did not necessarily find strong distinct jurisdictions to be antipathetic to their interests. And competition between the English crown and the French, important though it undoubtedly was in the centuries considered here, was not a competition between unified nation states, but between dynasties and their associated complexes of territories: most notably, in this connection, in the continuing relatively independent status, into the sixteenth century, of Brittany, and the identity of Normandy through the fifteenth and beyond.

It is important, therefore, not only to understand the struggles, conflicts, suffering and sacrifice which lie behind so many of the charters, but also to recognise that these are not exceptions to a rule, but part of not unfamiliar patterns in the world of the fourteenth, fifteenth, sixteenth and seventeenth centuries.

The intention here has been to present the charters, in their original form, in transcription and translation. Commentaries have been provided to suggest some of the context to their formation. It has not been the purpose here to consider the detailed nature of each document, in terms of its diplomatic history, although this might be a fruitful study in another context.[1] Nor has it been possible to spend as much time as might have been wished locating the charters amongst the other documents which record the development of Guernsey's difference – for example, the development of Guernsey's courts, and of the offices of bailiff and jurats, and the way in which the customary law, reorganised when Normandy and the Islands had the same ruler, emerged as the basis for the island's liberties.[2] Or, the process by which island litigation in English courts was eventually ended, as it was in Common Pleas in 1368.[3] Yet the emphasis here on the charters themselves, it can be argued, redresses a balance. It is, surely, extraordinary that so many of these documents have remained for so long unedited in print, or at least unavailable in translation; and it is clear enough that their symbolic significance and direct authority means that to ignore them in an account of the island's past is unjustified.[4] It is also to be hoped that the charters emerge as a little less routine and repetitive than some of their earlier students have suggested.[5]

---

[1] See, as an introduction, A. L. Brown, 'The Authorisation of Letters under the Great Seal', *BIHR*, 37 (1964), 125-55; H. C. Maxwell-Lyte, *Historical Notes on the Use of the Great Seal of England* (London: HMSO, 1926); V. H. Galbraith, *An Introduction to the Use of the Public Records* (Oxford: Clarendon Press, 1934), pp. 23-6; J. Otway-Ruthven, *The King's Secretary and the Signet Office in the XV Century* (Cambridge University Press, 1939).

[2] Le Patourel, *Channel Islands*, pp. 88-99, 104-7, 110.

[3] Le Patourel, *Channel Islands*, p. 113.

[4] They are mentioned little in, for example, Le Patourel, *Channel Islands*, or, with the exception of the 1560 charter, in A. J. Eagleston, *The Channel Islands under Tudor Government, 1485-1642: A Study in Administrative History* (Cambridge: published for the Guernsey Society at the University Press, 1949).

[5] H. de Sausmarez (ed.), 'The Earlier Charters of Guernsey: with Particular Reference to those of 15 Edward III and 1 Henry VII', *TSG*, x (1928); John le Patourel, 'The Charters and Privileges, Laws and Customs of the Island of Guernsey', *Guernsey Society Bulletin*, 2:1 (1946), 3-8.

Where possible, the edition is from the charter preserved in the Greffe, Royal Court House, Guernsey; the remaining editions are from the PRO text in the Jersey Prison Board Case papers (Prison Board). Abbreviations have been silently expanded; there has been no attempt, for the most part, to reproduce the forms of punctuation found in the Latin documents. In the transcriptions, there has been an attempt to reproduce the capitalisation found in the originals; in the translations, I have tended to keep capitalisation to a minimum. In the transcriptions and translations, the longer charters have been divided into numbered paragraphs – this has been done purely for convenience, and the interpolated numbering has been provided in parentheses.

Edward III

Commentary

The 1341 charter was born of a long struggle, and a short-term court crisis.

For almost a century after the loss of Normandy by John in 1204, relative peace had obtained between the kings of England and France. That peace had broken down seriously for the first time in the 1290s, when Edward I fought a war for his rights in south-west France, his duchy of Aquitaine. Guernsey's key role as a safe harbour on the long sea voyage between England and Aquitaine meant it was an important strategic part of this wider conflict. During the course of this struggle, Guernsey had suffered severely from French raids.[6] The period also saw the grant of the islands to Otto de Grandison – and Otto's increasingly ruthless attempts to impose his authority on the islands and extract the maximum return from them. This was most dramatically seen in a series of judicial Assizes.[7]

Even without Otto's interest, it is likely that Guernsey's rights would have been under threat. The English crown under Edward I and his son Edward II was notoriously keen to challenge the rights of anyone or any community which seemed to hinder the exercise of royal power. Their instrument was a legal proceeding driven by a writ of *quo warranto*, essentially asking by what warrant privileges were exercised.[8]

Yet from the accession of Edward III, the English crown became more and more focussed on its ambitions in France. Edward was the inheritor from his father of a claim to much French land as subject of the French king; but he was also, via his mother, a claimant to the French throne itself. In this capacity, he began a war which had direct implications for Guernsey.

---

[6] Marr, *Guernsey*, pp. 76, 136.
[7] Le Patourel, *Medieval Administration*, pp. 45-61; Marr, *Guernsey*, pp. 76-7.
[8] Donald W. Sutherland, *Quo Warranto Proceedings in the Reign of Edward I, 1278-1294* (Oxford: Clarendon Press, 1963).

The exiled claimant to the Scottish throne, David Bruce, raided the islands in 1336 and 1337, and in 1338 a French naval force attacked Guernsey, with Castle Cornet surrendering on 8 September.[9] English control of the Channel was reinforced thanks to a victory at Sluys in 1340, and in the autumn of that year Guernsey, though not Castle Cornet, was recaptured.[10]

The events of these years must have brought home to Edward the importance of Guernsey and Jersey. In 1341, with Castle Cornet still in the hands of the French, Edward faced one of his greatest crises. He had spent many months, and large sums of money, in the Low Countries, trying to assemble an alliance to take on the French king.[11] In parliament in 1340, he was subject to severe criticism. Returning to England, Edward dramatically attempted to make scapegoats of some of his ministers, but the result was further fierce criticism in parliament in the spring of 1341.[12] On top of this, David Bruce returned to Scotland from his French exile, and hostilities on the northern frontier resumed.

At this point an event occurred which represented both an opportunity and a threat. The death of Duke John III of Brittany on 30 April 1341 might have led to the accession there of Charles of Blois, thereby bringing the previously semi-independent duchy directly into the orbit of the French crown. On the other hand, John III's eleventh-hour decision to name his half-brother John de Montfort as heir gave Edward an opportunity to intervene in the politics of the duchy, concluding a treaty with him in October of that year. Edward seized his chance with both hands, but to do so he had to make concessions: one of these was to grant the communities of the Channel Islands, vital now in the war in Brittany, a blanket confirmation of their customs and laws, on 10 July 1341.

---

[9] Marr, *Guernsey*, pp. 77-8, 136-7.

[10] Marr, *Guernsey*, p. 137; Jonathan Sumption, *The Hundred Years' War* (2 vols; London: Faber, 1990-9), i: *Trial by Battle*, pp. 346, 363.

[11] W. M. Ormrod, *The Reign of Edward III: Crown and Political Society in England, 1327-1377* (New Haven: Yale University Press, 1990), p. 13.

[12] Michael Prestwich, *The Three Edwards: War and State in England, 1272-1377* (London: Weidenfeld and Nicolson, 1980), pp. 217-23.

EDWARD III 1341[13]

Edwardus Dei Gracia Rex Anglie et Francie et Dominus Hibernie Omnibus ad quos presentes litere pervenerint Salutem: Sciatis quod nos grata memoria recensentes quam constanter et magnanimiter dilecti et fideles nostri homines Insularum nostrarum de Jereseye Gernereye Serke et Aureneye in fidelitate nostra et progenitorum nostrorum Regum Anglie semper hactenus perstiterunt et quanta pro salvacione dictarum Insularum et nostrorum Jurium et honoris ibidem sustinuerunt tam pericula corporum quam suarum dispendia facultatum et proinde volentes ipsos favore prosequi gracioso concessimus pro nobis et heredibus nostris dictis hominibus Insularum predictarum quod ipsi heredes et successores sui omnia privilegia libertates immunitates exceptiones et consuetundines in personis rebus monetis et aliis eis virtute concessionum progenitorum nostrorum Regum Anglie vel alias legitime competentia habeant et teneant ac eis sine impedimento vel molestacione nostri heredum vel ministrorum quorumcunque plene gaundeant et utantur prout ipsi et eorum antecessores habitatores dictarum Insularum eis usi sunt racionabiliter et gavisi que jam illis in forma predicta generaliter confirmamus Volentes ea cum super hiis plene informati fuerimus prout justum fuerit specialiter confirmare. In cujus rei testimonium has literas nostras fieri fecimus Patentes. Teste me ipso apud Turrim Londonii decimo die Julii anno Regni nostri Anglie quinto decimo Regni vero nostri Francie secundo.

Per peticionem de Concilio in Parliamento

~ ~ ~

Edward, by the grace of God king of England and France and lord of Ireland, to all to whom these present letters shall come, greeting. Know ye that we recalling with grateful memory with what constancy and high spirit our beloved and faithful men of our islands of Jersey, Guernsey, Sark, and Alderney have always hitherto continued in their faithfulness to us and our progenitors kings of England and how great dangers to their bodies as well as costs to their property they have borne for the safety of the said islands and the conservation of our laws and honour therein, and in like manner desiring to follow after them with our gracious favour, we have granted for ourselves and our heirs to the said men of the aforesaid islands, that they themselves, their heirs and successors may have and hold all privileges,

---

[13] Prison Board.

liberties, immunities, exemptions, and customs in respect of their persons, goods, moneys, and other matters by virtue of the grant of our progenitors kings of England or otherwise lawfully by agreement, and, without impediment or molestation from us, our heirs or our officers whomsoever, may fully enjoy and use them according as they themselves and their predecessors, inhabitants of the said islands, have reasonably used and enjoyed them. Which things we do now confirm to them generally in the aforesaid form being willing after we have enquired into them to confirm them especially as may be just. In testimony whereof we have had these letters made patent, myself as witness, at the Tower of London the tenth day of July in the year of our reign in England the fifteenth, but of our reign in France the second.

By petition of the Council in Parliament.

Richard II

Commentaries

Edward III reigned for another thirty-six years after the grant of his charter to the bailiwicks. In that time, the English struggle against the French, which had provided the conditions for the original grant, went from one of desperation, through the heights of success in the battles of Crécy and Poitiers and the Treaty of Brétigny, to, once again, desperation. Edward's grandson, Richard II, inherited a position in which the English were struggling to maintain their lands in south-western France and in which their alliances in the north-west, especially in Brittany, on which the position of the islands so closely depended, were in tatters.

It was all the more urgent, then, that the rights and privileges of the islanders accepted by Edward III were confirmed, and the new king did so in November 1378 when he was at Gloucester.

Much had changed when Richard again came to act on the rights of the islanders. On 28 June 1394, Richard II granted a considerable increase to the rights of the communities of Guernsey and Jersey. In a brief charter issued from Westminster, he conceded to them the right to exemption from tolls, duties and customs in England, as if they were English. In conjunction with the grant of Edward III, earlier confirmed by Richard, this effectively gave Guernsey the financial privileges of being English while at the same time allowing the island its own customs and exemption from English laws.

The context of this charter is to be found in the king's policy towards the French, and more broadly in the way he attempted to reformulate English royal authority in what turned out to be the last five years of his reign. Richard's preference for peace with the French had already become clear by 1394. Following disastrous years of campaigning since the breakdown of the peace agreed at Bré-tigny,[14] a three-year truce in 1389 had been followed by negotiations

---

[14] Marr, *Guernsey*, pp. 141-3.

5

in search of a final peace. This proved elusive: a major sticking point was the possible return of Calais to the French, which was unacceptable to the English, and the possible surrender of the islands, also desired by the French, also represented an obstacle to the English. Eventually a truce was agreed, allowing for the long term of twenty-eight years, and Richard married the French princess Isabella.[15]

Later in 1394 Richard was to embark on an expedition to Ireland which was to prove a success. On his return he began a period of assertion of royal rights which some have seen as a tyranny. One key element of that assertion was the role of the non-English territories over which Richard ruled. Whether through systematic policy, or through their own reassertion of their rights and influence, Richard became particularly associated with Cheshire, Ireland, and others, including Guernsey.[16]

Sir Hugh de Calverley, who had been warden until 1393, was succeeded by Sir John de Golafre of Langley, who held office during the years 1393-6, and then by Edward, earl of Rutland. Golafre, a chamber knight, was apparently very close to the king, who had him buried at Westminster immediately beside his own tomb.[17] Rutland also possessed a close relationship with Richard. Soon to be promoted to the duchy of Aumale, he was the son and heir of the duke of York, and one well informed observer noted that there was no-one 'whom Richard loved better'.[18]

Richard's reign had already in 1394 seen exceptional internal political division. Given their close association with Richard's key supporters, their strengthened privileges and existing status, it is not surprising that the islands were to serve as a place of exile and imprisonment for one of Richard's bitterest enemies. From the time

---

[15] Marr, *Guernsey*, p. 79. Cf. J. J. N. Palmer, 'The Anglo-French Peace Negotiations, 1390-6', *Transactions of the Royal Historical Society*, 5th ser., 16 (1966), 81-94, esp. p. 93 (local objections, not English intransigence, as the obstacle to settlement); idem, 'The Background to Richard II's Marriage to Isabel of France (1396)', *BIHR*, 44 (1971), 1-17.

[16] Michael J. Bennett, 'Richard II and the Wider Realm', in Anthony Goodman and James L. Gillespie (eds.), *Richard II: The Art of Kingship* (Oxford: Clarendon, 1999), pp. 187-204 (although he mentions none of the Channel Islands in this connection).

[17] N. E. Saul, 'The Fragments of the Golafre Brass in Westminster Abbey', *Transactions of the Monumental Brass Society*, XV, i (1992), 19-32.

[18] 'Translation of a French Metrical History of the Deposition of Richard II', ed. J. T. Webb, *Archaeologia*, 20 (1824), 309; Saul, *Richard II*, p. 345 (for the idea that Richard possibly saw him as his heir).

when he had replaced Sir Simon de Burley as Richard's tutor or personal guardian, through his prominent membership of the commissions and councils which had attempted to restrain the king in 1385-6, John, Lord Cobham had become ever more clearly a man hated by Richard.[19] When the time came for Richard to assert his personal control, Cobham was clearly a marked man. On the same day, in September 1397, when another of Richard's bêtes noires, Richard Fitzalan, earl of Arundel, was arrested and executed, Cobham's trial was ordered, and he was convicted during the second, Shrewsbury, session of that parliament – and sent into exile in Jersey.[20]

It is therefore unsurprising that once Richard was deposed, and his supporters were being challenged in their turn, Cobham was active and Aumale his target. When on Friday 17 October 1399 the question was put whether the three dukes of Surrey, Exeter and Aumale should be arrested, Cobham was the first to reply, emphasising 'the evils of recent years'.[21]

RICHARD II 1378[22]

Richardus Dei Gratia Rex Anglie et Francie et Dominus Hibernie Omnibus ad quos presentes litere pervenerint Salutem. Inspeximus literas patentes quas dominus Edwardus nuper Rex Anglie avus noster fieri fecit in hec verba Edwardus dei gratia Rex Anglie et Francie et dominus Hibernie Omnibus ad quos presentes litere peruenerint salutem. Sciatis quod nos grata memoria recensentes quam constanter et magnanimiter dilecti et fideles nostri homines Insularum nostrarum de Jereseye Gernereye Serke et Aureneye in fidelitate

---

[19] J. S. Roskell, *The Impeachment of Michael de la Pole Earl of Suffolk in 1386 in the Context of the Reign of Richard II* (Manchester University Press, 1984), pp. 24, 61, 74; T. F. Tout, *Chapters in the Administrative History of Medieval England: The Wardrobe, the Chamber and the Small Seals* (6 vols., Manchester University Press, 1920-33), iii. 349; Anthony Tuck, *Richard II and the English Nobility* (London: Edward Arnold, 1973), pp. 43-4, 76, 100, 106-7; *RP*, iii. 204b, 221; *SR*, ii. 39-43.

[20] *Historia vitae et regni Ricardi Secundi*, ed. George B. Stow, Jr ([Philadelphia]: University of Pennsylvania Press, 1977), p. 144; Chris Given-Wilson (ed.), *Chronicles of the Revolution, 1397-1400: The Reign of Richard II* (Manchester University Press, 1993), pp. 60, 126, 174.

[21] 'Annales Ricardi Secundi et Henrici Quarti Regis Angliae', in *Chronica Monasterii S. Albani: Johannis de Trokelowe, et Henrici de Blaneforde . . . Chronica et Annales*, ed. H. T. Riley (Rolls Series 28(3); London: Longman's, Green, Reader, and Dyer, 1866), pp. 153-420, at pp. 306-7; Given-Wilson (ed.), *Chronicles of the Revolution*, pp. 204-5.

[22] Prison Board.

nostra et progenitorum nostrorum Regum Anglie semper hactenus perstiterunt et quanta pro salvacione dictarum Insularum et nostrorum Jurium et honoris ibidem sustinuerunt tam pericula corporum quam suarum dispendia facultatum et proinde volentes ipsos favore prosequi gracioso concessimus pro nobis et heredibus nostris dictis hominibus Insularum predictarum quod ipsi heredes et successores sui omnia privilegia libertates immunitates exemptiones consuetudines in personis rebus monetis et aliis eis virtute concessionum progenitorum nostrorum Regum Anglie vel alias legitime competentia habeant et teneant ac eis sine impedimento vel molestacione nostri heredum vel Minstrorum quorumcumque plene gaudeant et utantur prout ipsi et antecessores habitatores dictarum Insularum eis usi sunt rationabiliter et gavisi que jam illis in forma predicta generaliter confirmamus volentes ea cum super hiis plene informati fuerimus prout justum fuerit specialiter confirmare In cujus rei testimonium has literas nostras fieri fecimus patentes. Teste me ipso apud Turrim Londonii decimo die Julii Anno regni nostri Anglie quintodecimo regni vero nostri Francie secundo Nos autem concessiones confirmacionem privilegia libertates immunitates exempciones et consuetudines predicta rata habentes et grata ea pro nobis et heredibus nostris quantum in nobis est acceptamus approbamus ratificamus et ea predictis hominibus Insularum huiusmodi heredibus et successoribus suis concedimus et confirmamus prout litere predicte plenius testantur et prout ipsi et eorum antecessores habitatores dictarum Insularum eis usi sunt racionabiliter et gavisi In cujus rei testimonium has literas nostras fieri fecimus Patentes. Teste me ipso apud Gloucestriam decimo die Nouembris anno Regni nostri secundo.

~ ~ ~

Richard by the grace of God king of England and France and lord of Ireland to all those to whom these present letters shall come, greeting. We have inspected the Letters Patent which the Lord Edward lately king of England our grandfather caused to be made in these words. Edward, by the grace of God king of England and France and lord of Ireland, to all to whom these present letters shall come, greeting. Know ye that we recalling with grateful memory with what constancy and high spirit our beloved and faithful men of our islands of Jersey, Guernsey, Sark, and Alderney have always hitherto continued in their faithfulness to us and our progenitors kings of England and how great dangers to their bodies as well as costs to their property they have borne for the safety of the said islands and the conservation of our laws and honour therein, and in like manner desiring to follow after them with our gracious favour, we have granted for ourselves and our heirs to the said men of the aforesaid islands, that they them-selves, their heirs and successors may have and hold all privileges, liberties, immunities, exemptions, and customs in respect of their persons, goods, moneys, and other matters by virtue of the grant of our progenitors kings of England or otherwise lawfully by agreement, and, without impediment or molestation from us, our heirs or our officers whomsoever, may fully enjoy and use them according as they themselves and their predecessors, inhabitants of the said islands, have reasonably used and enjoyed them. Which things we do now confirm to them generally in the aforesaid form being willing after we have enquired into them to confirm them especially as may be just. In testimony whereof we have had these letters made pat-ent, myself as witness, at the Tower of London the tenth day of July in the year of our reign in England the fifteenth, but of our reign in France the second. We, moreover, holding the concessions, confirmations, privileges, liberties, immunities, and customs to be reasonable and seasonable, accept, approve, and ratify them for us and our heirs, as far as in us lies, and con-cede and confirm them to the aforesaid men of the islands in the same manner to their heirs and successors as the aforesaid Letters more fully testify and as they and their predecessors inhabitants of the said Islands have reasonably used and enjoyed them. In witness whereof we have had these our Letters made Patent. Myself as witness at Gloucester the tenth day of November in the second year of our reign.

RICHARD II 1394[23]

Richardus dei gracia Rex Anglie et ffrancie et Dominus Hibernie Omnibus ad quos presentes litere peruenerint Salutem Sciatis quod considerantes bonum gestum et magnam fidelitatem quam in ligeis et fidelibus nostris gentibus et Communitatibus Insularum nostrarum de Gerneseye Jereseye Serk et Aureneye indies inuenimus de gracia nostra speciali concessimus pro nobis et heredibus nostris quantum in nobis est eisdem gentibus et Commu-nitatibus quod ipse [sic] ac heredes et successores sui imperpetuum sint liberi et quieti in omnibus Ciuitatibus villis mercatoriis et portubus infra regnum nostrum Anglie de omnimodis theoloniis exaccionibus et custumis taliter et eodem modo quo fideles ligei nostri in regno nostro predicto existunt. Ita tamen quod dicte gentes et Communitates nostre ac heredes et successores sui predicti bene et fideliter se gerant erga nos et dictos heredes nostros imper-petuum. In cuius rei testimonium has literas nostras fieri fecimus patentes.

---

[23] Greffe.

Teste me ipso apud Westmonasterium vicesimo octavo Julii anno regni nostri decimo octavo.
   Hertilpole
   Per breve de priuato sigillo.

~ ~ ~

Richard, by the grace of God king of England and France and lord of Ireland, to all to whom these present letters may come, greeting. Know ye that we in consideration of the good behaviour and the great loyalty which we have ever found in our liege and faithful peoples and communities of our islands of Guernsey, Jersey, Sark and Alderney, have of our special grace granted for ourselves and our heirs, as far as in us lies, to the said peoples and communities, that they, their heirs and successors shall for ever be free and quit from all tolls, duties, and customs of whatsoever kind in all our cities, market towns, and ports within our kingdom of England, in the same manner as our faithful liege people in our aforesaid kingdom are. Provided always, however, that our said peoples and communities, their heirs and successors aforesaid shall well and faithfully conduct themselves towards us and our said heirs for ever. In witness whereof we have caused these our Letters to be made patent. Witness myself at Westminster this twenty-eighth day of July in the eighteenth year of our reign.

   Hertilpole

   By warrant of the Privy Seal

Henry IV

Commentary

Richard II returned from a second expedition to Ireland in the summer of 1399 and during August was taken into custody by his rival Henry of Bolingbroke, duke of Lancaster. He resigned the throne in September. Bolingbroke, soon to be crowned as King Henry IV, condemned many aspects of his predecessor's rule; but in the May of 1400 he confirmed the privileges which had been granted by Edward III in 1341 and confirmed by Richard in 1378.

The time was one dominated by concerns for security, with Richard II only recently dead, and preparations afoot for war against the Scots. Henry faced rebellion almost immediately and remained insecure for many years.

Not long after Henry's accession the French confirmed the truce with England which had been instigated by Richard II, although they avoided acknowledging Henry as king.[24] Relations with the French soon deteriorated, however, with raiding along the channel coast and affecting the islands.[25] Henry's regime needed the support of the bailiwicks, and the precedent of Edward III was an obvious one to follow.

Yet Henry's hostility to Richard's policies, and the specific possibility that the experience of John, Lord Cobham in Jersey may have been prominently canvassed, seems to have worked against a renewal of Richard's augmentation of the islands' privileges.[26] The 1394 charter was not confirmed. Guernseymen and their neighbours lost, for the moment, their right to be treated as Englishmen in terms of customs and other tolls.

---

[24] Anthony Tuck, 'Henry IV and Europe: A Dynasty's Search for Recognition', in R.H. Britnell A.J. Pollard (eds.), *The McFarlane Legacy, Studies in Late Medieval Politics and Society* (Stroud: Alan Sutton Publishing, 1995), pp. 107-25, esp. pp. 107-9; J.L. Kirby, *Henry IV of England* (London: Constable, 1970), pp. 80, 119-20.

[25] C.J. Ford, 'Piracy and Policy: the Crisis in the Channel, 1400-1403', *TRHS*, 5th series, XXIX (1979), pp. 63-78.

[26] Above, pp. 6-7.

HENRY IV 1400[27]

Rex Omnibus ad quos &c., salutem. Inspeximus literas patentes domini Ricardi nuper Regis Anglie secundi post conquestum de confirmacione factas in hec verba. Ricardus Dei gratia Rex Anglie et Francie et Dominus Hibernie Omnibus ad quos presentes litere pervenerint salutem. Inspeximus literas patentes quas dominus Edwardus nuper Rex Anglie avus noster fieri fecit in hec verba Edwardus Dei gratia Rex Anglie et Francie et Dominus Hibernie. Omnibus ad quos presentes litere pervenerint salutem. Sciatis quod nos grata memoria recensentes quam constanter et magnanimiter dilecti et fideles nostri homines Insularum nostrarum de Jereseye Gerneseye Serk et Aureneye in fidelitate nostra et progenitorum nostrorum Regum Anglie semper hactenus perstiterunt et quanta pro salvacione dictarum Insularum et nostrorum conservacione jurium et honoris ibidem sustinuerunt tam pericula corporum quam suarum dispendia facultatum et proinde volentes ipsos favore prosequi gracioso concesssimus pro nobis et heredibus nostris dictis hominibus Insularum predictarum quod ipsi heredes et successores sui omnia privilegia libertates immunitates exempciones consuetudines in personis rebus monetis et aliis eis virtute concessionum progenitorum nostrorum Regum Anglie vel alias legitime competencia habeant et teneant ac eis sine impedimento vel molestacione nostri heredum vel Ministrorum nostrorum quorumcumque plene gaudeant et utantur prout ipsi et eorum antecessores habitatores dictarum Insularum eis usi sunt rationabiliter et gavisi que jam eis in forma predicta generaliter confirmamus volentes ea cum super hiis plene informati fuerimus prout justum fuerit confirmare. In cujus rei testimonium has literas nostras fieri fecimus patentes Teste me ipso apud Turrim Londonii decimo die Julij anno regni nostri Anglie quinto decimo regni vero nostri Francie secundo. Nos autem concessiones confirmacionem privilegia libertates immunitates et consuetudines predicta rata habentes et grata ea pro nobis et heredibus nostris quantum in nobis est acceptamus approbamus ratificamus et ea predictis hominibus Insularum hujusmodi heredibus et successoribus suis concedimus et confirmamus prout litere predicte plenius testantur et prout ipsi et eorum antecessores habitatores dictarum Insularum eis usi sunt rationabiliter et gavisi. In cujus rei testimonium has literas nostras fieri fecimus patentes. Teste me ipso apud Gloucestriam decimo die Novembris anno regni nostri secundo. Nos autem concessiones confirmacionem privilegia libertates immunitates et consuetudines predicta rata habentes et grata ea pro nobis et heredibus nostris

---

[27] Prison Board.

quantum in nobis est acceptamus approbamus ratificamus et ea dilectis nobis nunc hominibus Insularum predictarum heredibus et successoribus suis de gratia nostra speciali concedimus et confirmamus prout litere predicte rationabiliter testantur et prout ipsi et eorum antecessores habitatores dictarum Insularum eis usi sunt rationabiliter et gavisi. In cujus &c Teste Rege apud Westmonasterium viij die Maii.

Per breve de privato sigillo et pro sex marcis solutis in Hanaperio.

~ ~ ~

Henry by the grace of God king of England and France and lord of Ireland to all to whom these present letters may come, greeting. We have inspected the Letters Patent of the Lord Richard lately king of England the second after the conquest in confirmation made in these words.

Richard by the grace of God king of England and France and lord of Ireland to all to whom these present letters may come, greeting. We have inspected the Letters Patent which the Lord Edward lately king of England our grandfather caused to be made in these words.

Edward, by the grace of God king of England and France and lord of Ireland, to all to whom these present letters shall come, greeting. Know ye that we recalling with grateful memory with what constancy and high spirit our beloved and faithful men of our islands of Jersey, Guernsey, Sark, and Alderney have always hitherto continued in their faithfulness to us and our progenitors kings of England and how great dangers to their bodies as well as costs to their property they have borne for the safety of the said islands and the conservation of our laws and honour therein, and in like manner desiring to follow after them with our gracious favour, we have granted for ourselves and our heirs to the said men of the aforesaid islands, that they themselves, their heirs and successors may have and hold all privileges, liberties, immunities, exemptions, and customs in respect of their persons, goods, moneys, and other matters by virtue of the grant of our progenitors Kings of England or otherwise lawfully by agreement, and, without impediment or molestation from us, our heirs or our officers whomsoever, may fully enjoy and use them according as they themselves and their predecessors, inhabitants of the said islands, have reasonably used and enjoyed them. Which things we do now confirm to them generally in the aforesaid form being willing after we have enquired into them to confirm them especially as may be just. In testimony whereof we have had these letters made patent, myself as witness, at the Tower of London the tenth day of July in the year of our reign in England the fifteenth, but of our reign in France the second.

We, moreover, holding the concessions, confirmations, privileges, liberties, immunities, and customs to be reasonable and seasonable, accept, approve, and ratify them for us and our heirs, as far as in us lies, and concede and confirm them to the aforesaid men of the islands in the same manner to their heirs and successors as the aforesaid Letters more fully testify and as they and their predecessors inhabitants of the said Islands have reasonably used and enjoyed them. In witness whereof we have had these our Letters made Patent. Myself as witness at Gloucester the tenth day of November in the second year of our reign.

We, moreover, holding the concessions, confirmations, privileges, liberties, immunities, and customs to be reasonable and seasonable, accept, approve, and ratify them for us and our heirs, as far as in us lies, and concede and confirm them, of our special favour, to the aforesaid men of the islands in the same manner to their heirs and successors as the aforesaid Letters more fully testify and as they and their predecessors inhabitants of the said Islands have reasonably used and enjoyed them. In witness whereof, &c.. Witness the King at Westminster the eighth day of May [in the first year of our reign].

By writ of privy seal and for six marks paid into the hanaper.

Henry V

Commentary

Henry V transformed English policy towards France. Henry IV in his later years had continued the policy of pursuing security for English interests in the south west of France, under terms akin to those of the Treaty of Brétigny. Henry V switched this to focus on the recovery of the old Norman-Angevin empire, including feudal superiority over Brittany. In January of 1414, in negotiation with the French he had seemed genuinely interested in marriage with the French princess Catherine, and agreed a truce for a year. But how far this was credible, given English demands for a dowry of one million crowns and the reassertion of their territorial ambitions, is highly questionable.[28] The confirmation of the islands' rights came in February of 1414. May 1414 saw the final meeting, in Guernsey, between English and Breton commissioners charged with making arrangements for the renewal of the truce with the Duke.[29] By the summer of the year, Henry was in complex negotiation with both of the rival French parties, the Burgundians and the Armagnacs, and skilfully seeking to play them off for the best advantage. This had a direct effect on the islands, for the new focus on the king's Norman inheritance obviously implied the redirection of English military efforts. When in the summer of 1415 war began, Henry commenced the siege of Harfleur. Yet although the islands might now find themselves adjacent once again to a Norman coast which acknowledged an English lord, Henry saw no reason to extend their privileges or return to them the rights they had briefly held under Richard II.

---

[28] Christopher Allmand, *Henry V* (London: Methuen, 1992), pp. 66-74.
[29] J. H. Wylie and W. T. Waugh, *The Reign of Henry V* (3 vols., Cambridge University Press, 1914-29), i. 102.

HENRY V 1414[30]

Henricus dei gracia Rex Anglie & ffrancie & Dominus Hibernie Omnibus ad quos presentes litere peruenerint Salutem. Inspeximus literas patentes domini Henrici nuper Regis Anglie patris nostri factas in hec verba Henricus dei gratia Rex Anglie et ffrancie et Dominus Hibernie Omnibus ad quos presentes litere peruerint salutem. Inspeximus literas patentes domini Ricardi nuper Regis Anglie secundi post conquestum de confirmacione factas in hec verba Ricardus dei gratia Rex Anglie et ffrancie et Dominus Hibernie Omnibus ad quos presentes litere peruenerint salutem. Inspeximus literas patentes quas dominus Edwardus nuper Rex Anglie avus noster fieri fecit in hec verba. Edwardus dei gratia Rex Anglie et ffrancie et Dominus Hibernie Omnibus ad quos presentes litere peruenerint salutem Sciatis quod nos grata memoria recensentes quam constanter et magnanimiter dilecti et fideles nostri homines Insularum nostrarum de Jereseye Gernesey Serk et Aureney in fidelitate nostra et progenitorum nostrorum Regum Anglie semper hactenus perstiterunt et quanta pro saluacione dictarum Insularum et nostrorum conservacione iurium et honoris ibidem sustinuerunt tam pericula corporum quam suarum dispendia facultatum et proinde volentes ipsos fauore prosequi gracioso concessimus pro nobis et heredibus nostris dictis hominibus Insularum predictarum quod ipsi heredes et successores sui omnia privilegia libertates immunitates exempciones consuetudines in personis rebus monetis et aliis eis virtute concessionum progenitorum nostrorum Regum Anglie vel alias legitime competencia habeant et teneant ac eis sine impedimento vel molestacione nostri heredum aut Ministrorum nostrorum quorumcumque plene gaudeant et utantur prout ipsi et eorum antecessores habitatores dictarum Insularum eis vsi sunt racionabiliter et gauisi que iam eis in forma predicta generaliter confirmamus volentes ea cum super hiis plene informati fuerimus prout iustum fuerit confimare. In cujus rei testimonium has literas nostras fieri fecimus patentes. Teste me ipso apud Turrim London' decimo die Julii anno regni nostri Anglie quintodecimo regni vero nostri ffrancie secundo. Nos autem concessiones confirmacionem priuilegia libertates immunitates et consuetudines predicta rata habentes et grata ea pro nobis et heredibus nostris quantum in nobis est acceptamus approbamus ratificamus et ea predictis hominibus Insularum huiusmodi heredibus et successoribus suis concedimus et confirmamus prout litere predicte plenius testantur et prout ipsi et eorum antecessores habitatores dictarum Insularum eis vsi sunt racionabiliter et gauisi. In cuius

---

[30] Prison Board.

rei testimonium has literas nostras fieri fecimus patentes. Teste me ipso apud Gloucestriam decimo die Nouembris Anno regni nostri secundo. Nos autem concessiones confirmacionem priuilegia libertates immunitates et consuetudines predicta rata habentes et grata ea pro nobis et heredibus nostris quantum in nobis est acceptamus approbamus ratificamus et ea dilectis nobis nunc homini- bus Insularum predictarum heredibus et successoribus suis de gracia nostra speciali concedimus et confirmamus prout litere predicte racionabiliter testantur et prout ipsi et eorum antecessores habitatores dictarum Insularum eis vsi sunt racionabiliter et gauisi. In cuius rei testimonium has literas nostras fieri fecimus patentes. Teste me ipso apud Westmonasterium octavo die Maii anno regni nostri primo. Nos autem concessiones confirmaciones privilegia libertates confirmation immunitates et consuetudines predicta rata habentes et grata ea pro nobis et heredibus nostris quantum in nobis est acceptamus approbamus ratificamus et ea dilectis nobis nunc hominibus Insularum predictarum heredi- bus et successoribus suis de gracia nostra speciali concedimus et confirmamus prout litere predicte racionabiliter testantur et prout ipsi et eorum antecessores habitatores Insularum predictarum eis vsi sunt racionabiliter et gauisi. In cujus rei testimonium has literas nostras fieri fecimus patentes. Teste me ipso apud Westmonasterium quartodecimo die ffebruarii Anno regni nostri primo

pro decem marcis solutis in Hanaperio.

Examinata per Ricardum Gabriell Johannem Clerk clericos.

~ ~ ~

Henry, by the grace of God king of England and France and lord of Ire- land, to all to whom these present letters may come, greeting. We have inspected the Letters Patent of the Lord Henry lately king of England, our father, made in these words. Henry, by the grace of God king of England and France and lord of Ireland, to all to whom these present letters may come, greeting. We have inspected the Letters Patent of the Lord Richard lately king of England the second after the conquest in confirmation made in these words:

Richard by the grace of God king of England and France and lord of Ireland to all to whom these present letters may come, greeting. We have inspected the Letters Patent which the Lord Edward formerly king of England our grandfather, caused to be made in these words: Edward, by the grace of God king of England and France and lord of Ireland, to all to whom these present letters shall come, greeting. Know ye that we recalling with grateful memory with what constancy and high spirit our beloved and faithful men of our islands of Jersey, Guernsey, Sark, and Alderney have always hitherto continued in their faithfulness to us and our progenitors kings of England and how great dangers to their bodies as well as costs to their property they have borne for the safety of the said islands and the conservation of our laws and honour therein, and in like manner desiring to follow after them with our gracious favour, we have granted for ourselves and our heirs to the said men of the aforesaid islands, that they themselves, their heirs and successors may have and hold all privileges, liberties, immunities, exemptions, and customs in respect of their persons, goods, moneys, and other matters by virtue of the grant of our progenitors Kings of England or otherwise lawfully by agreement, and, without impediment or molestation from us, our heirs or our officers whomsoever, may fully enjoy and use them according as they themselves and their predecessors, inhabitants of the said islands, have reasonably used and enjoyed them. Which things we do now confirm to them generally in the aforesaid form being willing after we have enquired into them to confirm them especially as may be just. In testimony whereof we have had these letters made patent, myself as witness, at the Tower of London the tenth day of July in the year of our reign in England the fifteenth, but of our reign in France the second.

We, moreover, holding the concessions, confirmations, privileges, liberties, immunities, and customs to be reasonable and seasonable, accept, approve, and ratify them for us and our heirs, as far as in us lies, and concede and confirm them to the aforesaid men of the islands in the same manner to their heirs and successors as the aforesaid Letters more fully testify and as they and their predecessors inhabitants of the said Islands have reasonably used and enjoyed them. In witness whereof we have had these our Letters made Patent. Myself as witness at Gloucester the tenth day of November in the second year of our reign.

We, moreover, holding the concessions, confirmations, privileges, liberties, immunities, and customs to be reasonable and seasonable, accept, approve, and ratify them for us and our heirs, as far as in us lies, and concede and confirm them, of our special favour, to the aforesaid men of the islands in the same manner to their heirs and successors as the aforesaid Letters more fully testify and as they and their predecessors inhabitants of the said Islands have reasonably used and enjoyed them. In witness whereof we have caused these our letters to be made patent. Witness myself at Westminster the eighth day of May in the first year of our reign.

We, moreover, holding the concessions, confirmations, privileges, liberties, immunities, and customs to be reasonable and seasonable, accept, approve, and ratify them for us and our heirs, as far as in us lies, and concede and confirm them, of our special favour, to the aforesaid men of the islands in the same manner to their heirs and successors as the aforesaid Letters more fully testify and as they and their predecessors inhabitants of the said Islands have reasonably used and enjoyed them. In witness whereof we have caused these our letters to be made patent. Witness myself at Westminster the fourteenth day of February in the first year of our Reign.

For ten marks paid into the hanaper

Examined by Richard Gabriell and John Clerk clerks

Henry VI

Commentary

In the eyes of his English subjects, and also of many Frenchmen, Henry VI inherited not just his father's English realm but that of France. Aged just over eight months old when he came to the throne in 1422, Henry was taken to France in 1430 and crowned the following year in Paris.[31] After a period of attempted compromises, by early 1441 rule by the royal council had been more or less abandoned, and any trace of the constraints of a royal minority had gone.[32] At this point he confirmed the privileges of many of his subjects and their communities, including those of the communities of the bailiwicks of Guernsey and Jersey on 10 February 1442.

Henry's grant to Guernsey and Jersey is particularly interesting, however, because, before reciting Henry V's confirmation of the sequence of charters beginning in 1341, it confirmed the grant by Richard II in 1394 of privileges in respect of English customs and tolls. This provision, ignored by Henry's father and grandfather, was a significant concession to the islanders, and the reasons for it can only be speculated upon. Henry's generosity in general is well attested, but there may have been other important factors operating in the decision.

One element may have been the gradual rehabilitation of Richard II in the reigns of Henry V and VI. At first buried at King's Langley, in 1413 he was re-interred, in the tomb Richard himself had always intended, in Westminster Abbey. A mixture of anxiety to prove Richard was truly dead, to atone for Henry IV's actions, and to claim, on

---

[31] Ralph A. Griffiths, *The Reign of Henry VI: The Exercise of Royal Authority, 1422-1461* (London: Benn, 1981), pp. 189-94; B. P. Wolffe, *Henry VI* (London: Eyre Methuen, 1981), pp. 54-62.

[32] J. L. Watts, 'When did Henry VI's Minority End?' in Dorothy J. Clayton, Richard G. Davies, and Peter McNiven (eds.), *Trade, Devotion and Governance: Papers in Later Medieval History* (Stroud: Sutton, 1994), pp. 116-39, esp. p. 129.

Henry V's part, to be in some sense Richard's heir, probably lay behind this.[33]

The islands themselves had passed out of the direct control of the crown early in Henry's reign. Most recently, Henry's uncle, Humphrey, duke of Gloucester had received the islands of Guernsey and Jersey in 1437 after the death of Humphrey's brother, John, duke of Bedford, in part fulfilment of a promise of lands to the value of 500 marks made by Henry V.[34]

Gloucester was antipathetic to the policies of many of those in the circle of courtiers around Henry as the king's independent rule developed. But this did not prevent the reassertion of the privileges of the islands. One trigger to this reassertion may well have been the events of the previous few months. The English government, acutely strapped for cash, had in 1440 first levied a tax on aliens: and had included amongst those liable Irishmen and Channel Islanders. This produced a significant protest, and one which was successful. In 1443, they were recognised as the king's subjects and so were henceforth exempt.[35] It may well have been the examination of Channel Island status in the aftermath of this act which led to the reintroduction of the grant by Richard II, in terms of allowance of rights in England as if they were Englishmen and women.

It might perhaps be suggested that these actions, in the charter and aliens' taxation, represented an integration of the islands into English structures of society and jurisdiction. Yet there is evidence that these privileges remained those of a distinct community. The rights granted in 1341 were retained, and indeed included for the first time in the same charter as those of 1394, and King Henry was soon to

---

[33] Saul, *Richard II*, p. 428; Paul Strohm, *England's Empty Throne: Usurpation and the Language of Legitimation, 1399-1422* (New Haven (CT) and London: Yale University Press, 1998), pp. 115-18.

[34] *Proceedings and Ordinances of the Privy Council of England*, ed. Harris Nicolas (7 vols., London: Record Commission, 1834-7), V (1835), p. 5; *48th Report of the Deputy Keeper of the Public Records* (London: HMSO, 1887), appendix, p. 317.

[35] *RP*, v. 38; R. A. Griffiths, 'The English Realm and Dominions and the King's Subjects in the Later Middle Ages', in J. G. Rowe (ed.), *Aspects of Late Medieval Government and Society: Essays Presented to J. R. Lander* (Toronto (Ont): published in association with the University of Western Ontario by University of Toronto Press, 1986), pp. 83-105, reprinted in R. A. Griffiths, *King and Country: England and Wales in the Fifteenth Century* (London: Hambledon, 1991), pp. 44-5.

demonstrate that he understood the value of territories under his control with a distinct identity – and the prestige this might bring.

On 24 November 1445, Henry VI granted the reversion of the lordship of the islands, still then held by Humphrey, duke of Gloucester, to Henry, duke of Warwick and his heirs.[36] Warwick was arguably Henry's closest friend, and the grant was clearly designed to bestow on him near-royal status, through the holding of a sovereign lordship under the king. In the event, Warwick predeceased Gloucester; he was therefore succeeded by Anne, Warwick's daughter and heir.[37] Yet Anne died less than three years after her father, leaving as heir her aunt, also called Anne.[38] She married Richard Neville, heir of Richard, earl of Salisbury, and Jersey and Guernsey were involved in the provisions made for the division of the Warwick inheritance.[39] Warwick acted as lord of the isles, in right of his wife, for example in letters patent issued on 18 January 1452.[40] The privileges of the islands might therefore be strengthened not just in the hands of members of the royal family, but in those of the king's closest friend, and even those of a nobleman without obvious direct ties to the crown.

HENRY VI 1442[41]

Henricus dei gracia Rex Anglie & ffrancie & Dominus Hibernie Omnibus ad quos presentes litere peruenerint salutem. Suspeximus literas patentes domini Ricardi nuper Regis Anglie secundi post conquestum factas in hec verba. Ricardus dei gracia Rex Anglie et ffrancie et Dominus Hibernie Omnibus ad quos presentes litere peruenerint salutem. Sciatis quod nos considerantes bonum gestum et magnam fidelitatem quam in ligeis et fidelibus nostris gentibus et Communitatibus Insularum nostrarum de Gerneseye Jereseye Serk et Aureneye indies inuenimus de gratia nostra speciali conces-

---

[36] *CPR, 1441-6*, p. 400.
[37] *CP*, xii/2, pp. 383-4; *CPR, 1446-52*, p. 42; *The Paston Letters*, ed. James Gairdner (reprinted Gloucester: Sutton, from the Library Edition of 1904, 1983), ii.. 78-9.
[38] Richard Beauchamp had had three daughters by his wife Elizabeth (Berkeley): Margaret, Eleanor and Elizabeth; by his other wife, Isabel, Baroness Burghersh, as well as his son Henry, he had had another daughter, the Anne in question here: *CP*, xii/2. 381-2; Griffiths, *Reign of Henry VI*, pp. 572-4.
[39] *CPR, 1446-52*, p. 262.
[40] *CPR, 1452-61*, pp. 571-2.
[41] Greffe.

simus pro nobis et heredibus nostris quantum in nobis est eisdem gentibus et Communitatibus quod ipse [sic] ac heredes et successores sui imperpetuum sint liberi & quieti in omnibus Ciuitatibus villis mercatoriis et portubus infra regnum nostrum Anglie de omnimodis theoloniis exaccionibus et custumis taliter et eodem modo quo fideles ligei nostri in regno nostro predicto existunt. Ita tamen quod dicte gentes et Communitates nostre ac heredes et successores sui predicti bene et fideliter se gerant erga nos et dictos heredes nostros imperpetuum. In cuius rei testimonium has literas nostras fieri fecimus patentes. Teste me ipso apud Westmonasterium vicesimo octauo die Julii anno regni nostri decimo octauo. Inspeximus eciam literas patentes domini Henrici nuper Regis Anglie patris nostri defuncti de confirmacione factas in hec verba. Henricus dei gratia Rex Anglie et ffrancie et Dominus Hibernie Omnibus ad quos presentes litere peruenerint salutem. Inspeximus literas patentes domini H[enrici] nuper Regis Anglie patris nostri defuncti de confirmacione factas in hec verba Henricus dei gratia Rex Anglie et ffrancie et Dominus Hibernie Omnibus ad quos presentes litere peruenerint salutem. Inspeximus literas patentes domini Ricardi nuper Regis Anglie secundi post conquestum de confirmacione factas in hec verba. Ricardus dei gratia Rex Anglie et Francie et Dominus Hibernie. Omnibus ad quos presentes litere peruenerint salutem. Inspeximus literas patentes quas Dominus Edwardus nuper Rex Anglie Auus noster fieri fecit in hec verba Edwardus dei gratia Rex Anglie et ffrancie et Dominus Hibernie Omnibus ad quos presentes litere peruenerint salutem Sciatis quod nos grata memoria recensentes quam constanter et magnanimiter dilecti et fideles nostri homines Insularum nostrarum de Jereseye Gerneseye Serk et Aureneye in fidelitate nostra et progenitorum nostrorum Regum Anglie semper hactenus perstiterunt et quanta pro saluacione dictarum Insularum et nostrorum conseruacione iurium et honoris ibidem sustinuerunt tam pericula corporum quam suarum dispendia facultatum et proinde volentes ipsos fauore prosequi gracioso concessimus pro nobis et heredibus nostris dictis hominibus Insularum predictarum quod ipsi heredes et successores sui omnia priuilegia libertates immunitates exempciones consuetudines in personis rebus monetis et aliis eis virtute concessionum progenitorum nostrorum Regum Anglie vel alias legitime competencia habeant et teneant ac eis sine impedimento vel molestacione nostri heredum aut Ministrorum nostrorum quorumcumque plene gaudeant et utantur prout ipsi et eorum Antecessores habitatores dictarum Insularum eis usi sunt rationabiliter et gauisi que iam eis in forma predicta generaliter confirmamus volentes ea cum super hiis plene informati fuerimus prout iustum fuerit confirmare In cuius rei testimonium has literas nostras fieri fecimus patentes. Teste me ipso apud Turrim Londonii decimo die Julii anno regni nostri Anglie quinto decimo regni vero nostri ffrancie secundo. Nos autem concessiones confirmacionem priuilegia libertates immunitates et consuetudines predicta rata habentes et grata ea pro nobis et heredibus nostris quantum in nobis est acceptamus approbamus ratificamus et ea predictis hominibus Insularum huiusmodi heredibus et successoribus suis concedimus et confirmamus prout litere predicte plenius testantur et prout ipsi et eorum antecessores habitatores dictarum Insularum eis vsi sunt racionaliter et gauisi. In cuius rei testimonium has literas nostras fieri fecimus patentes Teste me ipso apud Gloucestriam decimo die Novembris Anno regni nostri secundo. Nos autem concessiones confirmacionem priuilegia libertates immunitates et consuetudines predicta rata habentes et grata ea pro nobis et heredibus nostris quantum in nobis est acceptamus approbamus ratificamus et ea dilectis nobis nunc hominibus Insularum predictarum heredibus et successoribus suis de gracia nostra speciali concedimus et confirmamus prout litere predicte rationabiliter testantur et prout ipsi et eorum antecessores habitatores dictarum Insularum eis vsi sunt racionaliter et gauisi In cuius rei testimonium has literas nostras fieri fecimus patentes. Teste me ipso apud Westmonasterium octauo die Maii anno regni nostri primo. Nos autem concessiones confirmacionem privilegia libertates immunitates et consuetudines predicta rata habentes et grata ea pro nobis et heredibus nostris quantum in nobis est acceptamus approbamus ratificamus et ea dilectis nobis nunc hominibus Insularum predictarum heredibus et successoribus suis de gracia nostra speciali concedimus et confirmamus prout litere predicte racionabiliter testantur et prout ipsi et eorum antecessores habitatores Insularum predictarum eis vsi sunt rationabiliter et gauisi. In cuius rei testimonium has literas nostras fieri fecimus patentes Teste me ipso apud Westmonasterium quarto decimo die Februarii anno regni nostri primo. Nos autem literas predictas de huiusmodi quietanciis priuilegiis libertatibus immunitatibus exempcionibus et consuetudinibus minime revocatis de assensu dominorum spiritualium et temporalium in Parliamento nostro apud Westmonasterium Anno regni nostri primo tento existencium acceptamus approbamus & dilectis nobis nunc hominibus Insularum predictarum ratificamus et confirmamus prout litere predicte rationabiliter testantur et prout predicti nunc homines Insularum predictarum et antecessores sui habitatores earundem quietanciis priuilegiis libertatibus immunitatibus exempcionibus et consuetudinibus predictis a tempore confec-

cionis literarum predictarum semper hactenus rationabiliter vti et gaudere consueuerunt. In cuius rei testimonium has literas nostras fieri fecimus patentes. Teste me ipso apud Westmonasterium decimo die ffebruarii Anno regni nostri vicesimo.

Examinata per Johannem Bate Thomas Shipton clericos

~ ~ ~

Henry by the grace of God, king of England and France and lord of Ireland. To all those to whom these present letters shall come, greeting.

We have seen the Letters Patent of the Lord Richard late king of England the second after the Conquest, made in these words.

Richard, by the grace of God king of England and France and lord of Ireland, to all to whom these present letters may come, greeting. Know ye that we in consideration of the good behaviour and the great loyalty which we have ever found in our liege and faithful peoples and communities of our islands of Guernsey, Jersey, Sark and Alderney, have of our special grace granted for ourselves and our heirs, as far as in us lies, to the said peoples and communities, that they, their heirs and successors shall for ever be free and quit from all tolls, duties, and customs of whatsoever kind in all our cities, market towns, and ports within our kingdom of England, in the same manner as our faithful liege people in our aforesaid kingdom are. Provided always, however, that our said peoples and communities, their heirs and successors aforesaid shall well and faithfully conduct themselves towards us and our said heirs for ever. In witness whereof we have caused these our Letters to be made patent. Witness myself at Westminster this twenty-eighth day of July in the eighteenth year of our reign.

We have seen also the Letters Patent of confirmation of the Lord Henry late king of England our deceased father, made in these words. Henry by the grace of God king of England and France and lord of Ireland, to all those to whom these present Letters Patent shall come, greeting. We have seen the Letters Patent of the Lord Henry late king of England our father, made in these words. Henry by the grace of God king of England and France and lord of Ireland, to all those to whom these present Letters shall come, greeting. We have seen the Letters Patent of confirmation of the Lord Richard formerly king of England the second after the Conquest in these words.

Richard, by the grace of God, king of England and France and lord of Ireland, to all those to whom these present Letters Patent may come, greeting. We have inspected the Letters Patent which the Lord Edward late king of England our grandfather caused to be made in these words.

Edward, by the grace of God king of England and France and lord of Ireland, to all to whom these present letters shall come, greeting. Know ye that we recalling with grateful memory with what constancy and high spirit our beloved and faithful men of our islands of Jersey, Guernsey, Sark, and Alderney have always hitherto continued in their faithfulness to us and our progenitors kings of England and how great dangers to their bodies as well as costs to their property they have borne for the safety of the said islands and the conservation of our laws and honour therein, and in like manner desiring to follow after them with our gracious favour, we have granted for ourselves and our heirs to the said men of the aforesaid islands, that they themselves, their heirs and successors may have and hold all privileges, liberties, immunities, exemptions, and customs in respect of their persons, goods, moneys, and other matters by virtue of the grant of our progenitors kings of England or otherwise lawfully by agreement, and, without impediment or molestation from us, our heirs or our officers whomsoever, may fully enjoy and use them according as they themselves and their predecessors, inhabitants of the said islands, have reasonably used and enjoyed them. Which things we do now confirm to them generally in the aforesaid form being willing after we have enquired into them to confirm them especially as may be just. In testimony whereof we have had these letters made patent, myself as witness, at the Tower of London the tenth day of July in the year of our reign in England the fifteenth, but of our reign in France the second.

We, moreover, holding the concessions, confirmations, privileges, liberties, immunities, and customs to be reasonable and seasonable, accept, approve, and ratify them for us and our heirs, as far as in us lies, and concede and confirm them to the aforesaid men of the islands in the same manner to their heirs and successors as the aforesaid Letters more fully testify and as they and their predecessors inhabitants of the said Islands have reasonably used and enjoyed them. In witness whereof we have had these our Letters made Patent. Myself as witness at Gloucester the tenth day of November in the second year of our reign.

We, moreover, holding the concessions, confirmations, privileges, liberties, immunities, and customs to be reasonable and seasonable, accept, approve, and ratify them for us and our heirs, as far as in us lies, and concede and confirm them, of our special favour, to the aforesaid men of the islands in the same manner to their heirs and successors as the aforesaid Letters more fully testify and as they and their predecessors inhabitants of the said Islands have reasonably used and enjoyed them. In witness whereof we have caused these our letters to be made patent. Witness myself at Westminster the eighth day of May in the first year of our reign.

We, moreover, holding the concessions, confirmations, privileges, liberties, immunities, and customs to be reasonable and seasonable, accept, approve, and ratify them for us and our heirs, as far as in us lies, and concede and confirm them, of our special favour, to the aforesaid men of the islands in the same manner to their heirs and successors as the aforesaid Letters more fully testify and as they and their predecessors inhabitants of the said Islands have reasonably used and enjoyed them. In witness whereof we have caused these our letters to be made patent. Witness myself at Westminster the fourteenth day of February in the first year of our reign.

We, moreover, accept and approve the aforesaid letters, concerning acquittances, privileges, liberties, immunities, exemptions and customs (in no ways revoked), with the assent of the lords spiritual and temporal assembled in our parliament held at Westminster in the first year of our reign, and ratify and confirm the same now to our aforesaid beloved men of the said Islands, as the aforesaid letters rationally testify, and as the inhabitants of the aforesaid islands and their ancestors, inhabitants of the same, have possessed and enjoyed, those acquittances, privileges, liberties, immunities, exemptions, and customs from the time that the aforesaid Letters Patent were granted them. In witness whereof we have caused these our letters to be made patent. Witness myself at Westminster the tenth day of February the twentieth year of our reign.

Examined by John Bate and Thomas Shipton clerks

Edward IV

Commentary

Henry VI's reign ended in confusion, not least in Guernsey. There was confusion as a result of the fall of Lancastrian Normandy to the French king. As the final English positions in the Cotentin collapsed during 1450 the islands became a refuge for those fleeing – and they may for a time have been under serious threat themselves.[42] Another source of confusion was that the island's lord, Richard, earl of Warwick, moved into a stance of outright opposition to the crown, and by 1459 had been formally condemned for treason by parliamentary attainder. In 1460, and possibly earlier, his position in the Channel Islands was formally challenged by the Lancastrian regime.[43] So when, following his victory at Mortimer's Cross in February 1461, Edward, earl of March, son of the recently killed Richard, duke of York, was crowned, as Edward IV, the islands soon came under further threat. Although Edward's victory restored their lord, Richard, earl of Warwick, to a position of power, it deepened the confusion in the islands. Possibly with the agreement of the garrison, influenced by the decision of the displaced queen, Margaret of Anjou, to make concessions in return for French support against the new, Yorkist, king, Jersey was taken by Pierre de Brézé, comte de Maulévrier, grand seneschal of Normandy.[44]

Some months later, Louis XI wrote a sequence of letters on 3-5 December 1461 to the baillis of the Cotentin and of the isle of Jersey (or to the governor and jurats of Jersey) concerning the problems being experienced by French monasteries in asserting their rights in Jersey. This would seem to indicate that the seizure of the

---

[42] 'Ancient petitions of the Chancery and the Exchequer': ayant trait aux îles de la Manche, conservées au 'Public Record Office' à Londres (Société Jersiaise, publication spéciale; St.-Hélier, Jersey: Labey et Blampied, imprimeurs, 1902), pp. 89-90.

[43] Tim Thornton, 'The English King's French Islands: Jersey and Guernsey in English Politics and Administration, 1485-1642', in George W. Bernard and Steven J. Gunn (eds.), *Authority and Consent in Tudor England: Essays Presented to C. S. L. Davies* (Aldershot: Ashgate, 2002)

[44] Thornton, 'English King's French Islands', pp. 201-2.

island by de Brézé did not imply the simple absorption of Jersey by an assertive centralized French regime.[45] The negotiations between de Brézé and Margaret of Anjou implied that he would receive the islands in his own right, free from the sovereignty of the king of England.[46] There is no explicit mention of his intended relationship with the French crown. It may be that this was deliberate, as the French knew the sensitivity of the negotiations and wanted to retain the option of denying complicity - something which a direct claim to the islands would make impossible. More important, however, was the continuing strength of Norman autonomy. De Brézé was grand seneschal of the duchy and intimately connected to its traditions and structures; those who established his regime in Jersey, such as Jean de Carbonnel, seigneur of Sourdeval, were even more so. If some in Jersey, such as the St Martin family, plotted to support Brézé, or simply accepted his regime, it may be because they saw it as representing a secure expression of their Norman identity, not subjection to the French monarchy.

The silence regarding French sovereignty in Jersey was thrown into sharp relief by the Norman rebellion of 1465. De Brézé and his son supported Louis XI.[47] In the island, however, Jean de Carbonnel would not. Weak though the hold of the duke of Normandy might have been, he did attempt to revictual the island before it finally fell to the forces of Edward IV.[48] Another sign that de Brézé's regime might represent a Norman identity welcome to the islanders is to be found in the field of law, as it issued a set of ordinances which were to become an important part of the island's constitution. These were

---

[45] *Cartulaire des îles Normandes: recueil de documents concernant l'histoire de ces îles, conservés aux archives du département de la Manche et du Calvados, de la Bibliothèque nationale, du Bureau des rôles, du château de Warwick, etc* ([St. Hélier] Jersey: The Beresford library, limited, 1924 (ed. G.F.B. de Gruchy, R.R. Marett and E.T. Nicolle), pp. 272-7, items 192-3, and pp. 326-29, item 244.

[46] Thomas Basin, *Histoire des règnes de Charles VII et de Louis XI*, ed. J. Quicherat (4 vols., Paris: J. Renouard, 1855-9), iv. 358, pièce VIII. Jehan de Waurin, *Recueil des Croniques et anchiennes istories de la Grant Bretaigne, a present nomme Engleterre*, ed. William Hardy & Edward L.C.P. Hardy (5 vols.; Rolls Series, 39, London: Longman, 1864-91), v. 431-5, makes the motivation for Brézé's involvement no more than the jealousy of Louis XI.

[47] The agreement is printed in R. R. Lempriere, 'L'occupation de Jersey par le Comte de Maulévrier', *ABSJ*, X (1923-7), 181-3.

[48] 'L'occupation de Jersey par les Comtes de Maulévrier', pp. 184-8 (from Paris, Bibliothèque Nationale, MS 26,092, no. 764).

issued in his name alone: the sovereignty of Louis was not acknowledged.[49]

Neither was the tradition of autonomy represented by the lordship of the isles under English allegiance withering away. Richard Neville, earl of Warwick continued to aspire to the title of lord of the isles. He issued letters patent as lord throughout the period of Jersey's occupation.[50]

The grant of the charter to the bailiff, jurats and people of Guernsey and its bailiwick is therefore intriguing in its timing. Edward had not confirmed the privileges of the islanders at the beginning of his reign, perhaps because of the uncertainties surrounding the position of Jersey. The confirmation was issued, in March 1465, at the time of the rebellion against Louis IX, known as the League of the Public Weal, which was to emphasise the split between Jersey and the French crown, and ultimately its identification once again with the duke of Normandy. The charter itself was issued to the bailiff and jurats of Guernsey, and the communities of their bailiwick. Jersey was not mentioned in the confirmation clauses, although the English clerk who produced the version now held in the Greffe in Guernsey was so used to the collective formulation that he inadvertently included the name of Jersey and it had to be erased from the document.

Edward may also have repaid a personal debt in the grant of the charters. In his flight from defeat at the hands of Henry VI's supporters at Ludford Bridge in 1459, Edward, then earl of March, with the earl of Warwick, had passed through Devon and, en route for Calais, through the islands. As king, Edward enhanced the privileges of the fief in Guernsey, *le fieu Gallicien*, which belonged to the man who had brought him through the islands.[51] Edward made a point about

[49] 'L'occupation de Jersey par les Comtes de Maulévrier', pp. 179–80 - a *vidimus* of Maulévrier's letters patent, 21 Aug. 1462.
[50] T. W. M. de Guérin, 'An Account of the Families of de St Martin and de la Court (Seigneurs of Trinity)', *ABSJ*, IX (1919–22), 69, 83–4 (Thomas de la Court is granted the possessions of the de St Martin family in Jersey, 21 Mar. 1463). Of course, he also acted in this capacity in Guernsey, with more effect: *ibid.*, pp. 69–70 (letters patent 1 Apr. 1465); *List of Records in the Greffe, Guernsey*, vol. 2, ed. J. H. Lenfestey (List and Index Society, 11, 1978), p. 19 (no. 53, 30 Sept. 1466).
[51] G. J. Dupont, *Histoire du Cotentin et de ses îles* (Caen: F. Le Blanc-Hardel, 1870–85), ii. 644; Ferdinand Brock Tupper, *A History of Guernsey and its Bailiwick; with Occasional Notices of Jersey* (2nd edition, Guernsey: Le Lievre and London: Simpkin, Marshall & Co., 1876), p. 129.

his predecessors, too, in the charter. He chose to ignore the charters of Henry IV, V and VI, and instead to confirm directly the charters of 1378 and 1394 issued by Richard II.

Once Jersey had been recovered by the English crown, a further confirmation of charters was issued. This took the form of a reassertion, specifically to Jersey, then subsequently to Guernsey, of the previous grants of Richard II to the communities of both bailiwicks. The specific terms of the grant made, however, were slightly different. Although they confirmed the substance of Richard's charters, in granting the islands' laws and privileges, and exempting islanders from customs and other charges in English ports and markets, the charters did not simply recite and confirm the previous charters but used forms of words which, for example in the case of the exemption from customs, were much more complex and inclusive.

The context for this grant, the recent recovery of Jersey from occupation, needs to be seen in part in terms of the conflicts within the Yorkist regime. This came in the form of the dissention between the queen's Woodville connection, which was pro-Burgundian and anti-French, and the earl of Warwick and the Nevilles, who were pro-French. A key point in the falling out was the dismissal of archbishop Neville as chancellor on 8 June 1467, and the tournament of Lord Scales with the Bastard of Burgundy – a coup against the Nevilles which may in a sense have released the attack on Jersey.[52] The man who led the recovery mission, Richard Harliston, was not an adherent of Warwick but a long-standing Yorkist servant, with a father John who had been receiver of York's key honour of Clare as early as 1447/8 – he was therefore clearly distinguished from Warwick's previous regime in the islands.[53] Then, in spite of Warwick's claims to the lordship of both Jersey and Guernsey, the recaptured Jersey was granted to Anthony Woodville, Lord Scales, the queen's brother.[54] When the grant of the charter was made, in January 1469, relations between Edward and the Nevilles had reached crisis point, and in the spring of the year agents of the Nevilles were fomenting

---

Charles Ross, *Edward IV* (London: Eyre Methuen, 1974), p. 21, does not mention the possibility of passage through the islands.

[52] M. A. Hicks, *Warwick the Kingmaker* (Oxford and Malden, Mass.: Blackwell, 1998), p. 254.

[53] Johnson, *Duke Richard of York*, p. 233: receiver in 1447/8 and 1450/51.

[54] Hicks, *Warwick*, p. 264, thinks the grant to Scales tactless.

trouble in Yorkshire, trouble that would eventually lead to the flight of Edward and the re-adeption of Henry VI.[55]

It is this which helps explain the other significant departure in the charters of 1465-9. For the first time, a grant was made specifically to Guernsey; then, separate charters were issued for Guernsey and for Jersey. Undoubtedly the experience of 1461-8, and the previous experience of a charter issued just for the bailiwick of Guernsey, played a part in this separation. But in 1465 the separation was one necessitated by Jersey no longer acknowledging English rule; now in 1469 the English king was back in charge, but Guernsey and Jersey had found themselves under the control of opposing sides in an internecine struggle that was to destroy the house of Neville and bring the Yorkists to the nadir of their fortunes.

EDWARD IV 1465[56]

Edwardus dei gracia Rex Anglie & ffrancie & Dominus Hibernie Omnibus ad quos presentes litere peruenerint salutem. Inspeximus literas patentes domini Ricardi nuper Regis Anglie secundi post conquestum factas in hec verba.

 Ricardus dei gracia Rex Anglie et ffrancie et Dominus Hibernie Omnibus ad quos presentes litere peruenerint salutem. Inspeximus literas patentes quas Dominus Edwardus nuper Rex Anglie Auus noster fieri fecit in hec verba. Edwardus dei gratia Rex Anglie et ffrancie et Dominus Hibernie Omnibus ad quos presentes litere peruenerint salutem. Sciatis quod nos grata memoria recensentes quam constanter et magnanimiter dilecti et fideles nostri homines Insularum nostrarum de Gerneseye Jereseye Serk et Aureneye in fidelitate nostra et progenitorum nostrorum Regum Anglie semper hactenus perstiterunt et quanta pro saluacione dictarum Insularum et nostrorum conseruacione iurium et honoris ibidem sustinuerunt tam pericula corporum quam suarum dispendia facultatum et proinde volentes ipsos fauore prosequi gracioso conces-simus pro nobis et heredibus nostris dictis hominibus Insularum predictarum quod ipsi heredes et successores sui omnia priuilegia libertates immunitates exempctiones consuetudines in personis rebus monetis et aliis eis virtute concessionum progenitorum nostrorum Regum Anglie vel alias legitime competencia habeant et teneant ac eis sine impedimento vel molestacione

[55] Ross, *Edward IV*, pp. 125-30.
[56] Greffe.

nostri heredum vel Ministrorum nostrorum quorumcumque plene gaudeant et utantur prout ipsi et eorum antecessores habitatores dictarum Insularum eis vsi sunt racionabiliter et gauisi que iam eis in forma predicta generaliter confirmamus Volentes ea cum super hiis plene informati fuerimus prout iustum fuerit specialiter confirmare. In cujus rei testimonium has literas nostras fieri fecimus patentes Teste me ipso apud Turrim Londonii decimo die Julii Anno regni nostri Anglie quintodecimo regni vero nostri ffrancie secundo. Nos autem concessiones confirmacionem privilegia libertates immunitates exempciones et consuetudines predicta rata habentes et grata ea pro nobis et heredibus nostris quantum in nobis est acceptamus approbamus ratificamus et ea predictis hominibus Insularum huiusmodi heredibus et successoribus suis concedimus et confirmamus prout litere predicte plenius testantur et prout ipsi et eorum antecessores habitatores dictarum Insularum eis vsi sunt racionabiliter et gauisi. In cujus rei testimonium has literas nostras fieri fecimus patentes Teste me ipso apud Gloucestre decimo die Nouembris Anno regni nostri secundo. Inspeximus eciam alias literas patentes predicti domini Ricardi nuper Regis Anglie secundi post conquestum similiter factas in hec verba Ricardus dei gracia Rex Anglie et ffrancie et Dominus Hibernie Omnibus ad quos presentes litere peruenerint salutem. Sciatis quod nos considerantes bonum gestum et magnam fidelitatem quam in ligeis et fidelibus nostris gentibus et Communitatibus Insularum nostrarum de Gerneseye Jerseye Serk et Aureneye indies inuenimus de gracia nostra speciali concessimus pro nobis et heredibus nostris quantum in nobis est eisdem gentibus et Communitatibus quod ipse et heredes et successores sui imperpetuum sint libere et quieti in omnibus Ciuitatibus villis mercatoriis et portubus infra regnum nostrum Anglie de omnimodis theoloniis exaccionibus et custumis taliter et eodem modo quo fideles ligei nostri in regno nostro predicto existunt. Ita tamen quod dicte gentes et Communitates nostre ac heredes et successores sui predicti bene et fideliter se gerant erga nos et dictos heredes nostros imperpetuum. In cuius rei testimonium has literas nostras fieri fecimus patentes Teste me ipso apud Westmonasterium vicesimo octauo die Julii anno regni nostri decimo octauo. Nos autem literas predictas ac omnia et singula in eis contenta rata habentes et grata ea pro nobis et heredibus nostris quantum in nobis est acceptamus et approbamus ac nunc hominibus gentibus et Communitatibus Insularum Gerneseye Serk et Aureneye et successoribus suis ratificamus et confirmamus prout litere predicte racionabiliter testantur. In cuius rei testimonium has

literas nostras fieri fecimus patentes. Teste me ipso apud Westmonasterium vicesimo nono die Marcii Anno regni nostri quinto.
 Examinata per Johannem Pemberton Willielmum Morland clericos

[Pro viginti solidis solutis in Hanaperio.]

~ ~ ~

Edward by the grace of God king of England and France and lord of Ireland to all to whom these present letters may come, greeting. We have inspected the Letters Patent of Lord Richard lately king of England, the second after the Conquest, made in these words: Richard by the grace of God king of England and France and lord of Ireland to all those to whom these presents shall come, greeting. We have inspected the Letters Patent which the Lord Edward lately king of England our ancestor caused to be made in these words. Edward, by the grace of God king of England and France and lord of Ireland, to all to whom these present letters shall come, greeting. Know ye that we recalling with grateful memory with what constancy and high spirit our beloved and faithful men of our islands of Jersey, Guernsey, Sark, and Alderney have always hitherto continued in their faithfulness to us and our progenitors kings of England and how great dangers to their bodies as well as costs to their property they have borne for the safety of the said islands and the conservation of our laws and honour therein, and in like manner desiring to follow after them with our gracious favour, we have granted for ourselves and our heirs to the said men of the aforesaid islands, that they themselves, their heirs and successors may have and hold all privileges, liberties, immunities, exemptions, and customs in respect of their persons, goods, moneys, and other matters by virtue of the grant of our progenitors Kings of England or otherwise lawfully by agreement, and, without impediment or molestation from us, our heirs or our officers whomsoever, may fully enjoy and use them according as they themselves and their predecessors, inhabitants of the said islands, have reasonably used and enjoyed them. Which things we do now confirm to them generally in the aforesaid form being willing after we have enquired into them to confirm them especially as may be just. In testimony whereof we have had these letters made patent, myself as witness, at the Tower of London the tenth day of July in the year of our reign in England the fifteenth, but of our reign in France the second. We, moreover, holding the concessions, confirmations, privileges, liberties, immunities, and customs to be reasonable and seasonable, accept, approve, and ratify them for us and our heirs, as far as in us lies, and concede and confirm them to the aforesaid men of the islands in the same manner to their heirs and successors as the aforesaid Letters more fully testify and as they and their predecessors in-habitants of the said Islands have reasonably used and enjoyed them. In witness whereof we have had these our Letters made Patent. Myself as witness at Gloucester the tenth day of November in the second year of our reign.

We have also inspected other letters patent of the aforesaid Lord Richard formerly king of England the second after the Conquest similarly made in these words.

Richard, by the grace of God king of England and France and lord of Ireland, to all to whom these present letters may come, greeting. Know ye that we in consideration of the good behaviour and the great loyalty which we have ever found in our liege and faithful peoples and communities of our islands of Guernsey, Jersey, Sark and Alderney, have of our special grace granted for ourselves and our heirs, as far as in us lies, to the said peoples and communities, that they, their heirs and successors shall for ever be free and quit from all tolls, duties, and customs of whatsoever kind in all our cities, market towns, and ports within our kingdom of England, in the same manner as our faithful liege people in our aforesaid kingdom are. Provided always, however, that our said peoples and communities, their heirs and successors aforesaid shall well and faithfully conduct themselves towards us and our heirs aforesaid for ever. In witness whereof we have caused these our Letters to be made patent. Witness myself at Westminster this twenty-eighth day of July in the eighteenth year of our reign.

We, moreover, holding the aforesaid letters, and all and singular contained therein, to be reasonable and seasonable, accept and approve them for us and our heirs, as far as in us lies, and now ratify and confirm them to the men, peoples, and communities of the islands of Guernsey, Sark, and Alderney, and to their successors as the aforesaid Letters more fully testify. In witness whereof we have caused these our letters to be made patent. Witness myself at Westminster the twenty-ninth day of March in the fifth year of our reign.

Examined by John Pemberton William Morland Clerks

By payment of twenty shillings into the Hanaper

EDWARD IV 1469[57]

Edwardus dei gratia Rex Anglie et ffrancie et Dominus Hibernie Omnibus ad quos presentes litere peruenerint Salutem. Cum nobilissimus progenitor noster inclite memorie Ricardus quondam Rex Anglie et ffrancie et Dominus Hibernie post conquestum Secundus per literas suas patentes datas apud Westmonasterium octauo die Julii Anno regni sui decimo octauo in consideracione boni gestus et magne fidelitatis quos in ligeis et fidelibus suis gentibus et Communitatibus Insularum suarum de Guernesey Serk et Aureney indies inuenit de gracia sua speciali concessit pro se et heredibus suis quantum in eo fuit eisdem gentibus et Communitatibus suis quod ipsi et successores sui imperpetuum forent liberi et quieti in omnibus Ciuitatibus Villis mercatoriis et portubus infra Regnum Anglie de omnimodis Theoloniis exaccionibus et Custumis taliter et in eodem modo quo fideles ligei sui in Regno suo predicto extiterunt. Ita tamen quod dicte gentes et Communitates sue ac heredes et successores sui predicti bene et fideliter se gererent erga ipsum progenitorem nostrum et heredes suos imperpetuum prout in literis illis plenius continetur. Nos continuam fidelitatem gencium et Communitatum dictarum Insularum de Guernesey Serk et Aureney plenius intendentes litteras predictas et omnia et singula in eis contenta quo ad gentes et Communitates earundem Insularum de Guernesey Serk et Aureney acceptamus approbamus et eisdem gentibus et Communitatibus heredibus et successoribus suis per presentes ratificamus et confirmamus. Et ulterius nos memorie Reducentes quam valide viriliter et constanter dicte gentes et Communitates earundem Insularum de Guernesey Serk et Aureney nobis et progenitoribus nostris prestiterunt et quanta et pericula et perdita pro saluacione earundem Insularum et reduccione Castri nostri de Mount Orgill sustinuerunt de uberiori gracia nostra concessimus eisdem gentibus et Communitatibus quod ipse heredes et successores sui sint ita liberi et quieti in omnibus Ciuitatibus Burgis Villis Mercatoriis et aliis Villis portubus et locis infra Regnum nostrum Anglie et infra omnes terras et Insulas nostras citra vel vltra mare situata vel situatum de omnibus Theoloniis Custumis subsidiis Pontagiis Panagiis muragiis cariagiis fossagiis et aliis deueriis nobis et heredibus nostris in dicto Regno nostro Anglie quoquo modo soluendo seu faciendo sicut eedem Gentes et Communitates dictarum Insularum de Guernesey Serk et Aureney seu predecessores aut antecessores sui earundem Insularum sub obediencia aliquorum progenitorum nostrorum Regum Anglie existentum vmquam fuerunt. Et eciam quod dicte

---

[57] Taken from the inspeximus of this charter granted by Henry VII: Greffe.

Gentes et Communitates earundem Insularum de Guernesey Serk et Aure-
ney heredes et successores sui habeant et gaudeant omnia iura libertates et
franchesias sua infra easdem Insulas adeo libere et tam amplis modo et forma
sicut eedem gentes et Communitates siue predecessores aut antecessores sui
earundem Insularum sub obediencia aliquorum progenitorum nostrorum
Regum Anglie existentum vmquam habuerunt seu gauisi fuerunt absque fine
seu feodo pro premissis aut aliquo premissorum nobis in hanaperio nostro
soluendo seu faciendo. Eo quod expressa mencio de certitudine seu valore
annuo aut aliquo alio valore premissorum siue eorum alicuius aut de aliis
donis seu concessionibus per nos aut progenitores nostros eisdem gentibus et
Communitatibus ante hec tempora facta in presentibus minime facta existit.
Aut aliquo statuto actu siue ordinacione incontrarium editum non obstante.
In cuius rei testimonium has literas nostras fieri fecimus patentes. Teste me
ipso apud Westmonasterium vicesimo octauo die Januarii anno regni nostri
octauo.

~ ~ ~

Edward by the grace of God king of England and France and lord of Ireland to all to whom these present letters may come, greeting. Whereas our
most noble progenitor of glorious memory Richard the Second after the
Conquest, lately king of England and France and lord of Ireland, by his
Letters Patent given at Westminster on the eighth day of July in the eighteenth year of his reign in consideration of the good behaviour and great
loyalty which he always found in his liege and faithful peoples and communities of the islands of Guernsey, Sark and Alderney, of his special grace
granted for himself and his heirs, as far as in him lay, to these his same
peoples and communities that they themselves and their successors should
be for ever in all cities, market towns, and ports within the kingdom of
England free and quit of all tolls, duties, and customs of whatsoever kind in
such wise and in such manner as his own faithful lieges have continued in
his own aforesaid kingdom. Provided always that they his said people and
communities, their heirs and successors aforesaid should conduct themselves well and faithfully towards himself and his heirs for ever as is more
fully contained in those Letters. We considering more fully the continuous
loyalty of the said islands of Guernsey, Sark, and Alderney, the aforesaid
Letters and all and singular contained therein as regards the peoples and
communities of the same islands of Guernsey, Sark, and Alderney, do
accept approve and by these presents to these same people and community,
their heirs and successors, do ratify and confirm them. And, further, calling
to mind how valiantly, manfully and steadfastly the said peoples and com-

munities of the said islands of Guernsey, Sark, and Alderney have stood out for us and our progenitors and what great dangers and losses they have sustained for the safety of the said islands and for the recapture of our castle of Mont Orgueil, of our more abundant grace we have granted to the same people and community that they, their heirs and successors shall likewise be free and quit in all cities, boroughs, market towns, and other towns, ports, and places within our kingdom of England and within all our lands and islands lying or situated on this side or beyond the sea from all tolls, customs, subsidies, pontages, panages, murages, tallages, fossages, and other dues in whatever way to be discharged or made to us and our heirs in our said kingdom of England just as the same peoples and communities of the said islands of Guernsey, Sark, and Alderney, or their predecessors or ancestors of the same islands, living under the obedience of any of our progenitors the kings of England, have ever been. And further that the said peoples and communities, their heirs and successors, should have and enjoy all their rights, liberties, and franchises within the same islands as freely and in as full a manner and form as the same peoples and communities, or their predecessors and ancestors in the same islands living under the obedience of any of our progenitors the kings of England have ever had or enjoyed, without fine or fee in the premises or any of the premises to be paid or made to us in the hanaper; so far as express mention exists of the surety or annual value or any other value in the matter of the premises, or of any of them, or of other gifts or concessions by us or our progenitors to the same people and community, whether such mention has been made before these times or is expressly set forth in these presents, or any statute, act or ordinance published to the contrary, notwithstanding. In witness whereof we have caused these out Letters to be made Patent. Myself as witness at Westminster this twenty-eighth day of January in the eighth year of our reign.

Richard III

Commentary

Richard, duke of Gloucester, took the throne in the spring of 1483 in a move which dramatically reopened the dynastic conflict of the previous thirty years. Richard's impact on the islands was immediate.

Richard's first concern was the security of the Channel. The threat was real because of the presence there of Sir Edward Woodville, one of the kinsmen of Elizabeth Woodville, the late king's widow, with a fleet: one of those commissioned to arrest him was Edward Brampton, one of Edward IV's household men and since 1482 'captain' of Guernsey.[58] Then, after the initial Woodville threat was overcome, the exile in Duke Francis II's Brittany of Henry Tudor, emerging as the main opponent of the new king, meant Breton politics were a crucial concern for the king. Richard's immediate response in this case was in July 1483 to send Thomas Hutton, one of his clerks, to consider the issue of Breton piracy, the privileges of the Channel Islands in respect of their 'neutrality' in time of war, and the position of Woodville, and almost certainly Tudor, exiles in Brittany.[59]

In spite of this, Francis and his nobility supported Tudor's attempt to capitalise on the rebellion of Richard's erstwhile ally, the duke of Buckingham, in the autumn of 1483. But the rebellion failed, and Tudor made a somewhat forlorn attempt at a landing in the South West, before fleeing back across the Channel.[60] Richard turned his

---

[58] Cecil Roth, 'Perkin Warbeck and his Jewish Master', *Transactions of the Jewish Historical Society of England*, 9 (1918-20), 143-62; Rosemary Horrox, *Richard III: A Study in Service* (1989; corrected paperback edition, Cambridge University Press, 1991), pp. 102-3

[59] *Letters and Papers Illustrative of the Reigns of Richard III and Henry VII*, ed. James Gairdner (2 vols., Rolls Series, London: Longman, Green, Longman, and Roberts, 1861, 1863), i. 22; Ralph A. Griffiths and Roger S. Thomas, *The Making of the Tudor Dynasty* (Stroud: Alan Sutton, 1985; paperback edition 1993), p. 86; S. B. Chrimes, *Henry VII* (1972; corrected paperback edition, London: Eyre Methuen, 1977), p. 19; C. S. L. Davies, 'Richard III, Brittany and Henry Tudor', *Nottingham Mediaeval Studies*, 37 (1993), 110-26.

[60] Griffiths and Thomas, *Making of the Tudor Dynasty*, pp. 102-3; Chrimes, *Henry VII*, pp. 26-7; Horrox, *Richard III*, pp. 255-6; I. Arthurson and N. Kingwell, 'The Proclamation of Henry Tudor as King of England, 3 November 1483', *BIHR*, 63 (1990), 100-6.

naval forces towards a sustained assault on Breton interests, and, as this bore fruit, his diplomacy in the summer of 1484 shifted to an emphasis on the internal politics of Brittany, and especially to support for Pierre Landais, treasurer of Brittany and at that point in control of Duke Francis's government, who he hoped would hand over Tudor – only for the plan to be foiled by intelligence of the plan leaking, probably via Henry's mother Margaret Beaufort.[61]

It was in this period that Richard's confirmation of the islands' privileges occurred. In the December of 1483, Richard was reacting to the aftermath of Breton assistance for Henry Tudor. The islands were, of course, strategically crucial in the attempts to influence Brittany and retrieve Tudor. They acted as a forward listening post, a potential base from which to launch a kidnap.[62] The charter which Richard confirmed was that of 1465, however, and not that of 1469 – the more traditional and direct reassertion of the original grants of Richard II, without the more specific and extensive wording, and without the fulsome praises for the islanders' assistance in the recovery of Jersey and of Mont Orgueil. It was also, it should be noted, the charter which had been granted to the islands when his father-in-law, Richard Neville, had been undisputed lord, and not that which had been granted in connection with the recapture of Jersey and its grant to Anthony Woodville, an opponent whom Richard had recently executed in the most controversial of circumstances.

RICHARD III 1483[63]

Ricardus dei gracia Rex Anglie et ffrancie et Dominus hibernie omnibus ad quos presentes Litere peruenerint Salutem. Inspeximus Litteras Patentes Domini Edwardi nuper Regis Anglie quarti post conquestum fratris nostri factas in hec verba: Edwardus dei gracia Rex Anglie et ffrancie et Dominus

---

[61] Griffiths and Thomas, *Making of the Tudor Dynasty*, pp. 110-12; Chrimes, *Henry VII*, pp. 28-9; Charles Ross, *Richard III* (London: Eyre Methuen, 1991), pp. 196-9; Davies, 'Richard III, Brittany and Henry Tudor'.

[62] John Nesfield, trusted by Richard with the custody of Edward IV's queen, Elizabeth Woodville, had licence to visit Jersey in Dec. 1484, and in May 1485 Thomas Hutton returned: *British Library Harleian Manuscript 433*, ed. Rosemary Horrox and P. W. Hammond (4 vols., Upminster and Gloucester: Alan Sutton for the Richard III Society, 1979-83), ii. 178; *Foedera*, ed. Thomas Rymer (20 vols., London: A. & J. Churchill, 1704-35), xii. 269.

[63] Greffe.

Hibernie Omnibus ad quos presentes Litere peruenerint Salutem. Inspeximus literas patentes domini Ricardi nuper Regis Angliae Secundi post conquestum factas in hec verba. Ricardus dei gratia Rex Anglie et ffrancie et Dominus Hibernie Omnibus ad quos presentes litere peruenerint salutem. Inspeximus literas patentes quas Dominus Edwardus nuper Rex Anglie Auus noster fieri fecit in hec verba. Edwardus dei gratia Rex Anglie et ffrancie et Dominus Hibernie Omnibus ad quos presentes litere peruenerint salutem. Sciatis quod nos grata memoria recensentes quam constanter et magnanimiter dilecti et fideles nostri homines Insularum nostrarum de Gernesey Jereseye Serk et Aureneye in fidelitate nostra et progenitorum nostrorum Regum Anglie semper hactenus perstiterunt et quanta pro salvacione dictarum Insularum et nostrorum conservacione iurium et honoris ibidem sustinuerunt tam pericula corporum quam suarum dispendia facultatum et proinde volentes ipsos fauore prosequi gracioso concessimus pro nobis et heredibus nostris dictis hominibus Insularum predictarum quod ipsi heredes et successores sui omnia priuilegia libertates immunitates exempciones consuetudines in personis rebus monetis et aliis eis virtute concessionum Progenitorum nostrorum Regum Anglie vel alias legitime competencia habeant et teneant ac eis sine impedimento vel molestacione nostri heredum vel Ministrorum nostrorum quorumcumque plene gaudeant et vtantur prout ipsi et eorum antecessores habitatores dictarum Insularum eis vsi sunt racionabiliter et gauisi que iam eis in forma predicta generaliter confirmamus Volentes ea cum super hiis plene informati fuerimus prout iustum fuerit specialiter confirmare. In cuius rei testimonium has literas nostras fieri fecimus patentes Teste me ipso apud Turrim London' decimo die Julii anno regni nostri Anglie quintodecimo regni vero nostri ffrancie secundo. Nos autem concessiones confirmacionem priuilegia libertates immunitates exempciones et consuetudines predicta rata habentes et grata ea pro nobis et heredibus nostris quantum in nobis est acceptamus approbamus ratificamus et ea predictis hominibus Insularum huiusmodi heredibus et successoribus suis concedimus et confirmamus prout litere predicte plenius testantur et prout ipsi et eorum antecessores habitatores dictarum Insularum eis vsi sunt racionabiliter et gauisi. In cuius rei testimonium has literas nostras fieri fecimus patentes Teste me ipso apud Gloucestre decimo die Novembris Anno regni nostri secundo. Inspeximus eciam alias literas patentes predicti domini Ricardi nuper Regis Anglie secundi post conquestum similiter factas in hec verba. Ricardus dei gracia Rex Anglie et ffrancie et Dominus Hibernie Omnibus ad quos presentes litere peruenerint salutem. Sciatis quod nos considerantes bonum gestum et magnam fidelitatem quam in ligeis et fidelibus nostris gentibus et communitatibus Insularum nostrarum de Gerneseye Jerseye Serk et Aureneye indies inuenimus de gracia nostra speciali concessimus pro nobis et heredibus nostris quantum in nobis est eisdem gentibus et Communitatibus quod ipse ac heredes et successores sui imperpetuum sint libere et quiete in omnibus Ciuitatibus Villis mercatoriis et portubus infra regnum nostrum Anglie de omnimodis theoloniis exaccionibus et custumis taliter et eodem modo quo fideles ligei nostri in regno nostro predicto existunt. Ita tamen quod dicte gentes et Communitates nostre ac heredes et successores sui predicti bene et fideliter se gerant erga nos et dictos heredes nostros imperpetuum. In cujus rei testimonium has literas nostras fieri fecimus patentes Teste me ipso apud Westmonasterium vicesimo octavo die Julii anno regni nostri decimo octavo. Nos autem literas predictas ac omnia et singula in eis contenta rata habentes et grata ea pro nobis et heredibus nostris quantum in nobis est acceptamus et approbamus ac nunc hominibus Gentibus et Communitatibus Insularum de Gerneseye Jereseye Serk et Aureneye et successoribus suis ratificamus et confirmamus prout litere predicte rationabiliter testantur. In cuius rei testimonium has literas nostras fieri fecimus patentes. Teste me ipso Rege apud Westmonasterium vicesimo nono die Marcii. Nos autem Literas predictas ac omnia et singula in eis contenta rata habentes et grata ea pro nobis et heredibus nostris quantum in nobis est acceptamus et approbamus ac dilectis nobis et nunc hominibus gentibus et Communitatibus predictarum Insularum de Gerneseye Jereseye Serk et Aureneye heredibus et successoribus suis tenore presencium ratificamus et confirmamus prout litere predicte racionabiliter testantur. In cujus rei testimonium has literas nostras fieri fecimus patentes. Teste me ipso apud Westmonasterium quinto decimo die Decembris Anno regni nostri primo.

ELIOT

Per ipsum Regem et de data predicta auctoritate Parliamenti et pro viginti solidis solutis in hanaperio.

Examinata per Willielmum Morland Willielmum Kelet Clericos

~ ~ ~

Richard by the grace of God king of England and France and lord of Ireland to all to whom these present letters may come, greeting. We have inspected the letters patent of our lord Edward lately king of England our brother made in these words: Edward by the grace of God king of England and France and lord of Ireland to all to whom these present letters may come, greeting. We have inspected the Letters Patent of Lord Richard lately king of England, the second after the Conquest, made in these words: Richard by the grace of God king of England and France and lord of Ireland to all those to whom these presents shall come, greeting. We have inspected the Letters Patent which the Lord Edward lately king of England our ancestor caused to be made in these words. Edward, by the grace of God king of England and France and lord of Ireland, to all to whom these present letters shall come, greeting. Know ye that we recalling with grateful memory with what constancy and high spirit our beloved and faithful men of our islands of Guernsey, Jersey, Sark, and Alderney have always hitherto continued in their faithfulness to us and our progenitors kings of England and how great dangers to their bodies as well as costs to their property they have borne for the safety of the said islands and the conservation of our laws and honour therein, and in like manner desiring to follow after them with our gracious favour, we have granted for ourselves and our heirs to the said men of the aforesaid islands, that they themselves, their heirs and successors may have and hold all privileges, liberties, immunities, exemptions, and customs in respect of their persons, goods, moneys, and other matters by virtue of the grant of our progenitors Kings of England or otherwise lawfully by agreement, and, without impediment or molestation from us, our heirs or our officers whomsoever, may fully enjoy and use them according as they themselves and their predecessors, inhabitants of the said islands, have reasonably used and enjoyed them. Which things we do now confirm to them generally in the aforesaid form being willing after we have enquired into them to confirm them especially as may be just. In testimony whereof we have had these letters made patent, myself as witness, at the Tower of London the tenth day of July in the year of our reign in England the fifteenth, but of our reign in France the second. We, moreover, holding the concessions, confirmations, privileges, liberties, immunities, and customs to be reasonable and seasonable, accept, approve, and ratify them for us and our heirs, as far as in us lies, and concede and confirm them to the aforesaid men of the islands in the same manner to their heirs and successors as the aforesaid Letters more fully testify and as they and their predecessors inhabitants of the said Islands have reasonably used and enjoyed them. In witness whereof we have had these our Letters made Patent. Myself as witness at Gloucester the tenth day of November in the second year of our reign.

We have also inspected other letters patent of our aforesaid Lord Richard formerly king of England, the second after the Conquest, similarly made in these words.

Richard, by the grace of God king of England and France and lord of Ireland, to all to whom these present letters may come, greeting. Know ye that we in consideration of the good behaviour and the great loyalty which we have ever found in our liege and faithful peoples and communities of our islands of Guernsey, Jersey, Sark and Alderney, have of our special grace granted for ourselves and our heirs, as far as in us lies, to the said peoples and communities, that they, their heirs and successors shall for ever be free and quit from all tolls, duties, and customs of whatsoever kind in all our cities, market towns, and ports within our kingdom of England, in the same manner as our faithful liege people in our aforesaid kingdom are. Provided always, however, that our said peoples and communities, their heirs and successors aforesaid shall well and faithfully conduct themselves towards us and our heirs aforesaid for ever. In witness whereof we have caused these our Letters to be made patent. Witness myself at Westminster this twenty-eighth day of July in the eighteenth year of our reign.

We, moreover, holding the aforesaid letters, and all and singular contained therein, to be reasonable and seasonable, accept and approve them for us and our heirs, as far as in us lies, and now ratify and confirm them to the men, peoples, and communities of the islands of Guernsey, Jersey, Sark, and Alderney, and to their successors as the aforesaid Letters more fully testify. In witness whereof we have caused these our letters to be made patent. Witness myself at Westminster the twenty-ninth day of March in the fifth year of our reign. We, moreover, holding the aforesaid letters, and all and singular contained therein, to be reasonable and seasonable, accept and approve them for us and our heirs, as far as in us lies, and now ratify and confirm them to our beloved men, peoples, and communities of the aforesaid islands of Guernsey, Jersey, Sark, and Alderney, and to their successors as the aforesaid Letters reasonably testify. In witness whereof we have caused these our letters to be made patent. Witness myself at Westminster the 14th day of December in the first year of our reign.

ELIOT

By the king himself and according to the aforesaid authority of Parliament and for forty shillings paid into the hanaper.

Examined by William Morland William Kelet clerks

Henry VII

Commentary

Like Edward IV before him, Henry VII had a specific debt to repay in the islands when he became king of England. Henry's lengthy exile in Brittany had included at least one occasion when he may have been thankful for support given to him in the islands. Henry Tudor may have passed through the Channel Islands in 1471, as he escaped from Wales bound for a lengthy exile, as it turned out, in Brittany.[64] In 1483, he made an abortive attempt to land in the south west of England. There is a strong chance that on his return, across the Channel, he first found refuge in Jersey. His evident trust in Edmund Weston, Thomas St Martin and Clement le Hardy, appointed bailiff of Jersey not long after Bosworth, suggests a familiarity with these men which might have been gained during a visit there.[65] A later grant of office in Guernsey recalled St Martin and Weston's service to Henry at great personal cost.[66] It is possible that this referred to assistance given to Henry during his exile, and a later tradition tells of Clement le Hardy assisting Henry during that perilous return from England in November 1483. Perhaps Weston was also involved – le Hardy certainly seems later to have been one of the closest associates of Matthew Baker, a key supporter of Henry in the most difficult days of his time in Brittany and France.[67]

Henry trusted those who had aided him in his exile, and especially those whose Norman–French speech was familiar to him after his long years in Brittany and France. The circle of Henry's heir, Prince

---

[64] Griffiths and Thomas, *Making of the Tudor Dynasty*, p. 77; Chrimes, *Henry VII*, p. 17

[65] G. R. Balleine, *A Biographical Dictionary of Jersey* (London and New York: Staples Press, [1949]), pp. 398–401.

[66] *Materials for a History of the Reign of Henry VII. from Original Documents preserved in the Public Record Office*, ed. William Campbell (2 vols., RS 60, London: Longman & Co., 1873-5), i. 186 (28 Nov. 1485).

[67] Baker's appointment as captain in Jersey, 26 July 1488: *Materials for a History of the Reign of Henry VII.*, ii. 338-9; C. S. L. Davies, 'Richard III, Henry VII and the Island of Jersey', *The Ricardian*, 9 (1991-4), 334-42, at pp. 338, 340 (n. 8); cf. p. 337 on St Martin.

Arthur, was particularly influenced by the king's associates from the Channel Islands. The prince's premier usher was Thomas de St Martin; Edouard de Carteret was amongst the gentlemen carvers.[68] Jean Neele represents the clerical wing of this domination of the court in waiting. Born in Jersey, he had been educated in Paris before becoming treasurer to William Waynflete, bishop of Winchester. He was promoted by Henry VII to be Dean of the Chapel to Arthur, but he died in March 1498.[69]

Henry did, however, encounter some serious initial problems in the islands. Richard Harliston, since 1473 captain in chief of both Guernsey and Jersey, despite being initially confirmed by Henry in his role, rebelled, apparently looking for support to Margaret of Burgundy, sister of the Yorkist kings Edward IV and Richard III. Mont Orgueil held out for a period at the end of 1485 and in the early part of the following year. Eventually it fell,[70] however, and in the wake of this fall, the relationship of the islands to each other was further changed.

We have previously seen how in 1469, at least in part due to the recent occupation of Jersey and the chronic divisions within the regime of Edward IV, the two bailiwicks for the first time received separate charters of privileges. Since 1478, the islands had had different captains, although Richard Harliston retained the overall title of captain in chief. Now, with Harliston's fall, Henry allowed the position of the islands' separation to continue, in the shape of different captains.

Henry's choice of which charters to confirm is therefore doubly significant. Like Edward IV and Richard III before him, Henry made a point about his predecessors when he confirmed the charters. For he confirmed Edward IV's charters, ignoring Richard III's confirmation – and also thereby writing out of the story the Lancastrian kings. In Guernsey, as in so many other contexts, Henry was Edward IV's successor far more than he was a Lancastrian revivalist. But also, by choosing to confirm the most recently issued charters of Edward

---

[68] St Martin: *Materials for a History of the Reign of Henry VII.*, ii. 45 (already a gentleman usher of the chamber in 1486), 80, 141.
[69] *BRUO*, pp. 1340-1; Balleine, *Biographical Dictionary*, pp. 512-13; J. de la Croix, *Jersey: ses antiquités, ses institutions, son histoire* (3 vols., Jersey: C. Le Feuvre, 1859-61), iii. 174-5.
[70] Davies, 'Richard III, Henry VII and the Island of Jersey', pp. 336-7.

IV, rather than those of 1465, he ensured that the incipient separation of the bailiwicks was confirmed and reinforced.

In February 1486, when the charters were sealed, Mont Orgueil probably remained in the hands of Henry's opponents: there is therefore something of an irony to the charters' recitation of the sentiments of Edward IV's reign, which celebrate the contribution of the islanders to the recovery of the castle. But it was also a powerful incentive towards a policy which might be characterised as divide and rule: the Channel Islands were too important, especially given Henry's concerns with the duchy of Brittany and the fate of its heir Anne, to be allowed to be at the whim of one all-powerful political force.[71]

HENRY VII 1485[72]

Henricus dei gracia Rex Anglie et Francie et Dominus Hibernie Omnibus ad quos presentes litere peruenerint Salutem. Inspeximus literas patentes domini Edwardi nuper Regis Anglie quarti factas in hec verba: Edwardus dei gratia Rex Anglie et ffrancie et Dominus Hibernie Omnibus ad quos presentes litere peruenerint Salutem. Cum nobilissimus progenitor noster inclite memorie Ricardus quondam Rex Anglie et ffrancie et Dominus Hibernie post conquestum Secundus per literas suas patentes datas apud Westmonasterium octauo die Julii Anno regni sui decimo octauo in consideracione boni gestus et magne fidelitatis quos in ligeis et fidelibus suis gentibus et Communitatibus Insularum suarum de Guernesey Serk et Aureney indies inuenit de gracia sua speciali concessit pro se et heredibus suis quantum in eo fuit eisdem gentibus et Communitatibus suis quod ipsi et successores sui imperpetuum forent liberi et quieti in omnibus Ciuitatibus Villis mercatoriis et portubus infra Regnum Anglie de omnimodis Theoloniis exaccionibus et Custumis taliter et in eodem modo quo fideles ligei sui in Regno suo predicto extiterunt. Ita tamen quod dicte gentes et Communitates sue ac heredes et successores sui predicti bene et fideliter se gererent erga ipsum progenitorem nostrum et heredes suos imperpetuum prout in literis illis plenius continetur. Nos continuam fidelitatem gencium et Communitatum dictarum Insularum de Guernesey Serk et Aureney plenius intendentes litteras predictas et omnia et

---

[71] John M. Currin, 'Henry VII and the Treaty of Redon (1489): Plantagenet Ambitions and Early Tudor Foreign Policy', *History*, 81 (1996), 343-58

[72] Greffe.

singula in eis contenta quo ad gentes et Communitates earundem Insularum de Guernesey Serk et Aureney acceptamus approbamus et eisdem gentibus et Communitatibus heredibus et successoribus suis per presentes ratificamus et confirmamus. Et ulterius nos memorie Reducentes quam valide viriliter et constanter dicte gentes et Communitates earundem Insularum de Guernesey Serk et Aureney nobis et progenitoribus nostris prestiterunt et quanta et pericula et perdita pro saluacione earundem Insularum et reduccione Castri nostri de Mount Orgill sustinuerunt de uberiori gracia nostra concessimus eisdem gentibus et Communitatibus quod ipse heredes et successores sui sint ita liberi et quieti in omnibus Ciuitatibus Burgis Villis Mercatoriis et aliis Villis portubus et locis infra Regnum nostrum Anglie et infra omnes terras et Insulas nostras citra vel vltra mare situata vel situatum de omnibus Theoloniis Custumis subsidiis Pontagiis Panagiis muragiis cariagiis fossagiis et aliis deueriis nobis et heredibus nostris in dicto Regno nostro Anglie quoquo modo soluendo seu faciendo sicut eedem Gentes et Communitates dictarum Insularum de Guernesey Serk et Aureney seu predecessores aut antecessores sui earundem Insularum sub obediencia aliquorum progenitorum nostrorum Regum Anglie existentum vmquam fuerunt. Et eciam quod dicte Gentes et Communitates earundem Insularum de Guernesey Serk et Aureney heredes et successores sui habeant et gaudeant omnia iura libertates et franchesias sua infra easdem Insulas adeo libere et tam amplis modo et forma sicut eedem gentes et Communitates siue predecessores aut antecessores sui earundem Insularum sub obediencia aliquorum progenitorum nostrorum Regum Anglie existentum vmquam habuerunt seu gauisi fuerunt absque fine seu feodo pro premissis aut aliquo premissorum nobis in hanaperio nostro soluendo seu faciendo. Eo quod expressa mencio de certitudine seu valore annuo aut aliquo alio valore premissorum siue eorum alicuius aut de aliis donis seu concessionibus per nos aut progenitores nostros eisdem gentibus et Communitatibus ante hec tempora facta in presentibus minime facta existit. Aut aliquo statuto actu siue ordinacione incontrarium editum non obstante. In cuius rei testimonium has literas nostras fieri fecimus patentes. Teste me ipso apud Westmonasterium vicesimo octauo die Januarii anno regni nostri octauo. Nos autem litteras predictas ac omnia et singula in eisdem contenta Rata habentes et grata ea pro nobis et heredibus nostris quantum in nobis est acceptamus approbamus et prefatis gentibus et Communitatibus Insularum de Guernesey Serk et Aureney predictarum heredibus et successoribus suis tenore presencium ratificamus concedimus et confirmamus prout littere predicte in se racionabiliter testantur

In cuius rei testimonium has litteras nostras fieri fecimus patentes. Teste me ipso apud Westmonasterium decimo die ffebruarii Anno regni nostri primo.
HANNYNGTON

Per ipsum Regem et de data predicta auctoritate parliamenti et pro quad-raginta solidis solutis in Hanaperio.

Examinata per William Morland Ricardum Skypton clericos

~ ~ ~

Henry by the grace of God king of England and France and lord of Ireland, to all those to whom these present letters may come, greeting: we have inspected the Letters Patent of the Lord Edward the Fourth, lately king of England, made in these words: Edward by the grace of God king of England and France and lord of Ireland to all to whom these present letters may come, greeting. Whereas our most noble progenitor of glorious memory Richard the Second after the Conquest, lately king of England and France and lord of Ireland, by his Letters Patent given at Westminster on the eighth day of July in the eighteenth year of his reign in consideration of the good behaviour and great loyalty which he always found in his liege and faithful peoples and communities of the islands of Guernsey, Sark and Alderney, of his special grace granted for himself and his heirs, as far as in him lay, to these his same peoples and communities that they themselves and their successors should be for ever in all cities, market towns, and ports within the kingdom of England free and quit of all tolls, duties, and customs of whatsoever kind in such wise and in such manner as his own faithful lieges have continued in his own aforesaid kingdom. Provided always that they his said people and communities, their heirs and successors aforesaid should conduct themselves well and faithfully towards himself and his heirs for ever as is more fully contained in those Letters. We considering more fully the continuous loyalty of the said islands of Guernsey, Sark, and Alderney, the aforesaid Letters and all and singular contained therein as regards the peoples and communities of the same islands of Guernsey, Sark, and Alderney, do accept approve and by these presents to these same people and community, their heirs and successors, do ratify and confirm them. And, further, calling to mind how valiantly, manfully and steadfastly the said peoples and communities of the said islands of Guernsey, Sark, and Alderney have stood out for us and our progenitors and what great dangers and losses they have sustained for the safety of the said islands and for the recapture of our castle of Mont Orgueil, of our more abundant grace we have granted to the same people and community that they, their heirs and successors shall likewise be free and quit in all cities, boroughs, market towns, and other towns, ports, and places within our kingdom of England and within all our lands and islands lying or situated on this side or beyond the sea from all tolls, customs, subsidies, pontages, panages, murages, tallages, fossages, and other dues in whatever way to be discharged or made to us and our heirs in our said kingdom of England just as the same peoples and communities of the said islands of Guernsey, Sark, and Alderney, or their predecessors or ancestors of the same islands, living under the obedience of any of our progenitors the kings of England, have ever been. And further that the said peoples and communities, their heirs and successors, should have and enjoy all their rights, liberties, and franchises within the same islands as freely and in as full a manner and form as the same peoples and communities, or their predecessors and ancestors in the same islands living under the obedience of any of our progenitors the kings of England have ever had or enjoyed, without fine or fee in the premises or any of the premises to be paid or made to us in the hanaper; so far as express mention exists of the surety or annual value or any other value in the matter of the premises, or of any of them, or of other gifts or concessions by us or our progenitors to the same people and community, whether such mention has been made before these times or is expressly set forth in these presents, or any statute, act or ordinance published to the contrary, notwithstanding. In witness whereof we have caused these out Letters to be made Patent. Myself as witness at Westminster this twenty-eighth day of January in the eighth year of our reign.

We, moreover, holding the aforesaid letters, and all and singular contained therein, to be reasonable and seasonable, accept and approve them for us and our heirs, as far as in us lies, and now ratify and confirm them to the aforesaid peoples and communities of the islands of Guernsey, Sark, and Alderney, and to their heirs and successors, in the tenor of the present letters, as the aforesaid letters reasonably testify. In witness whereof we have caused these our letters to be made patent. Witness myself at Westminster this tenth day of February in the first year of our reign.

HANNYNGTON

By the king himself, and the aforesaid authority of parliament and for forty shillings paid into the hanaper

Examined by William Morland and Richard Skypton clerks

Henry VIII

Commentary

The accession of Henry VIII, though not without its tensions, was the smoothest the English crown had experienced for some years. It was smooth too in the Channel Islands, with the influence of the Weston family, founded in the early days of Tudor power, confirmed and indeed flourishing.

Sir Richard Weston was the son of Edmund Weston, who had gone to the islands in the company of Richard Harliston. [73] Edmund was the son of Peter Weston, of Boston (Lincolnshire), so the association with Harliston (from Humberstone in the same county) was probably at least in part a geographical one. Edmund married the widow of Renaud Lempriere, Catherine, the daughter of John Camel of Shapwick in Dorset. Their eldest son, the Richard in question here, was born at Rosel (Jersey) in 1469. Richard's success was made through Henry VII's favour for his followers from the Channel Islands. Within a few months of Bosworth, Edmund, first jointly and then alone, was made governor of Guernsey and appeared as an esquire for the body. [74] Richard appeared at court in 1502, winning at chess and the dice against the king. About this time he married one of the queen's gentlewomen, Anne, daughter of Oliver Sandys of Shere. Richard Weston demonstrated that the fate of others from Guernsey and Jersey, obscurity on the death of Arthur, was not inevitable. Before Henry VIII's coronation he had already succeeded his father as governor of Guernsey. [75] His eminence in the king's service is demonstrated by the offices he held – lieutenant of the forest and castle of Windsor (1508) and knight of the body (1518).

---

[73] General biographies can be found in S. T. Bindoff, *The House of Commons, 1509-1558* (3 vols., London: Secker & Warburg for the History of Parliament Trust, 1982), iii. 590-2; Balleine, *Biographical Dictionary*, pp. 612-14.

[74] *Materials for a History of the Reign of Henry VII.*, I, 186 (28 Nov. 1485; with Thomas de St Martin), 372-3 (8 Mar. 1486).

[75] *LP*, i. 54(71).

In these conditions, it is unsurprising that the new king confirmed the charter of his father, and did so before the end of his first year on the throne.

HENRY VIII 1510[76]

Henricus dei gratia Rex Anglie et Francie et Dominus Hibernie Omnibus ad quos presentes litere pervenerint Salutem. Inspeximus literas patentes domini Henrici nuper Regis Anglie septimi factas in hec verba: Henricus dei gratia Rex Anglie et Francie et Dominus Hibernie Omnibus ad quos presentes litere pervenerint Salutem. Inspeximus literas patentes domini Edwardi nuper Regis Anglie quarti factas in hec verba: Edwardus Dei gratia Rex Anglie et ffrancie et Dominus Hibernie Omnibus ad quos presentes litere pervenerint Salutem. Cum nobilissimus progenitor noster inclite memorie Ricardus quondam Rex Anglie et Francie et Dominus Hibernie post conquestum secundus per literas suas patentes datas apud Westmonasterium octavo die Julii Anno regni sui decimo octavo in consideracione boni gestus et magne fidelitatis quos in ligeis et fidelibus suis gentibus et Communitatibus Insularum suarum de Guernesey Serk et Aureney indies invenit de gracia sua speciali concessit pro se et heredibus suis quantum in eo fuit eisdem gentibus et Communitatibus suis quod ipsi et successores sui imperpetuum forent liberi et quieti in omnibus Civitatibus villis mercatoriis et portubus infra Regnum Anglie de omnimodo Theoloniis exaccionibus et Custumis taliter et eodem modo quo fideles ligei sui in Regno suo predicto extiterunt. Ita tamen quod dicte gentes et Communitates sue ac heredes et successores sui predicti bene et fideliter se gererent erga ipsum progenitorem nostrum et heredes suos imperpetuum prout in literis illis plenius continetur. Nos continuam fidelitatem gencium et Communitatum dictarum Insularum de Guernesey Serk et Aureney plenius intendentes literas predictas de omnia et singula in eis contenta quo ad gentes et Communitates earundem Insularum de Guernesey Serk et Aureney acceptamus approbamus et eisdem gentibus et Comunitatibus heredibus et successoribus suis per presentes ratificamus et confirmamus. Et ulterius nos memorie Reducentes quam valide viriliter et constanter dicte gentes et Communitates earundem Insularum de Guernesey Serk et Aureney nobis et progenitoribus nostris perstiterunt et quanta pericula et perdita pro salvacione earundem Insularum et reductione Castri nostri de Mount Orgill sustinu-

---

[76] Greffe.

erunt de uberiori gracia nostra concessimus eisdem gentibus et Communita-
tibus quod ipse heredes et successores sui sint liberi et quieti in omnibus
Civitatibus Burgis Villis Mercatoriis et aliis Villis portubus et locis infra
regnum nostrum Anglie et infra omnes terras et insulas nostras citra vel ultra
mare sint vel situatum de omnibus Theolonliis Custumis subsidiis pontagiis
panagiis muragiis cariagiis fossagiis et aliis deueris nobis et heredibus nostris
in dicto regno nostro Anglie quoquomodo solvendo seu faciendo sicut eedem
gentes et Communitates dictarum Insularum de Guernesey Serk et Aureney
seu predecessores ant antecessores sui earundem Insularum sub obediencia
aliquorum progenitorum nostrorum Regum Anglie existentum umquam
fuerunt. Et eciam quod dicte gentes et Communitates earundem Insularum de
Guernesey Serk et Aureney heredes et successores sui habeant et gaudeant
omnia jura libertates et franchesias sua infra easdem Insulas adeo libere et
tam amplis modo et forma sicut eedem gentes et communitates sive predeces-
sores aut antecessores sui earundem Insularum sub obediencia aliquorum
progenitorum nostrorum Regum Anglie existentum unquam habuerunt seu
gavisi fuerunt absque fine seu feodo per premissis ant aliquo premissorum
nobis in Hanaperio nostro solvendo seu faciendo. Eo quod expressa mencio de
certitudine seu valore annuo aut aliquo alio valore premissorum sive eorum
alicujus aut de aliquis donis seu concessionibus per nos aut progenitores
nostros eisdem gentibus et Communitatibus ante hec tempora facta in presen-
tibus minime facta existit. Aut aliquo statuto actu sive ordinacione
incontrarium editum non obstante. In cujus rei testimonium has literas nostras
fieri fecimus patentes. Teste me ipso apud Westmonasterium vicesimo octavo
die Januarii anno regni nostri octavo. Nos autem literas predictas ac omnia et
singula in eisdem contenta rata habentes et grata ea pro nobis et heredibus
nostris quantum in nobis est acceptamus approbamus et prefatis gentibus et
Communitatibus Insularum de Guernesey Serk et Aureney predictarum
heredibus et successoribus suis tenore presencium ratificamus concedimus et
confirmamus prout litere predicte in se racionabiliter testantur In cujus rei
testimonium has literas nostras fieri fecimus patentes. Teste me ipso apud
Westmonasterium decimo die Februarii anno regni nostri primo.

Nos autem literas predictas ac omnia et singula in eisdem contenta rata
habentes et grata ea pro nobis et heredibus nostris quantum in nobis est
acceptamus approbamus et prefatis gentibus et Communitatibus Iusularum de
Guernesey Serk et Aureney predictarum heredibus et successoribus suis tenore
presencium ratificamus concedimus et confirmamus prout litere predicte in se

racionabiliter testantur In cujus rei testimonium has literas nostras fieri fecimus patentes. Teste me ipso apud Westmonasterium quinto die Martii anno regni nostri primo.

   HANNYNGTON

Per ipsum Regem et de data predicta auctoritate parliamenti et pro quadraginta solidis solutis in Hanaperio.

Examinata per William Morland Francis Skipton clericos

~ ~ ~

Henry by the grace of God king of England and France and lord of Ireland: to all to whom these presents may come, greeting. We have inspected the Letters Patent of the Lord Henry the Seventh, lately king of England, made in these words: Henry by the grace of God king of England and France and lord of Ireland, to all those to whom these present letters may come, greeting. We have inspected the Letters Patent of the Lord Edward the Fourth, lately king of England, made in these words. Edward by the grace of God king of England and France and lord of Ireland to all to whom these present letters may come, greeting. Whereas our most noble progenitor of glorious memory Richard the Second after the Conquest, lately king of England and France and lord of Ireland, by his Letters Patent given at Westminster on the eighth day of July in the eighteenth year of his reign in consideration of the good behaviour and great loyalty which he always found in his liege and faithful peoples and communities of the islands of Guernsey, Sark and Alderney, of his special grace granted for himself and his heirs, as far as in him lay, to these his same peoples and communities that they themselves and their successors should be for ever in all cities, market towns, and ports within the kingdom of England free and quit of all tolls, duties, and customs of whatsoever kind in such wise and in such manner as his own faithful lieges have continued in his own aforesaid kingdom. Provided always that they his said people and communities, their heirs and successors aforesaid should conduct themselves well and faithfully towards himself and his heirs for ever as is more fully contained in those Letters. We considering more fully the continuous loyalty of the said islands of Guernsey, Sark, and Alderney, the aforesaid Letters and all and singular contained therein as regards the peoples and communities of the same islands of Guernsey, Sark, and Alderney, do accept approve and by these presents to these same people and community, their heirs and successors, do ratify and confirm them. And, further, calling to mind how valiantly, manfully and steadfastly the said peoples and communities of the said islands of Guernsey, Sark, and Alderney have stood out for us and our progenitors and what great dangers and losses they have sustained for the safety of the said islands and for the recapture of our castle of Mont Orgueil, of our more abundant grace we have granted to the same people and community that they, their heirs and successors shall likewise be free and quit in all cities, boroughs, market towns, and other towns, ports, and places within our kingdom of England and within all our lands and islands lying or situated on this side or beyond the sea from all tolls, customs, subsidies, pontages, panages, murages, tallages, fossages, and other dues in whatever way to be discharged or made to us and our heirs in our said kingdom of England just as the same peoples and communities of the said islands of Guernsey, Sark, and Alderney, or their predecessors or ancestors of the same islands, living under the obedience of any of our progenitors the kings of England, have ever been. And further that the said peoples and communities, their heirs and successors, should have and enjoy all their rights, liberties, and franchises within the same islands as freely and in as full a manner and form as the same peoples and communities, or their predecessors and ancestors in the same islands living under the obedience of any of our progenitors the kings of England have ever had or enjoyed, without fine or fee in the premises or any of the premises to be paid or made to us in the hanaper; so far as express mention exists of the surety or annual value or any other value in the matter of the premises, or of any of them, or of other gifts or concessions by us or our progenitors to the same people and community, whether such mention has been made before these times or is expressly set forth in these presents, or any statute, act or ordinance published to the contrary, notwithstanding. In witness whereof we have caused these out Letters to be made Patent. Myself as witness at Westminster this twenty-eighth day of January in the eighth year of our reign.

We, moreover, holding the aforesaid letters, and all and singular contained therein, to be reasonable and seasonable, accept and approve them for us and our heirs, as far as in us lies, and now ratify and confirm them to the aforesaid peoples and communities of the islands of Guernsey, Sark, and Alderney, and to their heirs and successors, in the tenor of the present letters, as the aforesaid letters reasonably testify. In witness whereof we have caused these our letters to be made patent. Witness myself at Westminster this tenth day of February in the first year of our reign.

We, moreover, holding the aforesaid letters, and all and singular contained therein, to be reasonable and seasonable, accept and approve them for us and our heirs, as far as in us lies, and now ratify, grant and confirm them to the aforesaid peoples and communities of the islands of Guernsey, Sark, and Alderney, and to their heirs and successors, in the tenor of the present letters, as the aforesaid letters reasonably testify. In witness whereof we have caused these our letters to be made patent. Witness myself at Westminster this fifth day of March in the first year of our reign.

HANNYNGTON

By the king himself, and the aforesaid authority of parliament and for forty shillings paid into the hanaper

Examined by William Morland and Francis Skypton clerks

Edward VI

Commentary

Edward VI's confirmation of the islands' privileges came on 6 March 1548. In many of its features it simply confirmed earlier documents, and this we will consider first. But then there are two major changes in the pattern of the document, when compared to earlier charters, which merit subsequent discussion.

The confirmation of earlier documents in the charter took the form of a confirmation of Henry VIII's confirmation of his father's confirmation of the Edward IV charter of 1469 which summarised the grants of Richard II. The specific charters to which it referred were actually those for Jersey, but in its summarising and confirming clauses Edward VI's charter reintegrates the bailiwicks, referring to the privileges both of Jersey, and of Guernsey, Sark and Alderney.

Why this reintegration might have occurred, after nearly eighty years of separation, is suggested by the first element in the document to depart distinctly from the contents of its predecessors. This is a mention of Edward Seymour, duke of Somerset, the king's uncle and Protector of the realm. He is mentioned as the man on whose advice the king was making the grant. Seymour's interest in the islands went beyond his general responsibilities as Protector, and predated the accession of his nephew. His connection with the islands had begun back in July 1536, and he appears to have paid more than average attention to them. Specifically, for the first time since the 1480s, one man had achieved a dominant position over both islands, and this meant a return to grants of privileges for both bailiwicks.[77]

The second is the mention of a custom charged against the merchants of Jersey. This was apparently at the rate of 3 $s.$ 6 $d.$, in the

---

[77] *LP*, ix. 202(22), 385(16). See, for example, his invitation to send representatives to parliament: *Actes des Etats de l'Ile de Jersey 1524-1596* (St. Helier: 12e publication de la Société Jersiaise, 1897), pp. 9-10; A. J. Eagleston, *The Channel Islands under Tudor Government, 1485-1642: A Study in Administrative History* (Cambridge: published for the Guernsey Society at the University Press, 1949), p. 34.

islands' currency, per quarter of grain – and was now to be held at one shilling only. A custom on wool was to be levied at no more than 3 *s.* 6 *d.* per 150 pounds of wool.

The third is a reassertion of the privilege of the islands in terms of their neutrality in any conflict, and their right to continue trading with all parties, whether friends or enemies of the king of England. This had of course been set down in a papal bull in the 1480s; the break with Rome had resulted in a question mark hanging over the islands' status, but Henry VIII had resolved this with a charter confirming the terms of the bull.[78] Edward's regime, however, adamant in its rejection of any papal pretensions, chose to restate the privilege, but without the slightest acknowledgement of any part of the papal contribution to its development.

This was the charter, then, of island communities which retained so many of the distinctive features of the previous two centuries: trading vigorously, often at the heart of conflict. Somerset's regime had, indeed, reaffirmed the highly aggressive foreign policy of the last years of Henry VIII's reign, and tension with France was not to be ended until the treaty of late March 1550.[79] The threat to the islands was evidently appreciated by the regime early in 1548, for the Privy Council warranted the delivery of ordnance to Helier Carteret for the defence of Jersey in the February of the year.[80] The charter suggests, however, a new ingredient: the rejection of Rome and the emergence of Protestantism in the islands, which at the time had made little impact there, but was to be a potent factor in years to come.

EDWARD VI 1549[81]

Rex Omnibus ad quos &c. Salutem Inspeximus literas patentes domini Henrici nuper Regis Anglie octavi patris nostri precharissimi de confirmacione factas in hec verba Henricus Dei gracia Rex Anglie et Francie et Dominus Hibernie Omnibus ad quos presentes litere pervenerint salutem. Inspeximus

---

[78] A copy is to be found in the Greffe: 1 May 1510.

[79] Michael L. Bush, *The Government Policy of Protector Somerset* (London: Edward Arnold, 1975), pp. 6–39, esp. pp. 9–10; Jennifer Loach, *Edward VI* (New Haven and London: Yale University Press, 1999), p. 107.

[80] *APC 1547-50*, p. 171.

[81] Prison Board.

literas patentes domini Henrici nuper Regis Anglie patris nostri de confirma-
cione factas in hec verba Henricus Dei gracia Rex Anglie et Francie et
Dominus Hibernie Omnibus ad quos presentes litere pervenerint salutem.
Inspeximus literas patentes domini Edwardi nuper Regis Anglie quarti factas
in hec verba Edwardus Dei gracia Rex Anglie et Francie et Dominus Hi-
bernie Omnibus ad quos presentes litere pervenerint salutem Cum
nobilissimus progenitor noster inclite memorie Ricardus quondam Rex Anglie
et Francie et Dominus Hibernie post conquestum secundus per literas suas
patentes datas apud Westmonasterium octavo die Julii anno regni sui decimo
octavo in consideracione boni gestus et magne fidelitatis quos in ligeis et
fidelibus suis gentibus et communitatibus Insularum de Jersey Guernesey
Scerke et Aureney indies invenit de gracia sua concessit pro se et heredibus
suis quantum in eo fuit eisdem gentibus et communitatibus suis quod ipsi
successores sui imperpetuum forent liberi et quieti in omnibus Civitatibus
villis mercatoriis et portubus infra Regnum Anglie de omnimodis theoloniis
exaccionibus et custumis taliter et in eodem modo quo fideles ligei sui in
Regno suo predicto extiterunt Ita semper quod dicti gentes et communitates
sue ac heredes et successores sui predicti bene et fideliter se gererent erga ipsum
progenitorem nostrum et heredes suos imperpetuum prout in literis illis
plenius continetur Nos continuam fidelitatem gentis et communitatis dicte
Insule de Jersey plenius intendentes literas predictas ac omnia et singula in eis
contenta quoad gentem et communitatem ejusdem Insule de Jersey acceptamus
approbamus et eisdem gentibus et communitati heredibus et successoribus suis
per presentes ratificamus et confirmamus. Et ulterius nos memorie reducentes
quam valide viriliter et constanter dicta gens et communitas ejusdem Insule de
Jersey nobis et progenitoribus nostris perstiterunt et quanta pericula et perdita
pro salvacione ejusdem Insule et reduccione Castri nostri de Mount Orgyll
sustinuerunt de uberiori gracia nostra concessimus eisdem gentibus et commu-
nitati quod ipsi heredes et successores sui sint ita liberi et quieti in omnibus
Civitatibus Burgis villis mercatoriis et aliis villis portubus et locis infra
Regnum nostrum Anglie et infra omnes terras et Insulas nostras citra vel ultra
mare sitas vel situatas de omnibus theoloniis custumis subsidiis pontagiis
pannagiis muragiis cariagiis fossagiis et aliis deveriis nobis et heredibus nostris
in dicto Regno nostro Anglie quoquo modo solvendis seu faciendis sicut
eedem gens et communitas dicte Insule de Jersey seu predecessores aut antecess-
sores sui ejusdem Insule sub obediencia aliquorum progenitorum nostrorum
Regum Anglie existentes unquam fuerunt Et eciam quod dicta gens et
communitas ejusdem Insule de Jersey heredes et successores sui habeant et

munitas ejusdem Insule de Jersey heredes et successores sui habeant et gaudeant omnia jura libertates et franchesias sua infra eandem Insulam adeo libere ac in tam amplis modo et forma sicut eedem gens et communitas sive predecessores aut antecessores sui ejusdem Insule sub obediencia aliquorum progenitorum nostrorum Regum Anglie existentium unquam habuerunt seu gavisi fuerunt absque fine seu feodo pro premissis aut aliquo premissorum nobis in hanaperio nostro solvendo seu faciendo Eo quod expressa mencio de certitudine seu valore annuo aut de aliquo alio valore premissorum vel eorum alicujus Aut de aliis donis sive concessionibus pro nos aut progenitores nostros eisdem gentibus et comunitati ante hec tempora factis in presentibus minime factis existit aut aliquo statuto actu sive ordinacione in contrarium edita non obstantibus. In cujus rei testimonium has literas nostras fieri fecimus patentes. Teste me ipso apud Westmonasterium vicesimo die Januarii Anno regni nostri octavo. Nos autem literas predictas ac omnia et singula in eisdem contenta rata habentes et grata ea pro nobis et heredibus nostris quantum in nobis est acceptamus et approbamus et prefatis gentibus et communitati Insule de Jersey predicte heredibus et successoribus suis tenore presencium ratificamus concedimus et confirmamus prout litere predicte in se racionabiliter testantur. In cujus rei testimonium has literas nostras fieri fecimus patentes. Teste me ipso apud Westmonasterium decimo die Februarij Anno regni nostri primo. Nos autem literas predictas ac omnia et singula in eisdem contenta rata habentes et grata ea pro nobis et heredibus nostris quantum in nobis est acceptamus et approbamus et prefatis gentibus et communitati Insule de Jersey predicte heredibus et successoribus suis tenore presencium ratificamus concedimus et confirmamus prout litere predicte in se racionabiliter testantur. In cujus rei testimonium has literas nostras fieri fecimus patentes. Teste me apud Westmonasterium vicesimo sexto die Februarii Anno regni nostri primo. Nos autem literas predictas ac omnia et singula in eisdem contenta rata habentes et grata ea pro nobis et heredibus nostris quantum in nobis est acceptamus et approbamus ac ea tam prefatis gentibus et communitati Insule de Jersey quam prefatis gentibus et communitatibus Insularum de Guernesey Serke et Aureney heredibus et successoribus suis tenore presencium ratificamus concedimus et confirmamus prout litere predicte in se racionabiliter testantur

[2] Et insuper nos volentes cum gentibus et communitatibus Insularum graciam facere ampliorem ac memorie reducentes quam valide viriliter et constanter dicti gentes et communitates earundem Insularum nobis et progenitoribus nostris perstiterunt et quanta pericula et perdita pro salvacione

60

earundem Insularum et reduccione et defensione Castri nostri de Mount Orgyll sustinuerunt de gracia nostra speciali ac ex certa sciencia et mero motu nostris de avisamento et consensu precharissimi Avunculi nostri Edwardi Ducis Somerset persone nostre gubernatoris ac Regnorum Dominiorum et Subditorum nostrorum protectoris ceterorumque Consiliariorum nostrorum concessimus ac per presentes concedimus prefatis gentibus et communitatibus Insularum predictarum et earum cuiuslibet quod ipsi heredes et successores sui ita libere et quiete in omnibus Civitatibus Burgis villis mercetis mercatoriis et aliis villis portubus infra Regnum nostrum Anglie ac infra omnes terras et Insulas nostras citra vel vltra mare sitas vel situatas de omnibus theoloniis custumis subsidiis pontagiis pannagiis muragiis cariagiis fossagiis et aliis deueriis nobis et heredibus nostris in dicto Regno nostro Anglie quoquo modo solvendis vel faciendis sicut eedem gentes et communitates dictarum Insularum seu predecessores aut antecessores sui sub obediencia aliquorum progenitorum nostrorum Regum Anglie existentium vnqam fuerunt.

[3] Et eciam quod dicte gentes et communitates earundem Insularum heredes et successores sui habeant et gaudeant omnia jura libertates et franchesias sua infra easdem Insulas et earum quamlibet adeo libere et in tam amplis modo et forma prout eedem gentes et communitates sive predecessores aut antecessores sui sub obediencia aliquorum progenitorem nostrorum Regum Anglie existentem unquam habuerunt et gavisi fuerunt

[4] Ac insuper cum datum est nobis intelligi quod quedam exaccio nuper levato fuerit de inhabitantibus et gentibus Insule nostre de Jersey et de mercatoribus et aliis illuc confluentibus contra antiquam extentam et consuetudinem ibidem usitatam videlicet per quolibet quarterio frumenti vel alterius grani extra Insulam illam exportato tres solidos et sex denarios monete currentis infra eandem Insulam ubi illa extenta antehac ad tantam summam se non extendebat ut accepimus Et cum dicti Inhabitantes et gentes Insule de Jersey predicte soliti fuerint similiter solvere ad usum nostrum per quibuslibet Centum et quinquaginta libris lane extra Insulam illam exportatis juxta extentam ibidem usitatam quatuor denarios monete currentis infra eandem Insulam Nos de avisamento et consensu predicto volumus ac per presentes concedimus pro nobis et heredibus nostris prefatis Inhabitantibus et gentibus Insule nostre de Jersey predicte quod ipsi et omnes alii mercatores illuc confluentes non plus nec majorem summam exnunc deinceps imperpetuum solvere teneantur ad usum nostrum quam duodecim denarios monete currentis infra

eandem Insulam de Jersey per quolibet quarterio frumenti sive alterius generis grani extra eandem Insulam posthac exportando Ita semper et sub condicione quod iidem Inhabitantes et gens Insule de Jersey predictas ac omnes alii mercatores et extranei illuc confluentes solvere debeant et teneant posthac imperpetuum ad usum nostrum per quibus libet Centum et quinquaginta libris lane extra Insulam illam exportandis tres solidos et dimidium monete currentis infra eandem Insulam

[5] Et cum diverse alie libertates in presentibus non expresse a progenitoribus nostris prefatis gentibus et communitatibus Insularum predictarum concesse extiterint e quibus una est quod tempore belli omnium nacionum gentes possint tam libere tute et secure accedere ac frequentare dictas nostras Insulas cum Navibus et mercandisis suis tam pro evitandis tempestatibus quam pro aliis suis licitis negociis inibi peragendis sicut in tempore pacis potuissent absque dampnificacione seu molestacione alicujus subditorum nostrorum vel in corporibus suis vel in bonis tam infra dictas Insulas quam in portubus et haffuris earundem quam concessionem seu prerogativam Nos pro commodo subditorum nostrorum Insularum predictaram ratam gratamque habentes eam pro nobis et heredibus nostris quantum in nobis est acceptamus et approbamus ac tam prefatis gentibus et communitatibus earundem Insularum heredibus et successoribus suis imperpetuum concedimus et confirmamus

[6] Et ideo omnibus nostris subditis firmiter injungendo precipimus ne hanc nostram concessionem et prerogativam donacionem infringere vel violare attemptent Et si quis ausu temerario contrafecerit volumus quod restituat non solum ablata sed quod eciam pro dampno interesse et expensis ad plenam compensacionem compellatur severeque puniatur ut nostri mandati contemptor temerarious

[7] Proviso semper quod aliqua clausula articulus sive aliquod aliud in presentibus literis nostris patentibus expressis et specificatis non exponantur interpretentur nec se extendant ad aliquod quod sit vel fieri possit nobis vel heredibus nostris prejudiciale quoad aliqua terras tenementa redditus vel hereditamenta nostra infra Insulas predictas sive earum aliquam.

[8] Et volumus ac per presentes concedimus quod dicte gentes et communitates habeant has literas nostras patentes sub magno sigillo nostro Anglie debito modo factas et sigillatas absque fine seu feodo nobis in hanaperio nostro seu

alibi ad usum nostrum per premissis solvendis vel faciendis Eo quod expressa mencio etc In cujus etc T. R. apud Westmonsterium vj die Marcij.

Per breve de privato sigillo &c.

~ ~ ~

The king, to all to whom these present letters come, greeting. We have inspected the Letters Patent of the Lord Henry the Eighth, lately king of England, our most dearly beloved father, made in these words: Henry by the grace of God king of England and France and lord of Ireland, to all those to whom these present letters may come, greeting. We have inspected the Letters Patent of the Lord Henry the Seventh, our father, lately king of England, made in these words: Henry by the grace of God king of England and France and lord of Ireland, to all those to whom these present letters may come, greeting.

We have inspected the Letters Patent of the Lord Edward the Fourth, lately king of England, made in these words. Edward by the grace of God king of England and France and lord of Ireland to all to whom these present letters may come, greeting. Whereas our most noble progenitor of glorious memory Richard the Second after the Conquest, lately king of England and France and lord of Ireland, by his Letters Patent given at Westminster on the eighth day of July in the eighteenth year of his reign in consideration of the good behaviour and great loyalty which he always found in his liege and faithful peoples and communities of the islands of Jersey, Guernsey, Sark and Alderney, of his special grace granted for himself and his heirs, as far as in him lay, to these his same peoples and communities that they themselves and their successors should be for ever in all cities, market towns, and ports within the kingdom of England free and quit of all tolls, duties, and customs of whatsoever kind in such wise and in such manner as his own faithful lieges have continued in his own aforesaid kingdom. Provided always that they his said people and communities, their heirs and successors aforesaid should conduct themselves well and faithfully towards himself and his heirs for ever as is more fully contained in those Letters. We considering more fully the continuous loyalty of the said island of Jersey, the aforesaid Letters and all and singular contained therein as regards the people and community of the same island of Jersey, do accept, approve, and by these presents to these same people and community, their heirs and successors, do ratify and confirm them. And, further, calling to mind how valiantly, manfully and steadfastly the said people and community of the said island of Jersey have stood out for us and our progenitors and what great dangers and losses they have sustained for the safety of the said islands and for the recapture of our castle of Mont Orgueil, of our more abundant favour we have granted to the same people and community that they, their heirs and successors shall likewise be free and quit in all cities, boroughs, market towns, and other towns, ports, and places within our kingdom of England and within all our lands and islands lying or situated on this side or beyond the sea from all theolonies, customs, subsidies, pontages, panages, murages, tallages, fossages, and other dues in whatever way to be discharged or made to us and our heirs in our said kingdom of England just as the same people and community of the said island of Jersey, or their predecessors or ancestors of the same island, living under the obedience of any of our progenitors the kings of England, have ever been. And further that the said people and community, their heirs and successors, should have and enjoy all their rights, liberties, and franchises within the same island as freely and in as full a manner and form as the same people and community, or their predecessors and ancestors in the same island living under the obedience of any of our progenitors the kings of England have ever had or enjoyed, without fine or fee in the premises or any of the premises to be paid or made to us in the hanaper; so far as express mention exists of the surety or annual value or any other value in the matter of the premises, or of any of them, or of other gifts or concessions by us or our progenitors to the same people and community, whether such mention has been made before these times or is expressly set forth in these present letters, or any statute, act or ordinance published to the contrary, notwithstanding. In witness whereof we have caused these out Letters to be made Patent. Myself as witness at Westminster this twentieth day of January in the eighth year of our reign.

We, moreover, holding the aforesaid letters, and all and singular contained therein, to be reasonable and seasonable, accept and approve them for us and our heirs, as far as in us lies, and now ratify and confirm them to the aforesaid people and community of the island of Jersey, and to their heirs and successors, in the tenor of the present letters, as the aforesaid letters reasonably testify. In witness whereof we have caused these our letters to be made patent. Witness myself at Westminster this tenth day of February in the first year of our reign.

We, moreover, holding the aforesaid letters, and all and singular contained therein, to be reasonable and seasonable, accept and approve them for us and our heirs, as far as in us lies, and now ratify, grant and confirm them to the aforesaid people and community of the island of Jersey, and to their heirs and successors, in the tenor of the present letters, as the aforesaid letters reasonably testify. In witness whereof we have caused these our letters to be made patent. Witness myself at Westminster this twenty-sixth day of February in the first year of our reign.

We, moreover, holding the aforesaid letters, and all and singular contained therein, to be reasonable and seasonable, accept and approve them for us and our heirs, as far as in us lies, and ratify, grant and confirm them both to the aforesaid people and community of the island of Jersey and to the aforesaid peoples and communities of the islands of Guernsey, Sark, and Alderney, and to their heirs and successors, in the tenor of the present letters, as the aforesaid letters in themselves reasonably testify.

[2] And above this, we wishing to show the peoples and communities of the islands our fuller favour, and calling to mind how valiantly, manfully and steadfastly the said peoples and communities of the same islands have stood out for us and our progenitors and what great dangers and losses they have sustained for the salvation of the same islands and the reduction and defence of our castle of Mount Orguyll, of our special grace, certain knowledge, and mere motion, on the advice and with the agreement of our dearest uncle Edward, duke of Somerset, governor of our person and Protector of our realms, lordships, and subjects, and of our other councillors we have granted and by these present letters we grant to the foresaid peoples and communities of the aforesaid islands, and to each of them, that they themselves, their heirs and successors, be as free and quit, in all the cities boroughs fairs, mart-towns and other towns and ports sited and situate within our kingdom of England and within all our lands and islands on this side of or beyond the sea, from all tolls, customs, subsidies, pontage, panage, murage, fossage, and all other duties to us and our heirs in our said kingdom of England, howsoever to be paid or made, as the same peoples and communities of the said islands or their predecessors or ancestors living under the obedience of any of our predecessors the kings of England ever were.

[3] And, furthermore, that the said peoples and communities of the said islands, their heirs and successors, should have and enjoy all their rights, liberties, and franchises within the same islands and any of them as freely and in as full a manner and form as the same peoples and communities or their predecessors and ancestors living under the obedience of any of our progenitors kings of England ever had and enjoyed them.

[4] And, above this, since it is given to us to understand that a certain exaction has recently been levied of the inhabitants and peoples of our island of Jersey and of merchants and others gathering there, against the ancient extent and custom used there, viz. for each quarter of wheat or

other grain exported out of that island three shillings and six pence of money current in the same island, where that extent previously did not extend to such a great sum, as we understand; and since the said inhabitants and peoples of the aforesaid island of Jersey have been accustomed similarly to pay to our use for each 150 pounds of wool exported out of that island, according to the extent used in that place, four pence of money current within the same island; we, by the advice and consent aforesaid will, and by the present letters grant, for us and our heirs, to the aforesaid inhabitants and peoples of our aforesaid island of Jersey that they themselves and all other merchants gathering there should not be held to pay more nor greater sum from now henceforth for ever to our use than twelve pence of money current within the same island of Jersey for each quarter of wheat or of other type of grain henceforth to be exported out of the same island. Thus always and on condition that the same inhabitants and people of the island of Jersey aforesaid and all other merchants and outsiders gathering there ought and hold to pay henceforth for ever to our use for each 150 pounds of wool exported out of the same island three and a half shillings of money current within the same island.

[5] And since various other liberties not expressed in the present letters exist, conceded by our progenitors to the aforesaid peoples and communities of the aforesaid island, of which one is that in time of war people of all nations have been able to visit and frequent our said islands with their ships and merchandise, both to escape storms and to conduct their other their lawful business there, as freely, safely, and securely as they have been able to in time of peace, without condemnation or interference from any of our subjects either in their bodies or in their goods, both within the said islands and in the ports and harbours of the same; finding this concession or prerogative reasonable and acceptable, for the benefit of our subjects of the aforesaid islands, we accept and approve, for us and our heirs, as far as in us lies, and we concede and confirm it both to the aforesaid peoples and communities of the same islands, and to their heirs and successors for ever.

[6] And therefore firmly enjoining all our subjects we order that they should not attempt to infringe or violate this our concession and prerogative grant; and if anyone, in their rashness and daring, should contravene it, we wish that he should not only restore that taken away but that he should be compelled to give full compensation for the costs, interest, and damages, and be severely punished for his audacious contempt of our order.

[7] Provided always that any clause, article or anything other expressed and specified in our present letters patent should not be set forth, interpreted or

extend itself to anything which should or could be prejudicial to us or our heirs in relation to any our lands, tenements, rents or inheritances within the foresaid islands or of any of them.

[8] And we wish and by these present [letters] we grant that the same peoples and communities should have these our letters patent under our great seal of England in due manner made and sealed, without fine or fee paid or made to us in our hanaper or elsewhere to our use by the premises. So that express mention, &c. In testimony whereof, &c. Witness the king at Westminster, 6 March

Mary

Commentary

Mary's accession in 1553 represented the start of a reversal of so many of her brother's policies – and her charter to Guernsey continued this trend. She confirmed not Edward's charter, but that of her father, Henry VIII. By doing this she abandoned Edward's incorporation of a strictly secular interpretation of the islands' neutrality. She also abandoned the return to joint treatment of Jersey and Guernsey – the charter she confirmed was that of 1510 specifically to Guernsey.

Mary's interest in doing this was at least in part because of the way her determination to break with the legacy of her brother had a very specific relevance in Guernsey. Somerset's influence had helped to support the position as governor of Sir Peter Mewtis, and he had become one of the closest supporters of Somerset's successor at the head of Edward's government, John Dudley, duke of Northumberland.[82] Mewtis had been pardoned for his role in Northumberland's attempt to place Jane Grey on the throne after Edward's death, but he had been swiftly replaced in the strategically sensitive governorship of Guernsey by Sir Leonard Chamberlain, whose religion and other ties made him a safe supporter of Mary.[83]

Chamberlain was appointed on 25 September 1553; the confirmation of the charter came on 6 December 1553. The restoration of the Roman Catholic order followed soon after.[84]

---

[82] D.M. Ogier, *Reformation and Society in Guernsey* (Woodbridge, The Boydell Press,1996) pp. 52, 55; J.H. le Patourel, *The Building of Castle Cornet Guernsey*: I, *Documents relating to the Tudor Reconstruction* [only one volume published] (St Peter Port, Guernsey: printed by the Guernsey Press Ltd, distributed by Manchester University Press, 1958), p. 10.

[83] A. H. Ewen, 'Essex Castle and the Chamberlain Family', *TSG*, xvi (1958 for 1957), 224–67, esp. pp. 233–44; Bindoff, *House of Commons, 1509-1558*, i. 616–17.

[84] Ogier, *Reformation and Society*, pp. 55-9.

MARY 1553[85]

Maria Dei gracia Anglie ffrancie et hibernie Regina fidei defensor et in terra ecclesie Anglicane et hibernice supremum caput Omnibus ad quos presentes littere peruenerint salutem Inspeximus litteras patentes Domini Henrici nuper Regis Anglie Octaui patris nostri precharissimi de confirmacione factas in hec verba. Henricus dei gracia Rex Anglie et ffrancie et Dominus Hibernie omnibus ad quos presentes littere peruenerint Salutem Inspeximus litteras patentes Domini Henrici nuper Regis Anglie patris nostri precharissimi de confirmacione factas in hec verba Henricus dei gracia Rex Anglie et ffrancie et Dominus hibernie Omnibus ad quos presentes littere peruenerint salutem Inspeximus litteras patentes domini Edwardi nuper Regis Anglie quarti factas in hec verba: Edwardus Dei gratia Rex Anglie et ffrancie et Dominus Hibernie Omnibus ad quos presentes littere pervenerint Salutem. Cum nobilissimus progenitor noster inclite memorie Ricardus quondam Rex Anglie et Francie et Dominus Hibernie post conquestum secundus per litteras suas patentes datas apud Westmonasterium octavo die Julii Anno regni sui decimo octavo in consideracione boni gestus et magne fidelitatis quos in ligeis et fidelibus suis gentibus et Communitatibus Insularum suarum de Guernesey Serk et Aureney indies invenit de gracia sua speciali concessit pro se et heredibus suis quantum in eo fuit eisdem gentibus et Communitatibus suis quod ipsi et successores sui imperpetuum forent liberi et quieti in omnibus Civitatibus villis mercatoriis et portubus infra Regnum Anglie de omnimodo Theoloniis exaccionibus et Custumis taliter et eodem modo quo fideles ligei sui in Regno suo predicto extiterunt. Ita tamen quod dicte gentes et Communitates sue ac heredes et successores sui predicti bene et fideliter se gererent erga ipsum progenitorem nostrum et heredes suos imperpetuum prout in litteris illis plenius continetur. Nos continuam fidelitatem gencium et Communitatum dictarum Insularum de Guernesey Serk et Aureney plenius intendentes Litteras predictas de omnia et singula in eis contenta quo ad gentes et Communitates earundem Insularum de Guernesey Serk et Aureney, acceptamus approbamus et eisdem gentibus et Communitatibus heredibus et successoribus suis ratificamus et confirmamus. Et ulterius nos memorie reductentes quam valide viriliter et constanter dicte gentes et Communitates earundem Insularum de Guernesey Serk et Aureney nobis et progenitoribus nostris perstiterunt et quanta pericula et perdita pro salvacione earundem Insularum et reductione Castri nostri de Mont Orgill sustinuerunt, de uberi-

---

[85] Greffe.

ori gracia nostra concessimus eisdem gentibus et Communitatibus quod ipsi heredes et successores sui sint liberi et quieti in omnibus Civitatibus Burgis Villis mercatoriis et aliis Villis et Portubus infra regnum nostrum Anglie et infra omnes terras et Insulas nostras citra vel ultra mare situm vel situatum de omnibus theoloniis custumis subsidiis pontagiis panagiis muragiis curiagiis fossagiis et aliis deueris nobis et heredibus nostris in dicto regno Anglie quoquomodo solvendo seu faciendo sicut eedem gentes et Communitates dictarum Insularum de Guernesey Serk et Aureneny seu predecessores aut antecessores sui earundem Insularum sub obedientia aliquorum progenitorum nostrorum Regum Anglie existentium vel qui ferunt. Et etiam quod dicte gentes et Communitates earundem Insularum de Guernensey Serk et Aureneny heredes et successores sui habeant et gaudeant omnia jura libertates et franchisias sua infra easdem Insulas adeo libere et tam amplius modo et forma prout eadem gentes et Communitates sue predecessores aut antecessores sui earundem Insularum sub obedientia aliquorum progenitorum nostrorum Regum Anglie existentium unquam habuerunt vel gavisi fuerunt absque fine sue feodo in premissis aut aliquo premissorum nobis in hanaperio nostro solvendo seu faciendo. Et quod expressa mencio de certitudine seu valore annuo aut aliquo valore premissorum sive eorum alicujus aut de aliquis donis seu concessionibus per nos aut progenitores nostros eisdem gentibus et Communitatibus ante hac tempora facta in presentibus minime facta existit. Aut aliquo statuto actu fine ordinacione in contrarium nonobstante. Nos autem literas predictas ac omnia et singula in eisdem contenta rata habentes et grata ea pro nobis et heredibus nostris quantum in nobis est acceptamus approbamus et prefatis gentibus et Communitatibus Insularum de Guernesey Serk et Aureney predictarum heredibus et successoribus suis tenore presentium ratificamus concedimus et confirmamus prout Litere predicte racionabiliter testantur. In cujus rei testimonium has litteras nostras fieri fecimus patentes. Teste me ipso apud Westmonasterium decimo die Februarii Anno Regni nostri primo.

Nos autem Literas predictas ac omnia et singula in eisdem contenta rata habentes et grata ea pro nobis et heredibus nostris quantum in nobis est acceptamus approbamus et prefatis gentibus et Communitatibus Insularum de Guernesey Serk et Aureney predicta heredibus et successoribus suis tenore presentium ratificamus et confirmamus prout Litere predicte racionabiliter testantur. In cujus rei testimonium has literas nostras fieri fecimus patentes. Teste me ipso apud Westmonasterium quinto die Martii Anno Regni nostri primo.

Nos autem litteras predictas ac omnia et singula in eisdem contenta rata habentes et grata ea pro nobis et heredibus nostris quantum in nobis est acceptamus approbamus et prefatis gentibus et Communitatibus Insularum de Guernesey Serk et Aureney predictarum heredibus et successoribus suis tenore presencium ratificamus concedimus et confirmamus prout littere predicte racionabiliter testantur. In cuius rei testimonium litteras nostras fieri fecimus patentes. Teste me ipsa apud Westmonasterium sexto die Decembris Anno Regni nostri primo.

Examinatum per nos Johannem Vaughan Williemum Shrimpton clericos Adams

~ ~ ~

Mary by the grace of God queen of England France and Ireland, Defender of the Faith, and on earth the supreme head of the Church of England and Ireland: to all to whom these presents may come Greeting: we have inspected the Letters Patent of the most dearly beloved Lord Henry the Eighth, lately king of England, our father, concerning the confirmation of the same, made in these words: Henry by the grace of God king of England and France and lord of Ireland: to all to whom these presents may come Greeting: we have inspected the Letters Patent of the most dearly beloved Lord Henry the Seventh, lately king of England, our father, concerning the confirmation of the same, made in these words: Henry by the grace of God king of England and France and lord of Ireland: we have inspected the Letters Patent of the Lord Edward the Fourth, lately king of England, made in these words: Edward by the grace of God king of England and France and lord of Ireland: to all to whom these presents may come Greeting: whereas our most noble progenitor of glorious memory Richard the Second after the Conquest, lately king of England and France and lord of Ireland, by his Letters Patent given at Westminster on the eighth day of July in the eighteenth year of his reign in consideration of the good behaviour and great loyalty which he always found among his liege and faithful peoples and communities of the islands of Guernsey, Sark and Alderney, of his special grace granted on behalf of himself and his heirs, as far as in him lay, to these his same peoples and communities that they themselves and their successors should be for ever in all cities, market towns, and ports within the kingdom of England free and quit of all tolls, taxes and customs of whatsoever kind in such wise and in such manner as his own faithful lieges have continued in his own aforesaid kingdom. Always provided that they his said people and communities and their heirs and successors aforesaid should conduct themselves well and faithfully towards himself and his heirs for ever as is more fully contained in those Letters. We considering more fully the continuous loyalty of the said islands of Guernsey, Sark and Alderney, the aforesaid Letters and all and singular contained therein as regards the peoples and communities of the same islands of Guernsey, Sark and Alderney, do accept approve and by these presents to these same peoples and communities their heirs and successors do ratify and confirm them. And further we calling to mind how valiantly, manfully and steadfastly the said people and communities of the said Islands of Guernsey, Sark and Alderney have stood out for us and our progenitors and what great dangers and losses they have sustained for the safety of the said islands and for the recapture of our castle of Mont Orgueil, of our more abundant grace have granted to the same peoples and communities that they, their heirs and successors shall likewise be free and quit in all cities, boroughs, market towns and other towns, ports and places within our kingdom of England and within all our lands and islands lying or situated on this side or beyond the sea from all tolls, customs, subsidies, pontages, panages, murages, tallages, fossages and other dues in whatever way to be discharged or made to us and our heirs in our said kingdom of England just as the same peoples and communities of the said islands of Guernsey, Sark, and Alderney or their predecessors, or ancestors of the same islands living under the obedience of any of our progenitors the kings of England have ever been. And further that the said peoples and communities, their predecessors and ancestors in the same islands living under the obedience of any of our progenitors the kings of England have ever had or enjoyed, without fine or fee in the premises or any of the premises to be paid or made to us in our treasury so far as express mention exists of the surety or annual value or any other value in the matter of the premises or of any of them or of other gifts or concessions by us or our progenitors to the same peoples and communities, whether such mention has been made before these times or is expressly set forth in these presents, or any statute, act or ordinance published to the contrary notwithstanding.

We moreover finding the aforesaid Letters reasonable and acceptable and all and singular therein contained, for ourselves and our heirs, as far as in us lies, accept approve and to our aforesaid peoples and communities of the islands of Guernsey, Sark and Alderney aforesaid their heirs and successors in the tenor of the present [letters] ratify grant and confirm, as the aforesaid letters reasonably testify. In witness whereof we have caused these our Letters to be made Patent. Witness myself at Westminster this tenth day of February in the first year of our reign.

We moreover, finding the aforesaid letters and all and singular therein contained reasonable and acceptable, for ourselves and our heirs as far as in us lies, accept, approve and to our aforesaid peoples and communities of the islands of Guernsey, Sark and Alderney aforesaid, their heirs and successors in the tenor of the present [letters] ratify, grant and confirm as the aforesaid Letters reasonably testify. In witness whereof we have caused these out Letters to be made Patent. Witness myself at Westminster this fifth day of March in the first year of our reign. We moreover finding the aforesaid letters and all and singular therein contained reasonable and acceptable, for ourselves and our heirs as far as in us lies, accept, approve and to our aforesaid peoples and communities of the islands of Guernsey, Sark and Alderney aforesaid, their heirs and successors, in the tenor of the present [letters] ratify, grant, and confirm as the aforesaid letters reasonably testify. In witness whereof we have caused these our Letters to be made Patent. Witness myself at Westminster this sixth day of December in the first year of our reign.

Examined by us John Vaughan William Shrimpton clerks

Adams

Elizabeth

Commentary

At the accession of the new queen, the island remained in the hands of Sir Leonard Chamberlain, who in conjunction with the bailiff Helier Gosselin had been enforcing Roman Catholicism with vigour. Very early in the new reign, an order was issued by the Privy Council that Sir Leonard should send the remaining 100 soldiers in Guernsey to Portsmouth. The messenger, who also had copies of proclamations for Guernsey and Jersey, was for some reason detained in Southampton. Perhaps as a result, in January of 1559 Sir Leonard seems to have written to the Privy Council requesting an increase in the forces at his disposal, and the right to come over to England to address the Council.[86] It is therefore unsurprising that Elizabeth's first charter to Guernsey was essentially a holding operation, which confirmed Mary's charter.

The inhabitants of the bailiwick sought additions to their rights early in the reign, however. On 13 October 1559 they were granted the right to import, duty free, 100 tuns of beer and other commodities for Castle Cornet. The right was explicitly equated to that enjoyed by Berwick, a part of the Scottish crown under English control. A very similar grant was made to Jersey later that year on 6 December.[87]

Elizabeth's second charter to Guernsey, granted on 15 March 1560, was the most significant redrafting of the island's privileges for more than a century. The new charter abandoned the pattern of simply confirming earlier documents and went into detail about aspects of the island's position which were expressed previously, and many which were not.

Why the need to abandon the previous confirmation, so recently obtained? Almost certainly, this reflected the outlook of those who

---

[86] *APC 1558-70*, pp. 6, 15, 45.
[87] *CPR 1558-60*, pp. 45, 247.

sought the confirmation and their determination to break with the Marian past. More specifically, the Marian charter was part of a tradition which relied on the papal bull to protect freedom of movement to and from the islands in time of war as in peacetime. The new charter, like that of Edward VI before it, did not base this set of privileges on the grant of the papacy.

Hence, first, the island's laws and customs were confirmed, then its freedom from English customs and duties; next, the privilege of neutrality and freedom of trade in times of war was reaffirmed. The jurisdiction of the bailiff and jurats and other officers was confirmed, as was the right to justice exclusively in the island, without threat of summons before any court in England.

The document is telling in two other respects of the mental world which produced it. The first is the reappearance of the assertion of the queen's right to the duchy of Normandy, not just in terms of a reference to the earlier control over Guernsey of kings of England and dukes of Normandy, but in terms of the islands as specifically part of the duchy.

Secondly, the document refers to authority granted by parliament. This was the reign of a queen regnant, and the authority of parliament was thereby enhanced. Specifically, those who sat in parliament, and many of the same men who also advised the queen in the crucial early months of the reign, had a clear perception of the place of the islands and of the duchy in the future of Europe.[88]

March 1560 was an exciting time to be a Protestant in England: Mary's death had delivered England into the hands of a Protestant queen, and England now seemed an instrument in the furtherance of Protestantism elsewhere. William Cecil, in particular, was involved in preparations for a campaign in Scotland which was to reinforce the success of the country's Reformation.[89] Just across the Channel, in Normandy, the period saw the flowering of Protestantism against the background of governmental and dynastic crisis.[90] Hopes were high that Normandy might be won convincingly for Protestantism – and

---

[88] Parliament had sat from 25 January to 8 May 1559.
[89] J. E. A. Dawson, 'William Cecil and the British Dimension of Early Elizabethan Foreign Policy', *History*, 74 (1989), 196–216.
[90] D. Nicholls, 'Social Change and Early Protestantism in France: Normandy, 1520–62', *European Studies Review*, x (1980), 279–308.

the territorial and religious ambitions of those around the queen were fired.

All this was to come to a head in the Newhaven expedition of 1563, in which the earl of Warwick, elder brother of the queen's favourite Robert Dudley, earl of Leicester, was commissioned, as captain general and governor, to rally the queen's subjects in the duchy of Normandy – and which was more specifically intended to ensure that the capture of Le Havre provided a bridgehead to supply Protestants there.[91]

Interpretations of these events have tended to emphasise the scepticism, especially of Cecil and Elizabeth, towards involvement in Normandy.[92] Yet the charter suggests that as early as 1560 there was a renewed interest in Guernsey as part of the duchy, and this seems to have grown, especially amongst the connections of Robert Dudley over the following years. Within this larger picture, the islands of Jersey and Guernsey played an obvious role. They were the surviving elements, the proof indeed, of the queen's ownership of Normandy.[93] They had also seen a high-profile confrontation between Catholicism and reform under Mary, which was now being settled decisively in favour of reform, and a reform strongly under Genevan influence and more radical than anything the queen would permit in England.[94]

While in so many ways the English regime allowed the existing elite to remain in place in Guernsey, an alternative view of the island was emerging. Matthieu Cauches, brother of Catherine Cauches who had so notoriously been burned for heresy under Mary, was already in (probably) December 1558 petitioning for justice. Back in Guernsey, a reforming party amongst the elite was proactively working for Reformation: Guillaume de Beauvoir, who had been in exile in Geneva, returned home and applied to Calvin himself for assistance. Calvin replied, on 26 December 1559, nominating Nicolas Baudouin as the minister of the church in Guernsey.

---

[91] *CPR 1560-1563*, pp. 252-3; Wallace T. MacCaffrey, 'The Newhaven Expedition, 1562-1563', *Historical Journal*, 40 (1997), 1–21.

[92] MacCaffrey is a case in point.

[93] Edward Coke, *The Fourth Part of the Institutes of the Laws of England: Concerning the Jurisdiction of Courts* (London: printed by M. Flesher for W. Lee and D. Pakeman, 1648), pp. 286-7.

[94] For this and the following paragraph, see Ogier, *Reformation and Society*, pp. 59-62.

The real driving force behind the early Reformation in Guernsey was, however, the interest of the triumphant Protestants of Jersey, and in particular the connections of Sir Hugh Paulet, the captain of Jersey.[95] When, early in Elizabeth's reign, a realisation of the desperate vulnerability of Guernsey, Sark and Alderney grew in England, the clearest voices to explain the situation and propose a remedy were those of the Paulets.[96] Paulet was keen to leave Wales and go to Jersey in the summer of 1559.[97] In January 1560, it was Paulet who supplied a sheet of news from Guernsey, including references to two priests who were maintaining Catholic rites in the island, and he implied that this was associated with obedience to Coutances and hence 'to foreyn obeissance'.[98]

Thanks to these influences, there are signs that the crown was coming to realise that the Royal Court had not co-operated with earlier demands for the dissolution of religious foundations in the island – and that this, and the broader issue of who held influence in the island, needed to be addressed. A series of commissions, the first appointed on 2 January 1561, was put in place, but the first actually to make a real impact in the island was that of 25 May 1563.[99]

The costs of obtaining the charter were eventually met when on 8 May 1566 the Royal Court agreed a tax of £60, partly accounted for by these charges.[100] The delay in imposing this tax implies that those who paid the costs of the new charter in 1560 had not then been in a position to recover them, and that they were part of the new establishment which emerged following the revolution in the membership of the Royal Court represented by the dismissal of seven jurats in 1565, and their replacement in such a way as to create

[95] For Paulet's contribution in Jersey, see 'Les Chroniques, &c., de l'île de Jersey', in G. Syvret (ed.), *Chroniques, des îles de Jersey, Guernesey, Auregny et Serk, auquel on a ajouté un abrégé historique des dites îles* (Guernsey: T.J. Mauger, 1832), chapter 26.

[96] In July 1560, Sir Hugh Paulet had been unwilling to allow his son Amias to go to Guernsey to work on a commission because of uncertainties over the negotiations in Scotland and what this might mean for war in the Channel: HMC, *Calendar of the Manuscripts of the Most Honorable Marquis of Salisbury Preserved at Hatfield House, Hertfordshire* (24 vols., London: HMSO, 1883-1976), i. 244.

[97] 25 June 1559: *CSPD 1547-80*, p. 132.

[98] Ogier, *Reformation and Society*, p. 76, quoting PRO, SP 15/9/53i.

[99] Ogier, *Reformation and Society*, pp. 64-7.

[100] Greffe: Jugements, Ordonnances et Ordres de Conseil, i. 248; Ogier, *Reformation and Society*, pp. 72-3;

a Protestant majority there.[101] The 1560 charter was, then, a manifesto for a party not yet in undisputed power either in England or in Guernsey itself, but at least in the island their time was not long in coming.

ELIZABETH 1559[102]

Elizabetha Dei gracia Anglie ffrancie et hibernie Regina fidei defensor &c. Omnibus ad quos presentes littere peruenerint salutem Inspeximus litteras patentes Domine Marie nuper Regine Anglie sororis nostre precharissime de confirmacione factas in hec verba. Maria Dei gracia Anglie ffrancie et hibernie Regina fidei defensor et in terra ecclesie Anglicane et hibernice supremum caput Omnibus ad quos presentes littere peruenerint salutem Inspeximus litteras patentes Domini Henrici nuper Regis Anglie Octaui patris nostri precharissimi de confirmacione factas in hec verba. Henricus dei gracia Rex Anglie et ffrancie et Dominus Hibernie omnibus ad quos presentes littere peruenerint Salutem Inspeximus litteras patentes Domini Henrici nuper Regis Anglie patris nostri precharissimi de confirmacione factas in hec verba Henricus dei gracia Rex Anglie et ffrancie et Dominus hibernie Omnibus ad quos presentes littere peruenerint salutem Inspeximus litteras patentes domini Edwardi nuper Regis Anglie quarti factas in hec verba: Edwardus Dei gratia Rex Anglie et ffrancie et Dominus Hibernie Omnibus ad quos presentes littere pervenerint Salutem. Cum nobilissimus progenitor noster inclite memorie Ricardus quondam Rex Anglie et Francie et Dominus Hibernie post conquestum secundus per litteras suas patentes datas apud Westmonasterium octavo die Julii Anno regni sui decimo octavo in consideracione boni gestus et magne fidelitatis quos in ligeis et fidelibus suis gentibus et Communitatibus Insularum suarum de Guernesey Serk et Aureney indies invenit de gracia sua speciali concessit pro se et heredibus suis quantum in eo fuit eisdem gentibus et Communitatibus suis quod ipsi et successores sui imperpetuum forent liberi et quieti in omnibus Civitatibus villis mercatoriis et portubus infra Regnum Anglie de omnimodo Theoloniis exaccionibus et Custumis taliter et eodem modo quo fideles ligei sui in Regno suo predicto extiterunt. Ita tamen quod dicte gentes et Communitates sue ac heredes et successores sui predicti bene et fideliter se gererent erga ipsum progenitorem nostrum et

---

[101] A. J. Eagleston, 'The Dismissal of the Seven Jurats in 1565', *TSG*, xii (1933-6), 508-16; Ogier, *Reformation and Society*, pp. 70-1.
[102] Greffe.

*heredes suos imperpetuum prout in litteris illis plenius continetur. Nos con-
tinuam fidelitatem gencium et Communitatum dictarum Insularum de
Guernesey Serk et Aureney plenius intendentes Litteras predictas de omnia
et singula in eis contenta quo ad gentes et Communitates earundem Insularum de Guernesey Serk et Aureney acceptamus approbamus et eisdem
gentibus et Communitatibus heredibus et successoribus suis ratificamus et
confirmamus. Et ulterius nos memorie reductentes quam valide viriliter et
constanter dicte gentes et Communitates earundem Insularum de Guernesey
Serk et Aureney nobis et progenitoribus nostris perstiterunt et quanta pericula
et perdita pro salvacione earundem Insularum et reductione Castri nostri de
Mont Orgill sustinuerunt, de uberiori gracia nostra concessimus eisdem
gentibus et Communitatibus quod ipsi heredes et successores sui sint liberi et
quieti in omnibus Civitatibus Burgis Villis mercatoriis et aliis Villis et Portubus infra regnum nostrum Anglie et infra omnes terras et Insulas nostras
citra vel ultra mare situm vel situatum de omnibus theoloniis custumis subsidiis pontagiis panagiis muragiis curiagiis fossagiis et aliis deueris nobis et
heredibus nostris in dicto regno Anglie quoquomodo solvendo seu faciendo
sicut eedem gentes et Communitates dictarum Insularum de Guernensey
Serk et Aureneny seu predecessores aut antecessores sui earundem Insularum
sub obedientia aliquorum progenitorum nostrorum Regum Anglie existentium
vel qui ferunt. Et etiam quod dicte gentes et Communitates earundem Insularum de Guernensey Serk et Aureneny heredes et successores sui habeant et
gaudeant omnia jura libertates et franchisias sua infra easdem Insulas adeo
libere et tam amplius modo et forma prout eadem gentes et Communitates
sue predecessores aut antecessores sui earundem Insularum sub obedientia
aliquorum progenitorum nostrorum Regum Anglie existentium unquam
habuerunt vel gavisi fuerunt absque fine sue feodo in premissis aut aliquo
premissorum nobis in hanaperio nostro solvendo seu faciendo. Et quod expressa mencio de certitudine seu valore annuo aut aliquo valore premissorum
sive eorum alicujus aut de aliquis donis seu concessionibus per nos aut progenitores nostros eisdem gentibus et Communitatibus ante hac tempora facta
in presentibus minime facta existit. Aut aliquo statuto actu fine ordinacione in
contrarium nonobstante. Nos autem literas predictas ac omnia et singula in
eisdem contenta rata habentes et grata ea pro nobis et heredibus nostris quantum in nobis est acceptamus approbamus et prefatis gentibus et
Communitatibus Insularum de Guernesey Serk et Aureney predictarum
heredibus et successoribus suis tenore presentium ratificamus concedimus et*

confirmamus prout Litere predicte racionabiliter testantur. In cujus rei testimonium has litteras nostras fieri fecimus patentes. Teste me ipso apud Westmonasterium decimo die Februarii Anno Regni nostri primo.

Nos autem Literas predictas ac omnia et singula in eisdem contenta rata habentes et grata ea pro nobis et heredibus nostris quantum in nobis est acceptamus approbamus et prefatis gentibus et Communitatibus Insularum de Guernesey Serk et Aureney predicta heredibus et successoribus suis tenore presentium ratificamus et confirmamus prout Litere predicte racionabiliter testantur. In cujus rei testimonium has literas nostras fieri fecimus patentes. Teste me ipso apud Westmonasterium quinto die Martii Anno Regni nostri primo.

Nos autem litteras predictas ac omnia et singula in eisdem contenta rata habentes et grata ea pro nobis et heredibus nostris quantum in nobis est acceptamus approbamus et prefatis gentibus et Communitatibus Insularum de Guernesey Serk et Aureney predictarum heredibus et successoribus suis tenore presencium ratificamus concedimus et confirmamus prout littere predicte racionabiliter testantur. In cuius rei testimonium litteras nostras fieri fecimus patentes. Teste me ipsa apud Westmonasterium sexto die Decembris Anno Regni nostri primo.

Nos autem litteras predictas ac omnia et singula in eisdem contenta rata habentes et grata ea pro nobis et heredibus nostris quantum in nobis est acceptamus approbamus et prefatis gentibus et Communitatibus Insularum de Guernesey Serk et Aureney predictarum heredibus et successoribus suis tenore presencium ratificamus concedimus et confirmamus prout littere predicte racionabiliter testantur. In cuius rei testimonium litteras nostras fieri fecimus patentes. Teste me ipsa apud Westmonasterium vicesimonono die Julii Anno Regni nostri primo.

Marten

Examinatum per nos Johannem Vaughan et Thomam Huycke

~ ~ ~

Elizabeth by the grace of God queen of England France and Ireland, Defender of the Faith, &c. To all to whom these presents may come, greeting. We have inspected the Letters Patent of the most dearly beloved Lady Mary, lately Queen of England, our sister, concerning the confirmation of the same, made in these words: Mary by the grace of God queen of England France and Ireland, Defender of the Faith, and on earth the supreme head of the Church of England and Ireland, to all to whom these presents may come, greeting. We have inspected the Letters Patent of the most dearly beloved Lord Henry the Eighth, lately King of England, our father, concerning the confirmation of the same, made in these words: Henry by the grace of God king of England and France and lord of Ireland, to all to whom these presents may come, greeting. We have inspected the Letters Patent of the most dearly beloved Lord Henry the Seventh, lately king of England, our father, concerning the confirmation of the same, made in these words: Henry by the grace of God king of England and France and lord of Ireland: we have inspected the Letters Patent of the Lord Edward the Fourth, lately king of England, made in these words: Edward by the grace of God king of England and France and lord of Ireland, to all to whom these presents may come, greeting. Whereas our most noble progenitor of glorious memory Richard the Second after the Conquest, lately king of England and France and lord of Ireland, by his Letters Patent given at Westminster on the eighth day of July in the eighteenth year of his reign in consideration of the good behaviour and great loyalty which he always found among his liege and faithful peoples and communities of the islands of Guernsey, Sark and Alderney, of his special grace granted on behalf of himself and his heirs, as far as in him lay, to these his same peoples and communities that they themselves and their successors should be for ever in all cities, market towns, and ports within the kingdom of England free and quit of all theolonian taxes and customs of whatsoever kind in such wise and in such manner as his own faithful lieges have continued in his own aforesaid kingdom. Always provided that they his said people and communities and their heirs and successors aforesaid should conduct themselves well and faithfully towards himself and his heirs for ever as is more fully contained in those Letters. We considering more fully the continuous loyalty of the said islands of Guernsey, Sark and Alderney, the aforesaid Letters and all and singular contained therein as regards the peoples and communities of the same islands of Guernsey, Sark and Alderney, do accept approve and by these presents to these same peoples and Communities their heirs and successors do ratify and confirm them. And further we calling to mind how valiantly, manfully and steadfastly the said people and communities of the said Islands of Guernsey, Sark and Alderney have stood out for us and our progenitors and what great dangers and losses they have sustained for the safety of the said islands and for the recapture of our castle of Mont Orgueil, of our more abundant grace have granted to the same peoples and communities that they, their heirs and successors shall likewise be free and quit in all cities, boroughs, market towns and other towns, ports and places within our kingdom of England and within all our lands and islands lying or situated on this side or beyond the sea from all theolonies, customs, subsidies, pontages, panages, murages, tallages, fossages, and other dues in whatever way to be discharged or made to us and our heirs in our said kingdom of England just as the same peoples and communities of the said islands of Guernsey, Sark, and Alderney or their predecessors, or ancestors of the same islands living under the obedience of any of our progenitors the kings of England have ever been. And further that the said peoples and communities, their predecessors and ancestors in the same islands living under the obedience of any of our progenitors the kings of England have ever had or enjoyed, without fine or fee in the premises or any of the premises to be paid or made to us in our treasury so far as express mention exists of the surety or annual value or any other value in the matter of the premises or of any of them or of other gifts or concessions by us or our progenitors to the same peoples and communities, whether such mention has been made before these times or is expressly set forth in these presents, or any statute, act or ordinance published to the contrary notwithstanding.

We moreover finding the aforesaid Letters reasonable and acceptable and all and singular therein contained, for ourselves and our heirs, as far as in us lies, accept approve and to our aforesaid peoples and communities of the islands of Guernsey, Sark and Alderney aforesaid their heirs and successors in the tenor of the present [letters] ratify grant and confirm, as the aforesaid letters reasonably testify. In witness whereof we have caused these our Letters to be made Patent. Witness myself at Westminster this tenth day of February in the first year of our reign.

We moreover, finding the aforesaid letters and all and singular therein contained reasonable and acceptable, for ourselves and our heirs as far as in us lies, accept, approve and to our aforesaid peoples and communities of the islands of Guernsey, Sark and Alderney aforesaid, their heirs and successors in the tenor of the present letters ratify, grant and confirm as the aforesaid Letters reasonably testify. In witness whereof we have caused these out Letters to be made Patent. Witness myself at Westminster this fifth day of March in the first year of our reign.

We moreover finding the aforesaid letters and all and singular therein contained reasonable and acceptable, for ourselves and our heirs as far as in us lies, accept, approve and to our aforesaid peoples and communities of the islands of Guernsey, Sark and Alderney aforesaid, their heirs and successors, in the tenor of the present letters ratify, grant, and confirm as the aforesaid letters reasonably testify. In witness whereof we have caused these our Letters to be made Patent. Witness myself at Westminster this sixth day of December in the first year of our reign.

We moreover finding the aforesaid letters and all and singular therein contained reasonable and acceptable, for ourselves and our heirs as far as in us lies, accept, approve and to our aforesaid peoples and communities of the islands of Guernsey, Sark and Alderney aforesaid, their heirs and successors, in the tenor of the present letters ratify, grant, and confirm as the aforesaid letters reasonably testify. In witness whereof we have caused these our Letters to be made Patent. Witness myself at Westminster this twenty-ninth day of July in the first year of our reign.

Marten

Examined by us John Vaughan and Thomas Huycke

ELIZABETH 1560[103]

ELIZABETH Dei Gracia Anglie ffrancie et Hibernie Regina Fidei Defensor &c. Omnibus ad quos presentes littere peruenerint Salutem.

Cum dilecti et fideles ligei et Subditi nostri Balliuus et Jurati Insule nostrae de Gernezey ac ceteri Incole et habitatores tam ipsius Insule quam Insularum nostrarum de Aureney alias Alderney et Sarke infra ducatum nostrum Normaniae et Predecessores eorum a tempore cujus contrarii memoria hominum non existit per seperales cartas concessiones confirmaciones et amplissima diplomata illustrium Progenitorum ac Antecessorum nostrorum tam Regum Anglie quam Ducum Normanie ac aliorum quamplurimis iuribus iurisdiccionibus priuilegiis immunitatibus libertatibus et franchesiis libere quiete et inuiolabiliter vsi freti et gauisi fuerunt tam infra Regnum nostrum Anglie quam alibi infra Dominia et loca ditioni nostre subiecta vltra citraque mare Quorum ope et beneficio predicte Insule ac loca maritima predicta in fide obedientia et seruitio tam nostro quam eorundem Progenitorum nostrorum constanter fideliter et inculpate perstiterunt ac perseuerarunt liberaque commercia cum Mercatoribus et aliis Indigenis ac Alienigenis tam pacis quam belli temporibus habuerunt et exercuerunt iudicia eciam et cogniciones omnium et omnimodarum causarum querelarum accionum et placitorum tam Ciuilium quam Criminalium et Capitalium ac iudicialem potestatem ea omnia tractandi decidendi discutiendi audiendi et terminandi atque in eisdem procedendi et in acta redigendi secundum leges et consuetudines Insularum et locorum predictorum ex antiquo receptas et approbatas preterquam in certis

---

[103] Greffe.

*casibus cognicioni nostre Regie reseruatis de tempore in tempus exercuerunt
executi sunt et peregerunt.*

*[2] Que omnia et singula cuius et quanti momenti sunt et fuerunt ad tute-
lam et conseruacionem Insularum et locorum maritimorum predictorum in
fide et obedientia Corone nostre Anglie Nos (ut equum est) perpendentes
neque non immemores quam fortiter et fideliter Insulani praedicti ac ceteri
Incole et habitatores ibidem nobis et progenitoribus nostris inseruierunt
Quantaque detrimenta dampna et pericula tam pro assidua tuicione earundem Insularum et locorum quam pro recuperacione et defensione Castri nostri
de Mount Orguill infra Insulam nostram de Gerzey sustinuerunt indiesque
sustinent non solum vt Regia nostra beneuolencia fauor et affectus erga
prefatos Insulanos illustri aliquo nostre beneficentie testimonio ac certis indiciis comprobetur verumeciam vt ipsi et eorum posteri deinceps imperpetuum
prout antea solitam et debitam obedienciam erga nos heredes et successores
nostros teneant ac inuiolabiliter obseruent has litteras nostras patentes magno
sigillo Anglie roboratas in forma que sequitur illis concedere dignati sumus.*

*[3] Sciatis igitur quod nos de gracia nostra speciali ac ex certa scientia et mero
motu nostris dedimus et concessimus ac pro nobis heredibus et successoribus
nostris per presentes damus et concedimus prefatis Balliuo et Juratis Insule
nostre predicte de Gernezey ac ceteris Incolis et habitatoribus tam ipsius
Insule quam predictarum Insularum nostrarum de Aureney alias Alderney et
Sarke quod ipsi et eorum quilibet, licet in presentibus non recitati seu cogniti
per specialia nomina sint semper in futurum ita liberi quieti et immunes in
omnibus Ciuitatibus Burgis Emporiis Nundinis mercatis villis mercatoriis et
aliis locis ac Portibus infra Regnum nostrum Anglie ac infra omnes prouincias
Dominia Territoria et loca ditioni nostre subiecta tam citra quam vltra mare,
de et ab omnibus Vectigalibus Theoloneis Custumiis Subsidiis Hidagiis
Tallagiis Pontagiis Pannagiis Muragiis Fossagiis Operibus Expedicionibus
bellicis (nisi in casu vbi corpus nostre prefate Regine haeredum vel successorum nostrorum (quod absit) in prisona detineatur) et de et ab omnibus aliis
contribucionibus et exaccionibus quibuscunque nobis heredibus et successoribus
nostris quouismodo debitis reddendis seu soluendis prout prefati Insulani seu
eorum aliquis virtute aliquarum cartarum concessionum confirmacionum siue
diplomatum per predictos Progenitores nostros quondam Reges Anglie et
Duces Normanie siue alios seu virtute aut vigore alicuius racionabilis et*

Richard II, 1394.

Edward IV, 1465.

Richard III, 1483.

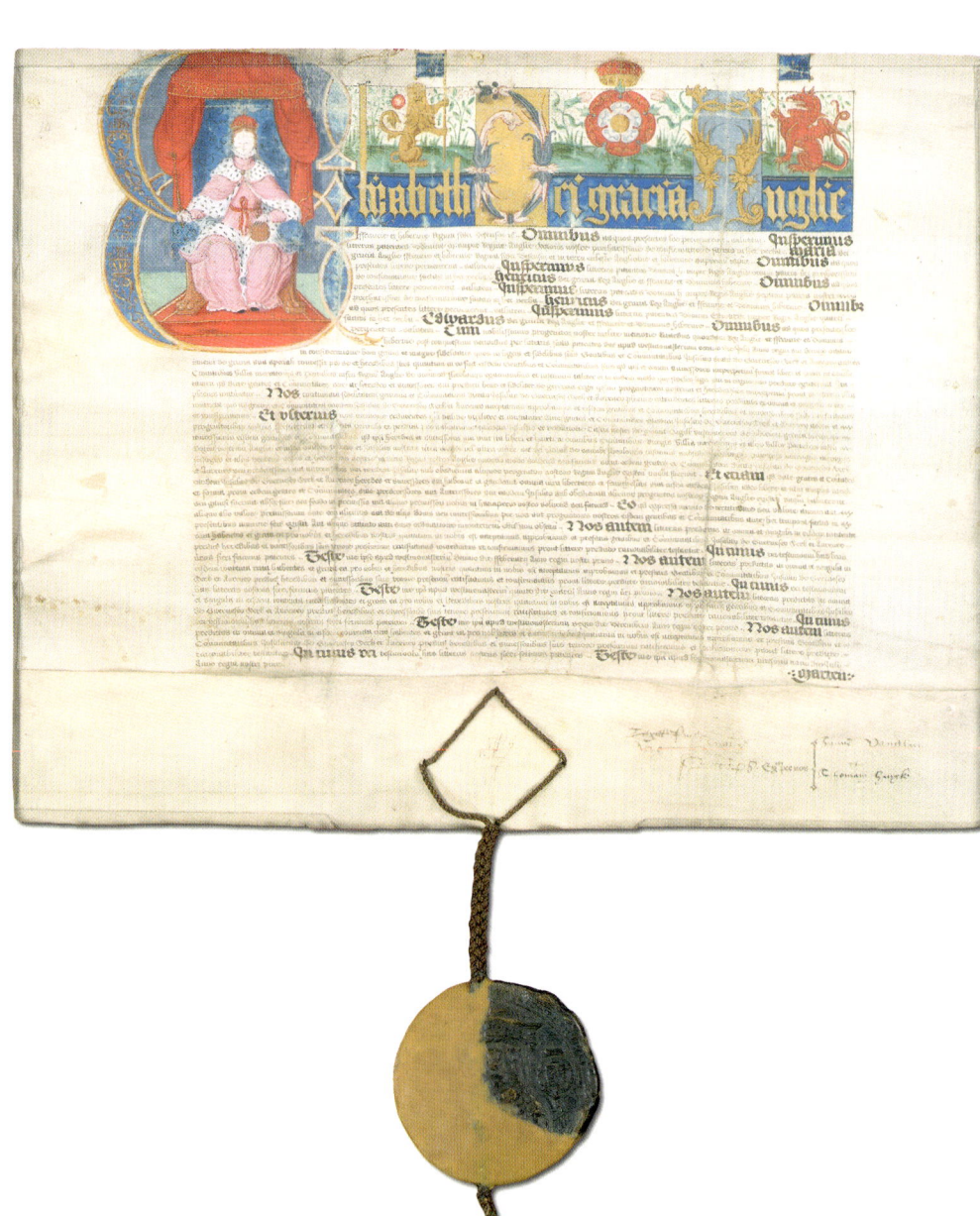

Elizabeth I, 1559.

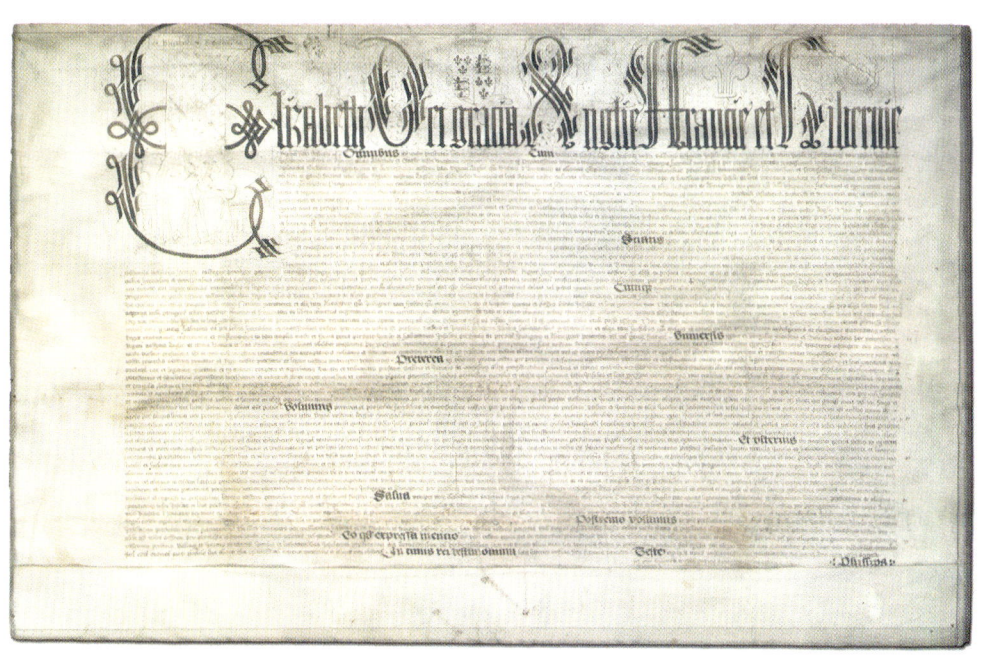

Elizabeth I, 1560.

James I, 1605.

Charles I, 1627.

Charles II, 1668.

legalis vsus prescripcionis vel consuetudinis vnquam aliquando fuerunt aut esse debuerunt vel potuerunt debuit vel potuit quouis modo.

[4] Cumque nonnulla alia priuilegia iurisdicciones immunitates libertates et franchesie per praedictos progenitores ac praedecessores nostros quondam Reges Anglie et Duces Normanie ac alios prefatis Insulanis indulta donata concessa et confirmata fuerunt ac a tempore cuius contrarii memoria hominum non existit infra Insulas et loca maritima predicta inuiolabiliter vsitata et obseruata fuerunt de quibus vnum est quod tempore belli omnium Nationum Mercatores et alii tam Alienigene quam Indigene tam hostes quam amici libere licite et impune queant et possint dictas Insulas et loca maritima cum Navibus mercibus et bonis suis tam pro euitandis tempestatibus quam pro aliis licitis suis negociis inibi peragendis adire accedere comeare et frequentari ac Iibera commercia negociacionem ac rem mercatoriam ibidem exercere ac tuto et secure commorari indeque remeare ac redire toties quoties absque dampno molestia seu hostilitate quacunque in rebus mercibus bonis aut corporibus suis idque non solum infra Insulas et loca maritima predicta ac procinctum eorundem verumeciam infra spacia vndique ab eisdem distantia usque ad visum hominis id est quatenus visus oculi possit assequi Nos eandem immunitatem impunitatem libertatem et privilegium ac caetera omnia premissa ultime recitata rata grataque habentes ea pro nobis heredibus et successoribus nostris quantum in nobis est prefatis Balliuo et Iuratis ac ceteris Incolis habitatoribus mercatoribus et aliis tam hostibus quam amicis et eorum cuilibet per presentes indulgemus ac elargimur auctoritateque nostra Regia renouamus reiteramus et confirmamus in tam amplis modo et forma prout predicte Incole et habitatores Insularum predictarum ac praedicti Indigene et Alienigene preantea vsi vel gauisi, fuerunt. Universis igitur et singulis Ministris et Subditis nostris per vniversum Regnum nostrum Anglie, ac cetera Dominia et loca ditioni nostre subiecta vbilibet constitutis per presentes denunciamus ac firmiter iniungendo precipimus ne hanc nostram donacionem concessionem et confirmacionem seu aliquid in eisdem expressum aut contentum temerare infringere seu quouis modo violare presumant Et si quis ausu temerario contrafecerit seu attemptauerit volumus et decernimus quantum in nobis est quod restituat non solum ablata aut erepta sed quod eciam pro dampno interesse et expensis ad plenariam recompensam et satisfacctionem compellatur per quecunque iuris nostri remedia seuereque puniatur ut Regie nostre potestatis ac legum nostrarum contemptor temerarius.

[5] Preterea ex uberiori gracia nostra per presentes ratificamus approbamus stabilimus et confirmamus omnes et singulas leges consuetudines infra Insulas et loca maritima predicta rite et legittime vsitatas et ex antiquo receptas et approbatas dantes et tribuentes praefatis Balliuo et Juratis ac omnibus aliis Magistratibus Ministris et ceteris quibuscunque ibidem in Officio aut functione aliqua constitutis plenam integram ac absolutam aucthoritatem potestatem et facultatem cognoscendi iurisdicendi et iudicandi de et super omnibus et omnimodis placitis processibus litibus accionibus querelis et causis quibuscunque infra Insulas et loca predicta emergentibus tam realibus personalibus et mixtis quam criminalibus et Capitalibus, eaque omnia et singula ibidem et non alibi placitandi et peragendi prosequendi et defendendi atque in eisdem vel procedendi vel supersedendi examinandi audiendi terminandi absoluendi condempnandi decidendi atque execucioni mandandi secundum leges et consuetudines Insularum et locorum maritimorum predictorum preantea vsitatas et approbatas absque prouocatione seu appellacione quacunque preterquam in casibus qui cognicioni nostre Regali ex vetusta consuetudine Insularum et locorum predictorum reseruantur. Quamquidem aucthoritatem potestatem et facultatem preterquam in iisdem casibus reseruatis nos pro nobis heredibus et successoribus nostris prefatis Balliuo et Iuratis ac aliis damus comittimus concedimus et confirmamus per presentes Adeo plene libere et integre prout praefati Balliuus et Iurati ac alii vel eorum aliquis vnquam antehac iisdem rite et legittime vsi functi aut giuisi sunt vel vti fungi et gaudere debuerunt aut licite potuerunt debuit aut potuit.

[6] Volumus preterea et pro nobis, heredibus et successoribus nostris per presentes concedimus prefatis Balliuo et Iuratis ac aliis Incolis et habitatoribus infra Insulas et loca marittima predicta quod nullus eorum de cetero per aliqua breuia seu processus ex aliquibus Curiis nostris infra Regnum nostrum Anglie emergentia sive eorum aliqua citetur euocetur in placitum trahatur seu quouis modo aliter respondere cogatur extra Insulas et loca maritima predicta coram quibuscunque Iudicibus Iusticiariis Magistratibus aut Officiariis nostris de aut super aliqua re lite materia seu causa quacumque infra Insulas praedictas emanente sed quod Insulani predicti et eorum quilibet huiusmodi breuibus et processibus non obstantibus impune valeant et possint valeat et possit infra Insulas et loca predicta residere comorari quiescere et iusticiam ibidem expectare absque aliqua pena corporali seu pecuniaria siue redempcione aut mulcta proinde incurrenda seu forisfacienda necnon absque aliqua offensione vel causa contemptus seu contumacie per nos heredes et successores

nostros illis seu eorum alicui aut aliquibus proinde infligendi irrogandi vel aliter adiudicandi Exceptis tantummodo huiusmodi casibus et non aliis qui per leges et consuetudines Insularum et locorum predictorum Regali nostre cognicioni atque examini reseruantur.

[7] Et vlterius de ampliori gracia nostra ac ex certa sciencia et mero motu nostris dedimus concessimus et confirmamus ac per has litteras nostras patentes pro nobis heredibus et successoribus nostris (quantum in nobis est) damus concedimus et confirmamus prefatis Balliuo et Iuratis ceterisque Incolis et habitatoribus Insularum et locorum marittimorum predictorum necnon mercatoribus et aliis eo confluentibus tot talia tanta huiusmodi et consimilia iura iurisdicciones immunitates impunitates indempnitates exempciones libertates et ffranchesias et priuilegia quecumque quot qualia quanta et que praefati Balliuus et Iurati ac ceteri Incole et habitatores mercatores et alii aut eorum aliquis antehac legittime et rite vsi freti seu gauisi fuerunt vsus fretus seu gauisus fuit ac omnia et singula quecumque alia in aliquibus cartis aut litteris patentibus nostris seu progenitorum nostrorum quondam Regum Anglie seu Ducum Normanie aut aliorum eis seu eorum predecessoribus antehac data concessa vel confirmata preantea vsa et non revocata seu abolita quocumque nomine aut quibuscumque nominibus iidem Balliuus Iurati ac ceteri Incole et habitatores earundem Insularum et locorum maritimorum predictorum aut eorum Predecessores seu eorum aliqui vel aliquis in eisdem litteris patentibus seu eorum aliquibus censeantur nuncupentur aut vocitentur seu censeri nuncupari aut vocitari debuerunt seu soliti fuerunt ac ea omnia et singula (licet in praesentibus minime expressa) prefatis Balliuo et Iuratis ac ceteris Incolis et habitatoribus Insularum et locorum maritimorum praedictorum necnon mercatoribus et aliis eo confluentibus Indigenis et Alienigenis per presentes confirmamus consolidamus et de integro ratificamus adeo plene libere et integre prout ea omnia et singula in eisdem litteris patentibus contenta modo perticulariter [sic] verbatim et expresse in presentibus litteris nostris patentibus recitata et declarata fuissent.

[8] Salua semper atque illabefactata Suprema Regia Potestate dominacione atque imperio Corone nostre Anglie tam quoad ligeanciam subieccionem et obedienciam Insulanorum predictorum ac aliorum quorumcumque infra Insulas et loca predicta commorancium siue degentium quam quoad Regalitates priuilegia res redditus vectigalia et cetera iura proficua commeditates et emolumenta quecumque infra Insulas et loca praedicta nobis heredibus et

successoribus nostris per prerogativam Corone nostre Anglie sive Ducatus Normanie seu aliter ex antiquo debita et consueta.

Salvis eciam appellacionibus et prouocacionibus quibuscumque Insulanorum predictorum ac aliorum ibidem commorancium siue degencium in omnibus eiusmodi casibus (et non aliis) que legibus et consuetudinibus Insularum et locorum predictorum Regali nostre cognicioni atque examini reservantur Aliqua sentencia clausula re aut materia quacumque superius in presentibus expressa siue specificata in contrarium in aliquo non obstantibus.

[9] Postremo volumus ac per presentes concedimus quod dicti Balliuus ac Iurati ac ceteri Incole et habitatores Insularum predictarum necnon mercatores et alii illuc comeantes seu confluentes habeant et de tempore in tempus habere possint has litteras nostras patentes sub magno sigillo nostro Anglie debito modo factas et sigillatas absque fine seu feodo magno vel parvo nobis in hanaperio nostro seu alibi ad vsum nostrum pro premissis quoquo modo reddendo solvendo vel faciendo.

[10] Eo quod expressa mencio de vero valore annuo aut de certitudine premissorum siue eorum alicuius aut de aliis donis siue concessionibus per nos vel per aliquem Progenitorum siue predecessorum nostrorum prefatis Balliuo et Iuratis ac ceteris Incolis et habitatoribus Insularum predictarum aut antecessoribus vel predecessoribus suis seu eorum alicui ante hec tempora factis in presentibus minime facta existit aut aliquo statuto actu ordinacione prouisione siue restriccione inde incontrarium facto edito ordinato siue prouiso aut aliqua alia re causa vel materia quacumque in aliquo non obstantibus.

In cuius rei testimonium has litteras nostras fieri fecimus Patentes.

Teste me ipsa apud Westmonasterium quintodecimo die Marcii Anno regni nostri secundo.

Per ipsam Reginam et de data predicta auctoritate parliamenti.

Phillips

~ ~ ~

ELIZABETH, by the grace of God, Queen of England, France, and Ireland, Defender of the Faith, &c

[1] To all to whom these present letters shall come, greeting. Whereas our beloved and faithful lieges and subjects, the bailiff and the jurats of our island of Guernsey, and the other sojourners in and inhabitants of both the same island and our islands of Aureneye, alias Alderney, and Sark, within our duchy of Normandy, and their predecessors, have from time beyond what the memory of men can reach, by virtue of several charters, grants, confirmations, and most ample writs, of our illustrious progenitors and ancestors, both kings of England and dukes of Normandy, and others, have used, enjoyed, and been in possession of very many rights, jurisdictions, privileges, immunities, liberties, and franchises, freely, quietly, and without any infringement of the same, both within the kingdom of England, and elsewhere within our dominions, and other places under our subjection on this side of, or beyond, the seas; by the aid and benefit of which grants, the aforesaid islands and the maritime places have stood out and continued constantly, faithfully, and unblameably in our faith, obedience, and service, and have enjoyed and gone on in their commerce and trade with merchants, both natives and aliens, as well in time of peace, as in time of war, and exercised and executed their duties in giving their decrees, and taking cognisance of all and every cause, quarrel, action, both civil and criminal, and capital pleas; and the right of jurisdiction they were vested with, to take into their consideration, to decide, discuss, hear, and determine, and to proceed in the premises, and keep records of their proceedings according to the laws and customs practised of old, and approved in the said islands and other places aforesaid; except in certain cases reserved from time to time to our royal cognisance.

[2] And we considering of how great advantage and moment all and singular the premises are, and have been, toward the safe-keeping and conservation of the said islands and other maritime places in their fidelity and allegiance to our crown of England; and being always mindful (as is just) how courageously and loyally the said islanders and inhabitants have behaved themselves in our own and in our progenitors' service, and considering what great detriments, losses and dangers they have sustained and do daily sustain, both for the constant safeguarding of the said islands and places, and for the recovery and defence of our Castle of Mont Orgueil, in our island of Jersey; to the end, not only to show some distinguished testimony and certain marks of our favour, affection, and royal beneficence towards the inhabitants aforesaid, but also to encourage them, and their posterity for ever, to persevere and continue inviolably in their accustomed and due obedience towards us, and our heirs and successors; we have

thought proper to grant to them these our royal letters patent, confirmed under the great seal of England, in form following.

[3] Know ye therefore, that we, of our special favour, certain knowledge, and mere motion, have given and granted, and for ourselves, our heirs and successors, we do by these present letters give and grant, to the said bailiff and jurats of our island of Guernsey aforesaid, and to the other sojourners and inhabitants, both of the same island, and of our other islands aforesaid, of Aureney, alias Alderney, and Sark; that they themselves and every one of them (though not herein stated or declared by their particular names) shall, for the time to come, be for ever free, exempted, and acquitted, in all our cities, boroughs, markets, and trading towns, fairs, mart-towns, and other places and ports, within our kingdom of England, and within all our provinces, dominions, territories, and other places under our subjection, this side of, or beyond, the seas, from and of all tributes, tolls, customs, subsidies, hidage, taylage, pontage, panage, murage, fossage, works, and warlike expeditions (except in case our body of ourself, the aforesaid Queen, her heirs and successors, should be held in prison (which God avert)), and of and from all other contributions and exactions whatsoever, that may be due from, to be rendered by, or be payable by, the said islanders, or any of them, to us, our heirs and successors, ever in any manner, by virtue of any charters, grants, confirmations, and writs of our said progenitors, formerly kings of England and dukes of Normandy, or others, or by virtue or reason of any reasonable and legal usage, prescriptions, or customs.

[4] And whereas some other privileges, jurisdictions, immunities, liberties, and franchises, were graciously given, granted, and confirmed by our progenitors and predecessors, formerly kings of England and dukes of Normandy, and others, to the aforesaid islanders, and have been used and observed constantly in the said islands and other maritime places, from the time whereof the memory of men reaches not to the contrary; one of which is, that in time of war merchants of all nations and others, both aliens and denizen, both enemies and friends, could and might freely, lawfully, without danger or punishment, come to, resort to, go to and fro, and frequent the said islands, and other aforesaid maritime places, with their ships, merchandise, and goods; both to avoid storms, and to conduct their other lawful business there, and to exercise there free commerce, business and trade, and securely, and without danger, remain there, and depart from thence, and return to the same, as often as they think fit, without any harm, molestation, or hostility whatsoever, in their goods, merchandise, or persons; and this not only within the said islands and maritime places, and all around the same, but likewise at such spaces and distances from the

islands as the sight of man goes to, that is as far as the eye of man can reach: We, by virtue of our royal authority, do, for ourselves, our heirs and successors, indulge and enlarge, and renew, reiterate, and confirm, by these present letters, as far as in us lies, the same immunities, impunities, liberties, and privileges, and all the other premisses last mentioned, finding them to be reasonable and seasonable, to the said bailiff and jurats, and the other sojourners, inhabitants and merchants, and others, whether enemies or friends, and to each of them, in as ample form and manner as heretofore they have used and enjoyed the same. In order therefore to prevent any violation or infraction of this our grant, concession, and confirmation, or any thing therein contained, in any manner whatsoever, we declare and give this warning by these present letters to all our officers and subjects in all parts of our kingdom of England, and throughout all our lordships and places under our obedience, wheresoever they lie, or are situated. And if any one of our said officers and subjects shall be so rash as to presume or attempt to transgress these our strict orders and commands, we order and decree (as far as in us lies), that he shall not only restore what has been taken or seized, but shall also be compelled to make a fuller restitution and satisfaction of all costs, interests, and damages, by whatever legal remedy, and he shall be severely punished for his audacious contempt of our royal power, and of our laws.

[5] Further, we, of our more gracious favour, do, by these present letters, ratify, approve, establish, and confirm, all and every one of the laws and customs which have been duly and legally from ancient times used, received, and approved within the aforesaid islands and maritime places; giving and granting to the aforesaid bailiff and jurats, and all other magistrates and officers of justice, and others who are appointed for performing the functions and executing the duties of any office, full and absolute authority, power, and faculty to have the cognisance, jurisdiction, and judgment concerning and touching all and all sorts of pleas, processes, lawsuits, actions, quarrels, and causes arising within the islands and maritime places aforesaid; both those actions which are real, personal, and mixed, and those which are criminal and capital, and to proceed in the said islands, and not elsewhere, in hearing the parties in their pleadings, and prosecutions of their processes, in their defence; and to hear, examine, and supersede the same, making decrees, determining, absolving, condemning, and putting their sentences in execution, according to the laws and customs previously practised and approved in the islands and maritime places aforesaid; without admitting any challenge or appeal, except in such cases as are reserved to our royal cognisance by the ancient customs of the islands and

places aforesaid. Which authority, power, and faculty (except in the cases reserved to us), we commit, give, grant, and confirm, for ourselves and our heirs and successors aforesaid, to the said bailiffs and jurats, and to the others, by these present letters, as freely, fully, and entirely, as the said bailiff and jurats, or others, or any of them, previously have rightfully and lawfully used, practised, and enjoyed, or might legally have used and enjoyed.

[6] Moreover, our will and pleasure is, and we grant, for ourselves, our heirs, and successors by these present letters, to the said bailiffs and jurats, and the other sojourners and inhabitants in the islands and maritime places aforesaid, that for the time to come, none of them be cited, or summoned, or drawn into any lawsuit, or forced in any manner by any writs or process, issued from any of our courts of the kingdom of England, to appear and answer before any judges, courts, or other officers of justice, out of any of the islands and maritime places aforesaid, touching or concerning any thing, dispute, causes, or matters in controversy whatsoever, arising in the aforesaid islands, but that the aforesaid islanders, and each of them, may lawfully, notwithstanding the said writs and processes, remain, reside quietly, and abide in the aforesaid islands, waiting for justice there; without incurring any punishment, corporal or pecuniary, by way of fine, mulct, ransom, or forfeiture, by reason of any offence, contempt, or contumacy, committed towards us, our heirs and successors, for which they might be sued, arraigned, or condemned; except only in the cases, and not others, which by the laws and customs of the islands and places aforesaid are reserved to our royal cognisance and determination.

[7] And moreover, of our more gracious favour, certain knowledge, and mere motion, we have given, granted, and confirmed, and by these our letters patent, for ourselves, our heirs and successors (as far as in us lies), we do give, grant, and confirm to the aforesaid bailiff and jurats, and other sojourners in, and inhabitants of, the aforesaid islands and maritime places; as also to merchants and others meeting there, the like, and as great, and as ample rights, jurisdictions, immunities, impunities, indemnities, exemptions, liberties, franchises, and privileges whatsoever, as the aforesaid bailiff and jurats, and other sojourners and inhabitants, and merchants and others, or any of them, have heretofore rightfully and legally used, practised, and enjoyed; and all and singular other things whatsoever that has been heretofore given, granted, and confirmed to them or their predecessors, in any charters or letters patent, of us or our progenitors, formerly kings of England, or dukes of Normandy, or others, and not revoked or abolished, by whatsoever name or names the same bailiff, jurats, and other sojourners in,

or inhabitants of, the same islands and maritime places aforesaid, or their predecessors, or any of them, may be supposed to have been comprised, called, or named, or ought to have been called or named, in the said letters patent, and all and singular which things, though not herein expressly mentioned, we do by these present letters confirm, consolidate, and ratify anew to the aforesaid bailiff and jurats, and other sojourners, and inhabitants, of the islands and maritime places aforesaid, and also merchants and others coming together there, those born there, and those born elsewhere, as fully, freely, and entirely, as if all and singular the things particularly mentioned and declared in the same letters patent were particularly and expressly recited and declared in these our present letters patent.

[8] Saving always entire and without detriment the regal and sovereign power, dominion, and empire of our crown of England, both as to what may concern the allegiance, subjection, and obedience of the aforesaid islanders, and others, whoever they may be, dwelling for a shorter or longer time in the same island; and also as to what may concern the regalities, privileges, incomes, revenues, tributes, and other rights, profits, commodities, and emoluments whatsoever, anciently due and accustomed to be paid to us, our heirs and successors, according to our royal prerogative as kings of England, or the prerogative of the duchy of Normandy, in the islands and places aforesaid; saving also to the aforesaid islanders, and others dwelling or being in the said islands, a right to appeal in all cases reserved to our cognisance and consideration by the laws and customs of the said island; but in no other case: Notwithstanding any sentence, clause, thing, or matter whatsoever expressed above, or specially contained to the contrary in these present letters.

[9] Lastly, our pleasure is, and by these present letters we grant, that the said bailiff and jurats, and other sojourners and inhabitants of the aforesaid islands; as also the merchants, and other persons who resort unto, and come there, may from time to time require and have these our letters patents made and sealed under our great seal of England, without rendering or paying to our use, any fine or fee, great or small, in our hanaper, or elsewhere to our use, for the same, in any way.

[10] And that although express mention of the true annual value, or of the certainty of the premises, or any of them, or of the other gifts or grants by us or any of our predecessors to the aforesaid bailiff and jurats, and other sojourners or inhabitants of the aforesaid islands, or their predecessors or ancestors, or to any of them, made before this time, is not mentioned in these present letters, or any statute, act, ordinance, proviso, or restriction to

the contrary thereof, made, ordained, or provided, or any other thing, cause, or matter whatsoever to the contrary notwithstanding.

In testimony whereof, we have caused these our letters to be made patent. Witness myself, at Westminster, the fifteenth day of March, in the second year of our reign. By the Queen herself, and by the aforesaid authority given by Parliament.

Phillips

James I

Commentary

James I, succeeding Elizabeth in March 1603, in his first charter to Guernsey did no more than confirm the terms of her grant of 1560. His charter did so without making specific reference to Elizabeth's grant, but its wording was almost precisely the same.

A year later, in a further charter, James confirmed Guernsey's rights with regard to customs etc., and then proceeded to recognise more specific rights which had in practice long been possessed by the islanders and their officers.

First, it granted Nicholas Baudouin, rector of St Peter Port, and his successors, 60 quarters of wheat per annum in perpetuity from the crown's possessions in the parish of St Saviour. This was a long-standing grant. Baudouin had been nominated by Calvin himself as minister in Guernsey, and had ever since played a central role in the Protestantism of the islands. The 1563 commissioners' report stated that they had granted Nicolas Baudouin sixty quarters of annual wheat rent; the Privy Council had ordered the same on 9 June 1563. Yet it seems he did not receive this, until in October 1567 a new commission granted him just over fifty-five quarters of annual wheat rent.[104]

The commission of 1563 had in a way bought local support for its Protestantising actions: on 20 August 1563 it had granted the Royal Court the significant revenues represented by the Petit Coutume.[105] By 1605, this had been employed on constructing a new harbour, and the charter recognised the grant and the legitimacy of the collection of the dues for a purpose considered worthy given its benefits

---

[104] Ogier, *Reformation and Society*, p. 73.

[105] Ogier, *Reformation and Society*, p. 65; *List of Records in the Greffe, Guernsey*: II, *Documents under Bailiwick Seal*, ed. J. H. Lenfestey (List and Index Society, special series, 11, 1978), p. 65, no. 447; Havilland de Sausmarez (ed.), *The Extentes of Guernsey 1248 and 1331: And Other Documents Relating to Ancient Usages and Customs in that Island* (Guernsey: La Société Guernsesiaise, 1934), p. 70.

to the security and prosperity of the islanders and those visiting for the purpose of trade.

Finally, the charter confirmed to the bailiff and jurats the right to administer the weights and measures in the islands, and the profits arising from this, in return for an annual payment of 20 shillings.

Although the appearance of the 1605 charter, in particular, is of a document which marks a new beginning in Guernsey's history, in reality there was a strong underlying continuity at work. This was seen in other respects: for example, the period saw the continuing governorship of Sir Thomas Leighton, who had been appointed as long ago as 1570 and who was to continue in the position until his death in 1610. His close alliance with both the aristocratic and ministerial wings of radical Protestantism, exemplified by his being married to a sister-in-law of Robert Dudley, earl of Leicester, and the patron of Thomas Cartwright, meant that the island's increasingly clear commitment to Presbyterianism in all its forms was not seriously challenged within the islands, and even when in 1613-16 James seems to have sanctioned a challenge from England it was not successful.[106]

JAMES I 1604[107]

JACOBUS Dei gratia Anglie Scotie ffrancie et Hibernie Rex fidei defensor etc Omnibus ad quos presentes litere peruenerint Salutem.

Cum dilecti et fideles ligei et subditi nostri Baliuus et Jurati Insule nostre de Garnezey ac ceteri Incole et habitatores tam ipsius Insule quam Insularum nostrarum de Aureney alias Alderney et Sarke infra Ducatum nostrum Normaniae, et predecessores eorum a tempore cuius contrarii memoria hominum non existit per Seperales Cartas concessiones confirmationes et amplissima diplomata illustrium Progenitorum et Antecessorum nostrorum tam Regum Anglie quam Ducum Normanie ac aliorum quamplurima Jura jurisdicciones priuilegia immunitates libertates exemptiones et franchesias libere quiete et inuiolabiliter vsi freti et gauisi fuerunt tam infra regnum nostrum Anglie quam alibi infra dominia et loca ditioni nostre Subjecta vltra

---

[106] Ogier, *Reformation and Society*, pp. 92-3; A. J. Eagleston, 'Guernsey under Sir Thomas Leighton (1570-1610)', *TSG*, xiii (1937-45), 72-108.
[107] Greffe.

citraque mare Quorum ope et beneficio predicte Insule et loca maritima predicta in fide obediencia et Seruicio tam nostri quam eorundem Progenitorum nostrorum constanter fideliter et inculpate perstiterunt ac perseuerarunt liberaque commercia cum mercatoribus et aliis indigenis et alienigenis tam pacis quam belli temporibus habuerunt et exercuerunt Judicia etiam et cognitiones omnium et omnimodo causarum querelarum accionum et placitorum tam ciuilium quam criminalium et capitalium ac judicialem potestatem ea omnia tractandi ordinandi decidendi discutiendi audiendi et terminandi atque in eisdem procedendi et in acta redigendi Secundum leges et consuetudines Insule et locorum predictorum ex antiquo receptas et approbatas preterquam in certis casibus cognitioni nostre regie reseruatis de tempore in tempus exercuerunt executi Sunt et peregerunt.

[2] Que omnia et Singula cuius et quanti momenti sunt et fuerunt ad tutelam et conseruationem Insularum et locorum maritimorum predictorum in fide et obediencia Corone nostre Anglie Nos vt equum est perpendentes neque non immemores quam fortiter et fideliter Insulani predicti ac caeteri Incole et habitatores ibidem nobis et progenitoribus nostris inseruierunt Quantaque detrimenta dampna et pericula tam pro assidua tuitione earundem Insularum et locorum quam pro recuperacione et deffencione Castri nostri de Mount Orguill infra Insulam nostram de Jersey Sustinuerunt indiesque Sustinent non Solum vt Regia nostra beneuolencia fauor et affectus erga prefatos Insulanos illustri aliquo nostre beneficencie testimonio ac certis Indiciis comprobetur verum eciam ut ipsi et eorum posteri deinceps imperpetuum prout antea Solitam et debitam obedientiam erga nos heredes et Successores nostros teneant et inuiolabiliter obseruent has literas nostras patentes magno Sigillo Anglie roboratas in forma qua Sequitur illis concedere dignati sumus.

[3] Sciatis igitur quod nos de gracia nostra Speciali ac ex certa Scientia et mero motu nostris dedimus et concessimus ac pro nobis heredibus et Successoribus nostris per presentes damus et concedimus prefatis Balliuo et Juratis Insule nostre predicte de Gernesey et ceteris Incolis et habitatoribus tam ipsius Insulae quam predictarum Insularum nostrarum de Aureney alias Alderney et Sarke Quod ipsi et eorum quilibet, licet in presentibus non recitati Seu cogniti per Specialia nomina Sint Semper infuturum ita liberi quieti et immunes in omnibus Ciuitatibus Burgis Emporiis Nundinis mercatis villis mercatoriis ac aliis locis ac portibus infra Regnum nostrum Anglie ac infra omnes Prouincias Dominia Territorias et loca dicioni nostre Subiecta tam citra

quam vltra mare de et ab omnibus vectigalibus Theoloneis Custumiis Subsidiis hidagiis tallagiis pontagiis pannagiis muragiis fossagiis operibus expeditionibus bellicis nisi in casu vbi corpus nostri heredum vel Successorum nostrorum (quod absit) in prisona detineatur et de et ab omnibus aliis contribucionibus et exactionibus in personis monetis rebus et aliis deueriis quibuscunque nobis heredibus et Successoribus nostris quouismodo debitis reddendis Seu Soluendis prout prefati Insulani Seu eorum aliquis virtute aliquarum Cartarum Concessionum confirmationum Siue diplomatum per predictos progenitores Siue antecessores nostros quondam Reges Anglie et Duces Normannie Siue alios Seu virtute et vigore alicuius racionabilis et legalis vsus prescriptionis vel consuetudinis vnquam aliquando fuerunt aut esse debuerunt vel potuerunt debuit vel potuit quouismodo.

[4] Cumque nonnulla alia priuilegia iurisdicciones immunitates libertates et franchesias per predictos progenitores et predecessores nostros quondam Reges Anglie et Duces Normannie ac alios prefatis Insulanis indulta donata concessa et confirmata fuerunt ac a tempore cuius contrarii memoria hominum non existit infra Insulas et loca maritima predicta inuiolabiliter vsitata et obseruata fuerunt de quibus vnum est Quod tempore belli omnium nacionum marcatores [sic] et alii tam Alienigene quam Indigene tam hostes quam amici libere licite et impune queant et possint dictas Insulas et loca maritima cum nauibus mercibus et bonis Suis tam pro euitandis tempestatibus quam pro aliis licitis Suis negotiis inibi peragendis adire accedere comeare et frequentare ac Iibera commercia negociacionem et rem mercatoriam ibidem exercere ac tuto et Secure comorari indeque remeare et redire toties quoties absque dampno molestia Seu hostilitate quacunque in rebus mercibus bonis aut corporibus Suis idque non Solum infra Insulas et loca maritima predicta ac procinctum eorundem verumeciam infra spacia vndique ab eisdem distantia vsque ad visum hominis id est quatenus visus oculi possit assequi Nos eandem immunitates impunitates libertates et priuilegia ac cetera omnia premissa vltime recitata rata grataque habentes ea pro nobis heredibus et Successoribus nostris quantum in nobis est prefatis Balliuo et Juratis ac ceteris Incolis habitatoribus mercatoribus et aliis tam hostibus quam amicis et eorum cuilibet per presentes indulgemus ac elargimur Authoritateque nostra regia renouamus reiteramus et confirmamus in tam amplis modo et forma prout predicti Incole et habitatores Insularum predictarum ac predicti Alienigene et indigene preantea vsi et gauisi fuerunt. Uniuersis igitur et Singulis ministris et subditis nostris per vniuersum Regnum nostrum Anglie ac cetera dominia et loca dicioni nostre

Subiecta vbilibet constitutis per presentes denunciamus et firmiter iniungendo praecipimus ne hanc nostram donacionem concessionem et confirmacionem Seu aliquid in eisdem expressum aut contentum temerarie infringere Seu quouismodo violare presumant Et Si quis ausu temerario contrafecerit Seu attemptauerit volumus et decernimus quantum in nobis est quod restituat non Solum ablata aut erepta Sed quod eciam pro dampno interesse et expensis ad plenariam recompensacionem et Satisfactionem compellatur per quecunque iuris nostri remedia Seuereque puniatur vt regie nostre potestatis ac legum nostrarum contemptor temerarius.

[5] Preterea ex vberiori gracia nostra per presentes ratificamus approbamus Stabilimus et confirmamus omnes et singulas leges ordinaciones constitutiones recorda inquisitiones et consuetudines infra Insulas et loca maritima predicta rite et legitime vsitatas compertas habitas et ex antiquo receptas et approbatas Dantes et tribuentes prefatis Balliuo et Juratis ac omnibus aliis magistratibus ministris et ceteris quibuscunque ibidem in officio et funcione [sic] aliqua constitutis plenam integram ac absolutam authoritatem potestatem et facultatem ordinandi cognoscendi iurisdicendi et iudicandi de et Super omnibus et omnimodis placitis processibus litibus accionibus querelis et causis quibuscunque infra Insulas et loca predicta emergentibus tam realibus personalibus et mixtis quam criminalibus et capitalibus eaque omnia et Singula ibidem et non alibi placitandi et peragendi prosequendi et defendendi atque in eisdem vel prosequendi vel supersedendi examinandi audiendi terminandi absoluendi condemnandi decidandi atque executioni mandandi Secundum leges et consuetudines Insularum et locorum maritimorum predictorum preantea vsitatas et approbatas absque prouocatione Seu appellatione quacunque preterquam in casibus qui cognicioni nostre regali ex vetustis in consuetudinibus Insularum et locorum predictorum reseruantur. Quam quidem authoritatem potestatem et facultatem preterquam in eisdem casibus reseruatis nos pro nobis heredibus et Successoribus nostris prefatis Balliuo et Juratis ac aliis damus comittimus concedimus et confirmamus per presentes adeo plene libere et integre prout prefati Balliuus et Jurati ac alii vel eorum aliquis vnquam antehac eisdem rite et legitime vsi functi aut gauisi Sunt vel vti fungi aut gaudere debuerunt aut licite potuerunt debuit aut potuit.

[6] Volumus preterea ac pro nobis heredibus et Successoribus nostris per presentes concedimus prefatis Balliuo et Juratis ac aliis Incolis et habitatoribus infra Insulas et loca maritima predicta quod nullus eorum decetero per aliqua

breuia Seu processus ex aliquibus Curiis nostris infra regnum nostrum Anglie emergencia Siue earum aliqua citetur euocetur in placito trahatur Seu quouismodo aliter respondere cogatur extra Insulas et loca maritima predicta coram quibuscunque Judicibus Justiciariis Magistratibus aut Officiariis nostris de aut Super aliqua re lite materia seu causa quacunque infra Insulas predictas emanante Sed quod Insulani predicti et eorum quilibet (huiusmodi breuibus et processibus non obstantibus) impune valeant et possint valeat et possit infra Insulas et loca maritima predicta residere comorari quiescere et Justiciam ibidem expectare absque aliqua pena corporali Seu pecuniario siue redempcione aut mulcta proinde incurrenda Seu forisfacienda Nec non absque aliqua offensione vel causa contemptus Seu contumacie per nos heredes et Successores nostros illis Seu eorum alicui aut aliquibus pro inde infligendi irrogandi vel aliter adiudicandi (exceptis tantumodo huiusmodi casibus et non aliis qui per leges et consuetudines Insularum et locorum predictorum regali nostre cognicioni atque examini reseruantur).

[7] Et Ulterius de ampliori gratia nostra ac ex certa Scientia et mero motu nostris dedimus concessimus et confirmauimus ac per presentes pro nobis heredibus et Successoribus nostris quantum in nobis est damus concedimus et confirmamus prefatis Balliuo et Juratis ceterisque Incolisque et habitatoribus Insularum et locorum maritimorum predictorum necnon mercatoribus et aliis eo confluentibus tot tanta talia huiusmodi et consimilia Jura ordinaciones - Jurisdicciones immunitates impunitates indempnitates exempciones libertates franchesias et priuilegia quecunque quot quanta qualia et que prefati Balliuus et Jurati ac ceteri Incole et habitatores mercatores et alii aut eorum aliquis antehac legitime et rite vsi freti seu gauisi fuerunt vsus fretus Seu gauisus fuit ac omnia et singula quecunque alia in aliquibus cartis aut literis patentibus nostris Seu progenitorum Siue predecessorum nostrorum quondam regum Anglie Seu Ducum Normannie aut aliorum eis Seu eorum predecessoribus antehac data concessa vel confirmata preantea vsa et non reuocata Seu abolita quocunque nomine aut quibuscunque nominibus iidem Balliuus Jurati et ceteri Incole et habitatores earundem Insularum et locorum maritimorum predictorum aut eorum predecessores Seu eorum aliqui vel aliquis in eisdem literis patentibus seu eorum aliquibus censeantur nuncupentur aut vocitentur Seu censeri nuncupari aut vocitari debuerunt Seu Soliti fuerunt ac ea omnia et singula licet in presentibus minime expressa prefatis Balliuo et Juratis ac ceteris Incolis et habitatoribus Insularum et locorum maritimorum predictorum Necnon mercatoribus et aliis eo confluentibus indigenis et alienigenis per

presentes confirmamus consolidamus et de integro ratificamus adeo plene libere et integre prout ea omnia et singula in eisdem literis patentibus contenta modo particulariter verbatim et expresse in presentibus recitata et declarata fuissent.

[8] Salua Semper atque illabefactata suprema regia potestate dominacione atque imperio corone nostre Anglie tam quoad ligeanciam Subieccionem et obedienciam Insulanorum predictorum ac aliorum quorumcunque [sic] infra Insulas et loca predicta comorancium Siue degencium quam quoad regalitatem priuilegia res redditus vectigalia ac cetera iura proficua commoditates et emolumenta quecunque infra Insulas et loca predicta nobis et heredibus et Successoribus nostris per prerogatiuam Corone nostre Anglie Siue Ducatus Normannie Seu aliter ex antiquo debita et consueta.

Saluis eciam appellacionibus et prouocacionibus quibuscunque Insulanorum predictorum ac aliorum ibidem comorancium Siue degencium in omnibus eiusmodi casibus et non aliis que legibus et consuetudinibus Insularum et locorum predictorum regali nostre cognitioni atque examini reseruantur Aliqua Sentencia clausula re aut materia quacunque Superius in presentibus expressa Siue Specificata in contrarium inde in aliquo non obstantibus.

[9] Postremo volumus ac per presentes concedimus Quod dicti Balliui et Jurati ac ceteri Incole ac habitatores Insularum predictarum Necnon mercatores et alii illuc comeantes Seu confluentes habeant et de tempore in tempus habere possint has literas nostras patentes sub magno Sigillo nostro Anglie debito modo factas et Sigillatas absque fine Seu feodo magno vel paruo nobis in hanaperio nostro Seu alibi ad vsum nostrum pro premissis quoquomodo reddendo soluendo vel faciendo.

[10] Eo quod expressa mentio de vero valore annuo vel certitudine premissorum Siue eorum alicuius aut de aliis donis siue concessionibus per nos aut per aliquem antecessorum Siue progenitorum nostrorum prefatis Balliuo et Juratis ac ceteris Incolis et habitatoribus Insularum predictarum ante hec tempora factis in presentibus minime facta existit aut aliquo Statuto Actu Ordinacione Prouisione Proclamatione Siue restriccione inde in contrarium ante hac habito facto edito ordinato Siue prouiso aut aliqua alia re causa vel materia quacunque in aliquo non obstantibus.

In cuius rei testimonium has literas nostras fieri fecimus patentes.

Teste me ipso apud Westmonasterium decimo octauo die Decembris Anno regni nostri Anglie ffrancie et hibernie Secundo et Scotie tricesimo octauo.

T. Rauenscrofte

per breue de priuato Sigillo

Examinata per me Thomam Marten

~ ~ ~

James, by the grace of God, king of England, Scotland, France, and Ireland, Defender of the Faith, etc.

[1] To all to whom these present letters shall come, greeting. Whereas our beloved and faithful lieges and subjects, the bailiff and the jurats of our Island of Guernsey, and the other sojourners in and inhabitants of both the same island and our islands of Aureneye, alias Alderney, and Sark, within our duchy of Normandy, and their predecessors, have from time beyond what the memory of men can reach, by virtue of several charters, grants, confirmations, and most ample writs, of our illustrious progenitors and ancestors, both kings of England and dukes of Normandy, and others, used, enjoyed, and been in possession of very many rights, jurisdictions, privileges, immunities, liberties, and franchises, freely, quietly, and without any infringement of the same, both within the kingdom of England, and elsewhere within our dominions, and other places under our subjection on this side of, or beyond, the seas; by the aid and benefit of which grants, the aforesaid islands and the maritime places have stood out and continued constantly, faithfully, and unblameably in our faith, obedience, and service, and have enjoyed and gone on in their commerce and trade with merchants, both natives and aliens, as well in time of peace, as in time of war, and exercised and executed their duties in giving their decrees, and taking cognisance of all and every cause, quarrel, action, both civil and criminal, and capital pleas; and the right of jurisdiction they were vested with, to take into their consideration, to take order, decide, discuss, hear, and determine, and to proceed in the premises, and keep records of their proceedings according to the laws and customs practised of old, and approved in the said islands and other places aforesaid; except in certain cases reserved from time to time to our royal cognisance:

[2] And we considering of how great advantage and moment all and singular the premises are, and have been, toward the safe-keeping and conservation of the said islands and other maritime places in their fidelity and allegiance to our crown of England; and being always mindful (as is

just) how courageously and loyally the said islanders and inhabitants have behaved themselves in our own and in our progenitors' service, and considering what great detriments, losses and dangers they have sustained and do daily sustain, both for the constant safeguarding of the said islands and places, and for the recovery and defence of our Castle of Mont Orgueil, in our island of Jersey; to the end, not only to show some distinguished testimony and certain marks of our favour, affection, and royal beneficence towards the inhabitants aforesaid, but also to encourage them, and their posterity for ever, to persevere and continue inviolably in their accustomed and due obedience towards us, and our heirs and successors; we have thought proper to grant to them these our royal letters patent, confirmed under the great seal of England, in form following.

[3] Know ye therefore, that we, of our special favour, certain knowledge, and mere motion, have given and granted, and for ourselves, our heirs and successors, we do by these present letters give and grant, to the said bailiff and jurats of our island of Guernsey aforesaid, and to the other sojourners and inhabitants, both of the same island, and of our other islands aforesaid, of Aureney, alias Alderney, and Sark; that they themselves and every one of them (though not herein stated or declared by their particular names) shall, for the time to come, be for ever free, exempted, and acquitted, in all our cities, boroughs, markets, and trading towns, fairs, mart-towns, and other places and ports, within our kingdom of England, and within all our provinces, dominions, territories, and other places under our subjection, this side of, or beyond, the seas, from and of all tributes, tolls, customs, subsidies, hidage, taylage, pontage, panage, murage, fossage, works, and warlike expeditions (except in case our body, or that of our heirs and successors, should be held in prison (which God avert)), and of and from all other contributions and exactions from their persons, money, goods and other duties whatsoever, that may be due from, to be rendered by, or be payable by, and claimed from, the said islanders, or any of them, to us, our heirs and successors, ever in any manner, by virtue of any charters, grants, confirmations, and writs of our said progenitors, formerly kings of England and dukes of Normandy, or others, or by virtue or reason of any reasonable and legal usage, prescriptions, or customs.

[4] And whereas some other privileges, jurisdictions, immunities, liberties, and franchises have been graciously given, granted, and confirmed by our progenitors and predecessors, formerly kings of England and dukes of Normandy, and others, to the aforesaid islanders, and have been used and observed constantly in the said islands and other maritime places, from the time whereof the memory of men reaches not to the contrary; one of

which is, that in time of war merchants of all nations and others, both aliens and denizen, both enemies and friends, could and might freely, lawfully, without danger or punishment, come to, resort to, go to and fro, and frequent the said islands, and other aforesaid maritime places, with their ships, merchandise, and goods; both to avoid storms, and to conduct their other lawful business there, and to exercise there free commerce, business and trade, and securely, and without danger, remain there, and depart from thence, and return to the same, as often as they think fit, without any harm, molestation, or hostility whatsoever, in their goods, merchandise, or persons; and this not only within the said islands and maritime places, and all around the same, but likewise at such spaces and distances from the islands as the sight of man goes to, that is as far as the eye of man can reach: We, by virtue of our royal authority, do, for ourselves, our heirs and successors, indulge and enlarge, and renew, reiterate, and confirm, by these present letters, as far as in us lies, the same immunities, impunities, liberties, and privileges, and all the other premises last mentioned, finding them to be reasonable and seasonable, to the said bailiff and jurats, and the other sojourners, inhabitants and merchants, and others, whether enemies or friends, and to each of them, in as ample form and manner as heretofore they have used and enjoyed the same. In order therefore to prevent any violation or infraction of this our grant, concession, and confirmation, or any thing therein contained, in any manner whatsoever, we declare and give this warning by these present letters to all our officers and subjects in all parts of our kingdom of England, and throughout all our lordships and places under our obedience, wheresoever they lie, or are situated. And if any one of our said officers and subjects shall be so rash as to presume or attempt to transgress these our strict orders and commands, we order and decree (as far as in us lies), that he shall not only restore what has been taken or seized, but shall also be compelled to make a fuller restitution and satisfaction of all costs, interests, and damages, by whatever legal remedy, and he shall be severely punished for his audacious contempt of our royal power, and of our laws.

[5] Further, we, of our more gracious favour, do, by these present letters, ratify, approve, establish, and confirm, all and every one of the laws, ordinances, constitutions, records, inquisitions, and customs which have been duly and legally from ancient times used, received, found, had, and approved within the aforesaid islands and maritime places; giving and granting to the aforesaid bailiff and jurats, and all other magistrates and officers of justice, and others who are appointed for performing the functions and executing the duties of any office, full and absolute authority, power, and

faculty to have the cognisance, jurisdiction, and judgment concerning and touching all and all sorts of pleas, processes, law-suits, actions, quarrels, and causes arising within the islands and maritime places aforesaid; both those actions which are real, personal, and mixed, and those which are criminal and capital, and to proceed in the said islands, and not elsewhere, in hearing the parties in their pleadings, and prosecutions of their processes, in their defence; and to hear, examine, and supersede the same, making decrees, determining, absolving, condemning, and putting their sentences in execution, according to the laws and customs previously practised and approved in the islands and maritime places aforesaid; without admitting any challenge or appeal, except in such cases as are reserved to our royal cognisance by the ancient customs of the islands and places aforesaid. Which authority, power, and faculty (except in the cases reserved to us), we commit, give, grant, and confirm, for ourselves and our heirs and successors aforesaid, to the said bailiffs and jurats, and to the others, by these present letters, as freely, fully, and entirely, as the said bailiff and jurats, or others or any of them, heretofore have rightfully and lawfully used, practised, and enjoyed, or might legally have used and enjoyed.

[6] Moreover, our will and pleasure is, and we grant, for ourselves, our heirs, and successors by these present letters, to the said bailiff and jurats, and the other inhabitants and sojourners in the islands and maritime places aforesaid, that for the time to come, none of them be cited, or summoned, or drawn into any lawsuit, or forced in any manner by any writs or process, issued from any of our courts of the kingdom of England, to appear and answer before any judges, courts, or other officers of justice, out of any of the islands and maritime places aforesaid, touching or concerning any thing, dispute, causes, or matters in controversy whatsoever, arising in the aforesaid islands, but that the aforesaid islanders, and each of them, may lawfully, notwithstanding the said writs and processes, remain, reside quietly, and abide in the aforesaid islands, waiting for justice there; without incurring any punishment, corporal or pecuniary, by way of fine, mulct, ransom, or forfeiture, by reason of any offence, contempt, or contumacy, committed towards us, our heirs and successors, for which they might be sued, arraigned, or condemned; except only in the cases, and not others, which by the laws and customs of the islands and places aforesaid are reserved to our royal cognisance and determination.

[7] And moreover, of our more gracious favour, certain knowledge, and mere motion, we have given, granted, and confirmed, and by our present letters, for ourselves, our heirs and successors (as far as in us lies), we do give, grant, and confirm to the aforesaid bailiff and jurats, and other so-

journers in, and inhabitants of, the aforesaid islands and maritime places; as also to merchants and others meeting there, the like, and as great, and as ample rights, ordinances, jurisdictions, immunities, impunities, indemnities, exemptions, liberties, franchises, and privileges whatsoever, as the aforesaid bailiff and jurats, and other sojourners and inhabitants, and merchants and others, or any of them, have heretofore rightfully and legally used, practised, and enjoyed; and all and singular other things whatsoever that has been heretofore given, granted, and confirmed to them or to their predecessors, in any charters or letters patent, of us or our progenitors, formerly kings of England, or dukes of Normandy, or others, and not revoked or abolished, by whatsoever name or names the same bailiff and jurats, and other sojourners in, or inhabitants of, the same islands and maritime places aforesaid, or their predecessors, or any of them, may be supposed to have been comprised, called, or named, or ought to have been called or named, in the said letters patent, and all and singular which things, though not herein expressly mentioned, we do by these present letters confirm, consolidate, and ratify anew to the aforesaid bailiff and jurats, and other sojourners, and inhabitants, of the islands and maritime places aforesaid, and also merchants and others coming together there, those born there, and those born elsewhere, as fully, freely, and entirely, as if all and singular the things particularly mentioned and declared in the same letters patent were particularly and expressly recited and declared in these our present letters patent.

[8] Saving always entire and without detriment the regal and sovereign power, dominion, and empire of our crown of England, as to what may concern the allegiance, subjection, and obedience of the aforesaid islanders, and others, whoever they may be, dwelling for a shorter or longer time in the same island; and also as to what may concern the regality, privileges, incomes, revenues, tributes, and other rights, profits, commodities, and emoluments whatsoever, anciently due and accustomed to be paid to us, our heirs and successors, according to our royal prerogative as kings of England, or the prerogative of the duchy of Normandy, in the islands and places aforesaid; saving also to the aforesaid islanders, and others dwelling or being in the said islands, a right to appeal in all cases reserved to our cognisance and consideration by the laws and customs of the said island; but in no other case: Notwithstanding any sentence, clause, thing, or matter whatsoever expressed above, or specially contained to the contrary in these present letters.

[9] Lastly, our pleasure is, and by these present letters we grant, that the said bailiff and jurats, and other sojourners and inhabitants of the aforesaid

islands; as also the merchants, and other persons who resort unto, and come there, may from time to time require and have these our letters patents made and sealed under our great seal of England, without rendering or paying to our use, any fine or fee, great or small, in our hanaper, or else-where to our use, for the same, in any way.

[10] And that although express mention of the true annual value, or of the certainty of the premises, or any of them, or of the other gifts or grants by us or any of our ancestors or progenitors to the aforesaid bailiff and jurats, and other sojourners or inhabitants of the aforesaid islands, made before this time, is not mentioned in these present letters, or any statute, act, ordi-nance, proviso, proclamation, or restriction to the contrary thereof before this time made, ordained, or provided, or any other thing, cause, or matter whatsoever to the contrary notwithstanding.

In testimony whereof, we have caused these our letters to be made patent. Witness myself, at Westminster, the eighteenth day of December, in the second year of our reign over England, France, and Ireland, and over Scotland the thirty-eighth.

T. Rauenscrofte

By writ of privy seal.

Examined by me Thomas Marten

~ ~ ~

JAMES I 1605[108]

Jacobus Dei gratia Anglie Scocie ffrancie et Hibernie Rex fidei defensor &c. Omnibus ad quos presentes litere peruenerint Salutem.

Sciatis quod nos ad humilem peticionem dilectorum et fidelium ligeorum et Subditorum nostrorum Balliui et Juratorum Insule nostre de Garnezey ac ceterorum Incolarum et Inhabitancium tam ipsius Insule quam Insularum nostrarum de Aureney alias Alderney et Sarke infra Ducatum nostrum Normanie de gracia nostra Speciali ac ex certa Scientia et mero motu nostris concessimus confirmauimus ratificauimus et approbauimus ac per presentes pro nobis heredibus et successoribus nostris concedimus et confirmamus ratificamus et approbamus prefatis Balliuo et Juratis Insule de Garnezey predicte ac

---

[108] Greffe.

ceteris Incolis et Inhabitantibus tam ipsius Insule de Garnezey quam predic-
tarum Insularum nostrarum de Aureney alias Alderney et Sarke predictarum
et Successoribus suis omnia et Singula tot tanta talia huiusmodi et consimilia
exoneraciones et acquietancias de et ab Solucione Toluete alias vocate petite
Custome ac de et ab omnibus aliis Tallagiis toluetis cariagiis consuetudinibus
riuagiis asponsagiis et omni wreck' achato et rechato Suo ac de recta prisa
nostra videlicet de vno dolio vini ante mallum et alio post mallum Necnon
tot tanta talia huiusmodi et consimilia libertates franchesie priuilegia Immu-
nitates exoneraciones ac acquietantias quecunque quot quanta qualia et que
iidem Balliuus et Jurati Insule de Garnezey predicte ac ceteri Incole et In-
habitantes tam ipsius Insule de Garnezey quam predictarum Insularum de
Aureney alias Alderney et Sarke predictarum per quodcunque nomen Incor-
poracionis Siue per quecunque nomina Incorporacionum antehac legittime
habuerunt tenuerunt aut vsi vel gauisi fuerunt aut habere tenere vti vel
gaudere debuerunt de Statu hereditario aut eorum aliquis antehac legittime
habuit tenuit vsus vel gauisus fuit aut habere tenere vti vel gaudere debuit de
Statu hereditario racione vel in pretextu aliquarum chartarum vel literarum
patentium per nos aut per aliquem progenitorum Siue Antecessorum nos-
trorum nuper regum aut reginarum Anglie eis aut predecessoribus Suis per
quodcunque Nomen Incorporacionis Siue per quecunque nomina Incorpora-
cionum antehac data concessa Seu confirmata aut racione vel pretextu alicuius
prescriptionis vsus Seu consuetudinis in eadem Insula de Garnezey ac in
predictis Insulis de Alderney et Sarke aut in earum aliqua antehac habitarum
vsitatarum Siue consuetarum aut aliquo alio legali modo iure Seu titulo
quocunque Habendum eis et Successoribus Suis imperpetuum Tenendum de
nobis heredibus et Successoribus nostris per talia eadem huiusmodi et con-
similia redditus et Seruitia per qualia et prout antehac de nobis aut de
domina Elizabeth nuper Regine Anglie tenebantur et non per alia

[2] Et Ulterius de abundanciori gracia nostra Speciali ac ex certa Sciencia et
mero [repeated] motu nostris concessimus ac per presentes pro nobis heredibus
et Successoribus nostris concedimus prefatis Balliuo et Juratis Insule nostre de
Garnezey ac ceteris Incolis et Inhabitantibus tam ipsius Insule quam Insu-
larum nostrarum de Alderney et Sarke predictarum et Successoribus Suis
Quod ipsi et Successores Sui decetero imperpetuum exonerati et acquietati
Sint erunt de et ab Solucione alicuius custume Subsidii tonnagii Siue ponda-
gii cuiuscunque nobis heredibus vel Successoribus nostris debito Siue Solubili
de aut pro aliquibus mercibus Siue merchandizis quibuscunque infra predictas

Insulas de Garnezey Alderney et Sarke crescentibus prouenientibus factis Siue operatis et que per prefatum Balliuium et Iuratos Insule de Garnezey aut ceteros Incolas et Inhabitantes tam ipsius Insule quam Insularum nostrarum de Alderney et Sarke predictarum aliquo tempore imposterum in hoc regno nostro Anglie aut aliquem portum Siue crecam eiusdem regni transportatis conueiatis Siue adductis erunt per presentes pro tali transportacione

[3] Et Ulterius volumus ac per presentes pro nobis heredibus et Successoribus nostris de gratia nostra Speciali ac ex certa Sciencia et mero motu nostris concedimus Nicholas Baudouyn Rectori Ecclesie parochialis Sancti Petri infra predictam Insulam nostram de Garnezey et Successoribus Suis annuatim imperpetuum ad et versus manutencionem Sustentacionem et releuamencionem eiusdem Rectoris et Successorum Suorum pro tempore existenti Sexaginta quarteria frumenti nostri percipienda capienda et recipienda eadem Sexaginta quarteria frumenti annuatim de redditibus reuencionibus et aliis proficuis nobis heredibus et Successoribus nostris annuatim prouenientibus debitis Siue Solubilis in parochia Sancti Saluatoris infra eandem Insulam de Garnezey racione fraternitatis obitum missarum et aliorum huiusmodi vigore aliquorum Actuum Parliamentorum infra hoc regnum Anglie in eo casu editorum et prouisorum aut aliquo alio titulo Siue iure quocunque eisdem modo et forma ac eisdem diebus et temporibus prout predictus Nicholaus Baudouyn eadem antehac percipere capere et recipere consueuit

[4] Cumque nos credibiliter informamur Quod Inhabitantes dicte Insule nostre de Garnezey magnis oneribus Sumptibus et expensis Suis edificare construere et erigere inchoauerunt quendam portum Siue le Peere in mare prope Insulam de Garnezey predictam qui quidem portus Siue le Peere iam pene perfectus et consummatus existit ad magnam Securitatem et emolumentum omnium mercatorum et aliorum in partes illas merchandizandi et negociandi causa confluentium

[5] Cumque eciam nos Similiter informamur Quod Balliuus et Jurati dicte Insule de Garnezey et predecessores Sui tempore regni domine Elizabeth nuper regine Anglie leuauerunt et perceperunt ac leuare et percipere consueuerunt ad et versus fabricam et Structuram Portus Siue le Peere quandam consuetudinem Siue custumam vulgariter vocatam pettie Custome de quibusdam merchandizis mercibus Nauibus et aliis rebus tam in eandem Insulam

de Garnezey de tempore in tempus adductis Siue importatis quam in eadem Insula crescentibus Siue operatis

[6] *Sciatis quod nos pro plenaria perfeccione et consummacione Portus Siue le Peere predicti ac pro perpetua reparacione Sustentacione et emendatione eiusdem Necnon pro Supportacione et manutencione aliorum publicorum expensarum et onerum eiusdem Insule de gracia nostra Speciali ac ex certa Sciencia et mero motu nostris dedimus et concessimus ac per presentes pro nobis heredibus et Successoribus nostris damus et concedimus plenam liberam et licitam potestatem facultatem et authoritatem prefatis Balliuo et Juratis et Successoribus Suis Quod ipsi et Successores Sui decetero imperpetuum libere licite et impune capere percipere et recipere possint et valeant ad plenam et perfectam construccionem et edificacionem predicti Portus Siue le Peere ac ad perpetuam reparacionem Sustentacionem et emendationem eiusdem Necnon ad Supportationem et manutencionem aliorum publicorum expensarum et onerum eiusdem Insule tam de et pro omnibus et Singulis Merchandizis mercibus nauibus et aliis rebus in eandem Insulam de tempore in tempus adductis Siue importatis adducendis Siue importandis quam de omnibus et Singulis merchandizis mercibus et aliis rebus in eadem Insula crescentibus Siue operatis crescituris Siue operandis tot tanta talia et huiusmodi denariorum Summas nomine parue custum Anglice pettie Custume quot quanta qualia et que tempore regni dicte nuper regine Elizabeth capere percipere Siue recipere ligitime [sic] consueuerunt*

[7] *Et vlterius de vberiori gracia nostra Speciali ac ex certa sciencia et mero motu nostris dedimus et concessimus ac per presentes pro nobis heredibus et Successoribus nostris damus et concedimus prefatis Balliuo et Juratis et Successoribus suis imperpetuum ponderacionem et mensuram omnium huiusmodi marchandizarum et aliarum rerum quarumcunque que antehac ponderari Seu mensurari Solebant apud le common Beame and measures gallice poids et mesures du Roy Insule predicte Ac omnia proficua commoditates et emolumenta quecunque pro huiusmodi ponderacione et mensuracione antehac vsualiter percepta habita Siue consueta in tam amplis modo et forma prout nos aut domina Elizabetha nuper regina Anglie Siue iidem Balliuus et Jurati habuimus percepimus Siue gauisi fuimus habuit percepit Siue gauisus fuit aut habuerunt perceperunt vel gauisi fuerunt Habendum tenendum et gaudendum predictam ponderacionem et mensuracionem ac proficua commoditates et emolumenta inde prefatis Balliuo et Juratis et Successoribus Suis imper-*

petuum ad Solum et proprium opus et vsum eorundem Balliuis et Juratorum et Successorum Suorum imperpetuum

[8] Reddendo inde annuatim nobis heredibus et Successoribus nostris annualem redditum Siue annualem Summam viginti Solidorum legalis monete Anglie per Annum ad manus Receptoris reuencionum nostrarum heredum et Successorum nostrorum dicte Insule de Garnezey ad festum Sancti Michaelis Archangeli Singulis Annis Soluendam imperpetuum

[9] Volumus et per presentes concedimus prefatis Balliuo et Juratis quod habeunt et habebunt has literas nostras patentes Sub magno Sigillo nostro Anglie debito modo factas et Sigillatas absque fine Seu feodo magno vel paruo nobis in hanaperio Cancellarum nostre Seu alibi ad usum nostrum quoquomodo reddendo Seu Soluendo

[10] Eo quod expressa mencio de vero valore annuo aut de aliquo alio valore vel certitudine premissorum siue eorum alicuius aut de aliis donis Siue concessionibus per nos Seu per aliquem Antecessorum Seu progenitorum nostrorum prefatis Balliuo et Juratis ante hec tempora factis in presentibus minime facta existit aut aliquo Statuto Actu ordinacione prouisione proclamacione Siue restriccione inde in contrarium antehac habito facto edito ordinato Siue prouiso aut aliqua alia re causa vel materia quacunque in aliquo non obstante

In cuius rei testimonium has literas nostras fieri fecimus patentes

Teste me ipso apud Westmonasterium quintodecimo die Junii Anno regni nostri Anglie ffrancie et Hibernie tercio et Scocie tricesimo octauo.

per breue de priuato Sigillo &c

T Ravenscrofte

~ ~ ~

James, by the grace of God, King of England, Scotland, France, and Ireland, Defender of the Faith, etc. To all those to whom these present letters come, greeting.

Know that we, at the humble petition of our beloved and faithful liege subjects, the bailiff and the jurats of our Island of Guernsey, and the other sojourners in, and inhabitants of the same Island, as well as of our Islands of Aureney, alias Alderney, and Sark, within our duchy of Normandy, of our special favour, certain knowledge, and mere motion, have given, confirmed, ratified and approved, and, for ourselves, our heirs and successors, do by these present letters give and confirm, ratify and approve, to the said bailiff and jurats of our Island of Guernsey aforesaid, and to the other sojourners and inhabitants, as well of the said Island, as of our other Islands aforesaid, of Aureney, alias Alderney, and Sark, and to their successors, all and singular, as many, as ample, and all the like exemptions and acquittances from and of the payment of taylage, tolls, carriage services, customs, rivages, asponsages, and all wreck, emption and redemption and of our rightful prise, viz. of one tun of wine *ante mallum* and another *post mallum*. And also the like, and as great, and as ample liberties, franchises, privileges, immunities, discharges, and acquittances whatsoever, as the said bailiff and jurats of the aforesaid island of Guernsey and the aforesaid other sojourners and inhabitants both of the same island of Guernsey and of the aforesaid islands of Aureney alias Alderney and Sark, by whatever name of incorporation or names of incorporations, or any of them, previously legitimately had, held or used or enjoyed, or ought to have had, held, used or enjoyed, of an hereditary state, by reason of, or on the grounds of, any charters or letters patent given, granted or confirmed by us or by any of our progenitors or predecessors formerly kings or queens of England to them or their predecessors by whatsoever name, incorporation or by whatsoever names or incorporations before this or by reason or on the grounds of any prescription, use or custom in the same island of Guernsey and in the aforesaid islands of Alderney and Sark or in any of them before this had, used or accustomed, or by any other legal manner, right or title whatsoever, to be had and held to them and their successors for ever, of us, our heirs and successors, by such, similar, equivalent and equal rent and service as they were previously held of us or of Lady Elizabeth formerly queen of England, and not otherwise.

[2] And further, of our fuller and special favour, certain knowledge and mere motion, we have granted and by these present letters for us, our heirs and successors, we grant to the aforesaid bailiff and jurats of our island of Guernsey and to the other sojourners and inhabitants, as of the same isle as of our aforesaid isles of Alderney and Sark and their successors, that for the time to come they themselves and their successors should perpetually henceforth be free and quit of and from the payment of any custom, subsidy, tonnage or poundage whatsoever kind owed or payable to us, our heirs or successors of or for any goods or merchandise of any kind growing, coming forth, made or produced within the aforesaid islands of Guernsey, Alderney and Sark and which were transported, conveyed, or brought by

the aforesaid bailiff and jurats of the island of Guernsey or other sojourners and inhabitants, both of the same island and of our islands of Alderney and Sark aforesaid at any time in the past in this our realm of England or any port or creek of the same realm, by the present letters, for such transport.

[3] And, moreover, our will and pleasure is, and, by these present letters, for ourselves, our heirs and successors, of our special favour, certain knowledge, and mere motion, we grant to Nicholas Baudouyn, rector of the parish church of St Peter in our aforesaid island of Guernsey and his successors annually for ever to and towards the maintenance, sustenance and relief of the same rector and his successors for the time being, sixty quarters of our wheat, the same sixty quarters of wheat to be had, taken and received annually from the rents, revenues and other profits issuing, owed or payable to us, our heirs and successors, from the parish of St. Saviour in the same island of Guernsey by reason of the fraternities, obits, masses and other similar things, by strength of certain acts of parliament in this realm of England ordained and provided for such a case, or by any other title or right whatsoever, in manner and form and at the same days and times as the aforesaid Nicholas Baudouyn has been accustomed to have, take and receive the same.

[4] And whereas we are credibly informed that the inhabitants of our said island of Guernsey have taken on to build, construct and erect, at their great charges, burdens and expenses, a certain harbour or the 'peere' in the sea beside the aforesaid island of Guernsey, the which harbour or 'peere' is now almost completed and finished, to the great security and prosperity of all the merchants and others coming to those parts to buy, sell and do business.

[5] And whereas, furthermore, we are similarly informed that the bailiff and jurats of the said island of Guernsey and their predecessors, in the time of the reign of the Lady Elizabeth formerly queen of England, levied and took, and were accustomed to levy and take, for and towards the fabric and structure of the harbour or 'peere', a certain duty or custom, commonly called 'pettie Custome', of certain merchandise, goods, ships, and other things, both those brought or imported into the same island of Guernsey from time to time and those growing or made, or to grow or be made, in the same island, of as many, as large, similar and like sums of money, by the name of the small custom, called in English 'pettie Custume' as in the time of the reign of the said former Queen Elizabeth they were accustomed legitimately to take, have or receive.

113

[6] Know that we, for the full completion and finishing of the aforesaid port or 'le Peere', and for the perpetual repair, maintenance, and improvement of the same, and also for the support and maintaining of other public expenses and works of the same island, of our special favour, certain knowledge and mere motion, we have granted and conceded, and by these present letters, for ourselves, our heirs and successors, we grant and concede full, free, and lawful power, right and authority to the aforesaid bailiff and jurats and their successors, that they themselves and their successors forever henceforth can and may freely, lawfully and without danger or punishment, take, have or receive the like, and as great, and as ample sums of money, by the name of the small custom, in English 'pettie Custume', as they were accustomed to take, have or receive in the time of the reign of said former Queen Elizabeth, towards the full and perfect construction and building of the aforesaid port or 'le Peere' and towards the repair, maintenance and improvement of the same for ever, and also towards the support and maintaining of other public expenses and works of the same island, both of and for all and singular merchandise, goods, ships and other things brought or imported, or to be brought or imported, into the same island from time to time, and of all and singular merchandise, goods and other things growing or made in the same island, or to grow or be made

[7] And moreover, of our more gracious special favour, certain knowledge, and mere motion, we have granted and conceded, and by these present letters, for our heirs and successors, we grant and concede, to the aforesaid bailiff and jurats and their successors for ever the weighing and measuring of all of this kind of merchandise and of whatever other things, which were accustomed to be weighed or measured at the 'common Beame and measures', in French 'poids et mesures du Roy', of the aforesaid island, and all profits, commodities and emoluments whatsoever usually taken, had or accustomed for this weighing and measuring, in as ample manner and form as we or Lady Elizabeth formerly queen of England or the same bailiff and jurats either had, received or enjoyed, or have had, received or enjoyed. To have, hold, and enjoy the aforesaid weighing and measuring, and the profits, commodities and emoluments therefore, to the aforesaid bailiff and jurats and their successors for ever, and to the sole and exclusive benefit and use of the same bailiff and jurats and their successors for ever.

[8] Rendering thence annually to us, our heirs and successors an annual rent or annual sum of twenty shillings of English legal tender, to be paid into the hands of the receiver of our revenues, and those of our heirs and successors of the said island of Guernsey at the feast of St Michael the Archangel each year in perpetuity.

[9] Our pleasure is, and by these present letters we grant, that the said bailiff and jurats should and will have these our letters patent made and sealed in due manner, without rendering or paying to our use or benefit, any fine or fee, great or small, in our hanaper in Chancery, or elsewhere to our use, for the same.

[10] And that although express mention of the true annual value, or of the certainty of the premises, or any of them, or of the other gifts or grants by us or any of our predecessors to the aforesaid bailiff and jurats, made before this time, is not mentioned in these present letters, or any statute, act, ordinance, proviso, proclamation or restriction to the contrary thereof, made, published, ordained, or provided, or any other thing, cause, or matter whatsoever to the contrary notwithstanding.

In testimony whereof, we have caused these our letters to be made patent. Witness myself, at Westminster, the fifteenth day of June, in the third year of our reign over England, France, and Ireland, and over Scotland the thirty-eighth.

By writ of privy seal.

T. Ravenscrofte

Charles I

Commentary

In 1627 Charles I confirmed the two previous grants of his father James I. In doing so he continued the tradition of rights and privileges which had been recreated by Elizabeth I. This charter's main additions to the tradition related to the secularised properties associated with churches, chapels, hospitals and schools, which were safeguarded in the custody of the bailiff and jurats, and also a specific allowance of commodities to be exported without custom or other charges for the security of Castle Cornet and the island itself.

Given Charles's well known interest in reducing the examples of jurisdictional and especially religious autonomy in his realms and dominions, it is perhaps surprising that the document continued so many of Guernsey's liberties. Although Baudouin's name has gone, for example (he died 16 April 1613), there is still the confirmation of the grant of 60 quarters of wheat for the minister of St Peter Port. It seems that, especially in 1627, Charles and his ministers were happy to allow Guernsey's regime to continue undisturbed. At that time, the English were at war with the French (1626-9), and Guernsey's position was too vulnerable, and its assistance too valuable, for there to be any incentive for major interference: and the Huguenots who might identify so closely with their co-religionists in Guernsey were potentially a vital ally for the English.[109]

This was to change, however.[110] Charles and Archbishop Laud, in spite of the views of their governor, the earl of Danby, looked to challenge the Presbyterianism of the islanders, endowing scholarships in Oxford to train ministers committed to their form of Anglicanism, and even considering at one point removing children from the island

---

[109] Thomas Cogswell, *The Blessed Revolution: English Politics and the Coming of War, 1621-1624* (Cambridge University Press, 1989); idem, 'Prelude to Ré: The Anglo-French Struggle over La Rochelle, 1624-1627', *History*, 71 (1986), 1-21.
[110] Conrad Russell, *The Causes of the English Civil War* (Oxford: Clarendon Press, 1990), pp. 112-13.

to an education elsewhere as the only way of breaking the religious commitment of the islanders.[111] There are, in fact, hints in the document of what lay in store. While the charter continues rights of free movement of goods, it is the most restrictive and cautious of the sequence in this respect. Quantities of goods are strictly limited, and customs officials are required to take sureties and keep records to ensure these limits are not exceeded. If in 1627 Charles was willing to go along with the islands' rights and privileges, it was perhaps already clear that this was on sufferance.[112]

CHARLES I 1627[113]

Carolus Dei gratia Anglie Scocie ffrancie et hibernie Rex fidei defensor &c.

Omnibus ad quos presentes litere pervenerint Salutem. Cum dilecti et fideles Subditi nostri Ballivus et Jurati Insule nostre de Garnezey ac ceteri Incole et Inhabitantes tam ipsius Insule quam Insularum nostrarum de Aureney alias Alderney et Sarke infra Ducatum nostrum Normannie et predecessores eorum a tempore cuius contrarii memoria hominum non existit per seperales Chartas Concessiones Confirmaciones et amplissima Diplomata illustrium Progenitorum et Antecessorum nostrorum tam Regum Anglie quam Ducum Normannie ac aliorum quamplurima jura jurisdicciones priuilegia immunitates libertates exempciones et franchesias libere et quiete inviolabiliter vsi freti et gauisi fuerunt tam infra Regnum nostrum Anglie quam alibi infra Dominia et loca dicioni nostre subiecta vltra citraque Mare, Quorum ope et beneficio predicte Insule et loca maritima predicta in fide obediencia et seruicio tam nostri quam eorundem Progenitorum nostrorum constanter fideliter et inculpate perstiterunt ac perseverarunt liberaque Commercia cum Mercatoribus ac aliis indigenis et alienigenis tam pacis quam belli temporibus habuerunt et exercuerunt iudicia eciam et cognicones omnium et omnimodo causarum querelarum accionum et placitorum tam civilium quam criminalium et capitalium ac iudicialem potestatem ea omnia tractandi ordinandi decidendi discuciendi audiendi et terminandi atque in eisdem procedendi et in acta redigendi secundum leges et consuetudines Insule et locorum predictorum ex

---

[111] Eagleston, *Channel Islands under Tudor Government*, pp. 141-2; *CSPD, 1632-3*, p. 288.
[112] For Charles and the customs, and the difficulties of interpretation for those at the time, see for example, Pauline Croft, 'Fresh Light on Bate's Case', *Historical Journal*, 30 (1987), 523-39.
[113] Greffe.

antiquo receptu [sic] et approbatas preterquam in certis casibus cogniconi nostre regie reservatis de tempore in tempus exercuerunt executi sunt et peregerunt

[2] Que omnia et singula cuius et quanti momenti sunt et fuerunt ad tutelam et conservacionem Insularum et locorum maritimorum predictorum in fide et obediencia Corone nostre Anglie. Nos vt equum est perpendentes neque non immemores quam fortiter et fideliter Insulani predicti ac ceteri Incole et habitatores ibidem nobis et progenitoribus nostris inservierunt Quantaque detrimenta damna et pericula tam pro assidua tuitione earundem Insularum et locorum quam pro recuperacone et defensione Castri nostri de Mount Orgueil infra Insulam nostram de Jersey sustinuerunt indiesque sustinent non solum vt regia nostra benvolencia fauor et affectus erga prefatos Insulanos illustri aliquo nostre beneficencie testimonio ac certis indicibus comprobetur verum eciam vt ipsi et eorum posteri deinceps imperpetuum prout antea solitum [sic] et debitam obedienciam erga nos heredes et Successores nostros teneant et inviolabiliter observent has literas nostras patentes magno Sigillo Anglie roboratas in forma qua sequitur illis concedere dignati sumus

[3] Sciatis igitur quod nos de gracia nostra speciali ac ex certa sciencia et mero motu nostris dedimus concessimus et confirmavimus ac per presentes pro nobis heredibus et Successoribus nostris damus concedimus et confirmamus prefatis Ballivo et Iuratis Insule nostre predicte de Gernezey et ceteris Incolis et habitatoribus tam ipsius Insule quam predictarum Insularum nostrarum de Aureney alias Alderney et Sarke et Successoribus suis, quod ipsi et eorum quilibet et eorum Successores licet in presentibus non recitati aut cogniti per specialia nomina sint semper in futur ita liberi quieti et immunes in omnibus Ciuitatibus Burgis Emporiis Nundinis Mercatis villis Mercatoriis et aliis locis ac Portubus infra Regnum nostrum Anglie ac infra omnes Provincias Dominia Territorum et loca dicioni nostre subiecta tam citra quam vltra Mare de et ab omnibus vectigalibus theoloneis custumiis subsidiis hidagiis tallagiis pontagiis pannagiis muragiis fossagiis operibus expedicionibus bellicis nisi in casu vbi Corpus nostr' heredum vel Successorum nostrorum (quod absit) in prisona detineatur et de omnibus aliis contribucionibus et exaccionibus in personis monetis rebus et aliis deveriis quibuscunque nobis heredibus vel Successoribus nostris quovismodo debitis reddendis seu solvendis prout prefati Insulani seu eorum aliquis virtute aliquarum Chartarum Concessionum Confirmacionum siue Diplomatum per predictos Progenitores siue Anteces-

sores nostros quondam Reges Anglie et Duces Normanie siue alios siue virtute et vigore alicuius racionabilis et legalis usus prescripcionis vel consuetudinis vnquam aliquando fuerunt aut esse debuerunt vel potuerunt debuit vel potuit quovismodo

[4] Cumque nonulla alia priuilegia iurisdicciones immunitates libertates et franchesias per predictos Progenitores et Predecessores nostros quondam Reges Anglie et Duces Normanie ac alios prefatis Insulanis indulta donata concessa et confirmata fuerunt ac a tempore cuius contrarii memoria hominum non existit infra Insulas et loca maritima predicta inviolabiliter vsitata et observata fuerunt de quibus vnum est Quod tempore belli omnium nacionum mercatores et alii tam alienigenie quam Indigine tam hostes quam Amici libere licite impune queant et possint dictas Insulas et loca maritima cum Nauibus Mercibus et bonis suis tam pro evitandis tempestatibus quam pro aliis licitis suis negociis inibi peragendis adire accedere commeare et frequentare ac libera Commercia negociacionem et rem mercatoriam ibidem exercere ac tuto et secure commorare indeque remeare et redire tocies quocies absque damno molestia seu hostilitate quacunque in rebus mercibus bonis aut corporibus suis idque non solum infra Insulas et loca maritima predicta ac precinctum eorundem verumeciam infra spacia vndique ab eisdem distantia usque ad visum hominum id est quatenus visus occuli possit assequi

Nos eadem immunitate impunitate libertate et priuileg ac cetera omnia premissa ultime recitata rata grataque habentes ea pro nobis heredibus et Successoribus nostris quantum in nobis est prefatis Balliuo et Iuratis ac ceteris Incolis habitatoribus Mercatoribus et aliis tam hostibus quam Amicis et eorum cuilibet per presentes indulgemus et elargimur Authoritateque nostra regia renovamus reiteramus et confirmamus in tam amplis modo et forma prout predicti Incole et Habitatores Insularum predictarum ac predicti Alienigene et Indigene preantea vsi et gauisi fuerunt

Universis igitur et singulis Ministris et subditis nostris per vniversum Regnum nostrum Anglie ac cetera Dominia et loca dicioni nostre subiecta vbilibet constituta per presentes denunciamus et firmiter iniungendo precipimus ne hanc nostram donacionem concessionem et confirmacionem seu aliquid in eisdem expressum aut contentum temerare infringere seu quovismodo violare presumant Et si quis ausu temerarie contrafecerit seu attemptauerit volumus et determinamus (quantum in nobis est) quod restituat non solum ablata et erepta sed quod eciam pro damno interesse et expensis ad plenariam recompensacionem et satisfaccionem compellatur per quecunque iuris nostri remedia Seuereque puniatur vt regie nostre potestatis ac legum nostrarum Contemptor temerarius

[5] Preterea ex uberiori gracia nostra per presentes ratificamus approbamus stabilimus et confirmamus omnes et singulas leges ordinaciones constituciones recorda inquisiciones et consuetudines infra Insulas et loca maritima predicta rite et legitime usitatas compertas habitas et ex antiquo receptas et approbatas dantes et tribuentes prefatis Ballivo et Juratis ac omnibus aliis Magistratibus Ministris et ceteris quibuscunque ibidem in officio et funccione aliqua consti-tutis plenam integram ac absolutam authoritatem potestatem et facultatem ordinandi cognoscendi iurisdicendi et iudicandi de et super omnibus et omni-modis placitis processibus libertatibus accionibus querelis et causis quibuscunque infra Insulas et loca predicta emergentibus tam realibus person-alibus et mixtis quam criminalibus et capitalibus Eaque omnia et singula ibidem et non alibi placitandi et peragendi prosequendi et defendendi atque in eisdem vel prosequendi vel supersedendi examinandi audiendi terminandi absolvendi condemnandi decidendi atque execucioni mandandi secundum leges et consuetudines Insularum et locorum maritimorum predictorum pre-antea vsitatas et approbatas absque provocacione seu appellacione quacunque preterquam in casibus qui cognicioni nostre regali ex vetustis consuetudinibus Insularum et locorum predictarum reservantur. Quamquidem authoritatem potestatem et facultatem (preterquam in eisdem casibus reservatis) nos pro nobis heredibus et Successoribus nostris prefatis Ballivo et Juratis ac aliis damus committimus concedimus et confirmamus per presentes adeo plene libere et integre prout prefati Ballivus et Jurati ac alii vel eorum aliquis vnquam antehac eisdem rite et legitime vsi functi et gauisi sunt vel vti fungi aut gaudere debuerunt aut licite debuerunt potuerunt aut potuit

[6] Volumus preterea ac pro nobis heredibus et Successoribus nostris per presentes concedimus prefatis Ballivo et Juratis ac aliis Incolis et Habitatoribus infra Insulas et loca maritima predicta quod nullus eorum de cetero per aliqua brevia seu processus ex aliquibus Curiis nostris infra Regnum nostrum An-glie emergencia siue earum aliqua citetur evocetur in placito trahetur [sic] seu quovismodo aliter respondere cogatur extra Insulas et loca maritima predicta coram quibuscunque Judicibus Justiciariis Magistratibus aut Ministris nostris de aut super aliqua re lite materia seu causa quacunque infra Insulas predic-

*tas emanente Sed quod Insulani predicti et eorum quilibet huiusmodi bre-
vibus et processibus non obstantibus impune valeant et possint valeat et possit
infra Insulas et loca maritima predicta residere comorari quiescere et Justiciam
ibidem expectare absque aliqua pena corporali siue pecuniaria siue redempcione aut mulcta proinde incurrenda seu forisfacienda Necnon absque aliqua
offensione vel causa contemptus seu contumacon per nos heredes aut Successores nostros illis seu eorum alicui aut aliquibus proinde infligendi irrogandi
vel aliter adiudicandi (exceptis tantummodo huiusmodi casibus et non aliis
qui per leges aut consuetudines Insularum et locorum predictorum regali
nostre cognicioni atque examini reservantur*

*[7] Cumque informamur quod Jurati et Ballivi Insule de Garnezey predicte
ac ceteri Incole et Inhabitantes tam ipsius Insule de Garnezey quam predictarum Insularum nostrarum de Aureney alias Alderney et Sarke antehac
exonerati et acquietati fuerunt de et ab solucione tolueti alias vocati petite
custum ac de et ab omnibus alias tallagiis toluetis cariagiis consuetudinibus et
consimilibus aspontagiis et omni wrecc' achato et rechato suo ac de recta prisa
nostra videlicet de vno dolio vini ante mallum et alio post mallum*

*[8] Sciatis quod nos de gracia nostra speciali ac ex certa sciencia et mero motu
nostris concessimus et confirmavimus ratificavimus et approbavimus ac per
presentes pro nobis heredibus et Successoribus nostris concedimus et confirmamus ratificamus et approbamus prefatis Ballivo et Juratis Insule de
Garnezey predicte ac ceteris Incolis et Inhabitantibus tam ipsius Insule de
Garnezey quam predictarum Insularum nostrarum de Aureney alias Alderney et Sarke predictarum et Successoribus suis exoneraciones vel
acquietancias de et ab solucione tolueti alias vocati petite Custome ac de et ab
omnibus aliis tallagiis toluetis cariagiis consuetudinibus et consimilibus asponsagiis et omni wrecc' achato et rechato suo ac de recta prisa nostra videlicet de
vno dolio vini ante mallum et alio post mallum*

*[9] Necnon tot tanta talia huiusmodi et consimilia alia libertates franchesie
priuilegia immunitates exoneraciones ac acquietancias quecunque quot quanta
qualia et que iidem Ballivus et Jurati Insule de Garnezey predicte ac ceteri
Incole et Inhabitantes tam ipsius Insule de Garnezey quam predictarum
Insularum de Aureney et Sarke predictarum per quodcunque nomen Incorporacionis siue per quecunque nomina Incorporacionum antehac legitime
habuerunt tenuerunt aut vsi vel gauisi fuerunt aut habere tenere vti vel*

gaudere debuerunt de statu hereditario aut eorum aliquis antehac legitime habuit tenuit vsus vel gauius fuit aut habere tenere vti vel gaudere debuerunt de statu hereditario racione vel pretextu aliquarum Chartarum vel literarum Patencium per nos aut per aliquem Progenitorum siue Antecessorum nostrorum nuper Regum aut Reginarum Anglie eis aut Predecessoribus suis per quodcunque nomen Incorporacionis siue per quecunque nomina Incorporacionum antehac datarum concessarum seu confirmatarum aut racione aut pretextu alicuius prescripcionis vsus seu consuetudinis in eadem Insula de Garnezey ac in predictis Insulis de Alderney et Sarke aut in earum aliqua antehac habitarum vsitatarum siue consuetarum aut aliquo alio legali modo iure seu titulo quocunque Habendum eis et Successoribus suis imperpetuum Tenendum de nobis heredibus et successoribus nostris per talia eadem hujusmodi et consimilia redditus et servicia per qualia et prout antehac de nobis aut precharissimo nuper patre nostro Domino Jacobo beate memorie aut Domina Elizabetha nuper Regina Anglie tenebantur et non per alia

[10] Et vlterius de abundanciori gracia nostra speciali ac ex certa sciencia et mero motu nostris concessimus ac per presentes pro nobis heredibus et successoribus nostris concedimus prefatis Ballivo et Juratis Insule nostre de Garnezey ac ceteris Insulis et Inhabitantibus tam ipsius Insule quam Insularum nostrarum de Alderney et Sarke predictarum et successoribus suis quod ipsi et successores sui de cetero imperpetuum exonerati et acquietati sint et erunt de et ab solucione alicuius Custume Subsidii tonnagii siue poundagii cuiuscunque nobis heredibus et successoribus nostris debiti siue solubili de aut pro aliquibus mercibus siue merchandizis quibuscunque infra predictas Insulas de Garnezey Alderney et sarke crescentibus prouenientibus factis siue operatis et que per prefatum Ballivum et Iuratos Insule de Garnezey aut ceteros Incolos [sic] et Inhabitantes tam ipsius Insule quam Insularum nostrarum de Alderney et Sarke predictarum aliquo tempore imposterum in hoc Regno Anglie aut aliquem Portum siue Crecam ejusdem Regni transportatis conveiatis sive adductis erunt pro tali transportacione

[11] Et vlterius volumus ac per presentes pro nobis heredibus et successoribus nostris de gracia nostra speciali et ex certa sciencia et mero motu nostris concedimus Rectori Ecclesie parochialis Sancti Petri infra predictam Insulam nostram de Garnezey et successoribus suis annuatim imperpetuum ad et versus manutencionem sustentacionem et relevamencionem ejusdem Rectoris et successorum suorum pro tempore existenti sexaginta quarteria frumenti

nostri percipiendi capiendi et recipiendi eadem sexaginta quarteria frumenti annuatim de redditibus revencionibus et aliis proficiis nobis heredibus et successoribus nostris annuatim provenientibus debitis siue solubilis in parocia Sancti Salvatoris infra eandem Insulam de Gernezey racione fraternitatis obitum missarum et huiusmodi vigore aliquorum Actuum Parliamentorum infra hoc Regnum Anglie in eo casu editorum et prouisorum dissolutorum aut aliquo alio titulo siue jure quocunque eisdem modo ac eisdem diebus et temporibus prout predictus Rector aut eius predecessor eadem antehac percipere capere et recipere consuevit

[12] Cumque nos credibiliter informamur quod Inhabitantes dicte Insule nostre de Garnezey magnis oneribus sumptibus et expensis suis edificare construare et erecti sunt quendam portum sive le Peere in Mare prope Insulam de Garnezey predictam qui quidem portus sive le Peere pene perfectus et consummatus fuit ad magnam securitatem et emolumentum omnium Mercatorum et aliorum in partes illas merchandizandi et negociandi causa confluentium

[13] Cumque eciam nos similiter informamur quod Ballivus et Jurati dicte Insule de Gernezey et Predecessores sui tempore Regni Domine Elizabethe nuper Regine Anglie levaverunt et reciperunt [sic] ac levare percipere consueverunt ad et versus fabricam et structuram portus sive le Peere quandam consuetudinem siue custumam vulgariter vocatam pettie Custome de quibusdam Merchandizis Mercibus Nauibus et aliis rebus tam in eandem Insulam de Garnezey te [sic, for de] tempore in tempus adductis siue importatis quam in eadem Insula crescentibus siue operatis

[14] Sciatis quod nos pro perpetua reperacone sustentacione et emanedacione eiusdem Portus siue le Peere, necnon pro supportacione et manutencione aliorum publicorum expensuum et onerum eiusdem Insule de gracia nostra speciali ac ex certa sciencia et mero motu nostris dedimus et concessimus ac per presentes pro nobis heredibus et successoribus nostris damus et concedimus plenam liberam et licitam potestatem facultatem et authoritatem prefatis Ballivo et Juratis et Successoribus suis quod ipsi et successores sui de cetero imperpetuum libere licite et impune capere percipere et recipere possint et valeant ad perpetuam reperacionem sustentacionem et emandacionem predicti Portus siue le Peere, necnon ad supportacionem et manutencionem aliorum publicorum expensuum et onerum eiusdem Insule tam de et pro omnibus et

singulis merchandizis mercibus Nauibus et aliis rebus in eandem Insulam de tempore in tempus adductis siue importtatis adducendis siue importandis quam de omnibus et singulis merchandizis et aliis rebus in eadem Insula crescentibus siue operatis crescendis siue operandis tot tanta talia et huiusmodi denariorum summas parve Custume anglice pettie Custome quot quanta qualia et que tempore Regni dicte nuper Regine Elizabethe capere percipere siue recipere legitime consueuerunt

[15] Et ulterius de vberiori gracia nostra speciali ac ex certa sciencia et mero motu nostr dedimus et concessimus ac per presentes pro nobis heredibus et successoribus nostris damus et concedimus prefatis Ballivo et Juratis et sucessoribus suis imperpetuum ponderacionem et mensuram omnium huiusmodi merchandizarum et aliarum rerum quarumcunque que antehac ponderari seu mensurari solebant apud le comon Beame and Measures galice poid et mensures du Roy Insule predicte ac omnia proficua commoditates et emolumenta quecunque pro huiusmodi ponderacione et mensuracione antehac usualiter percepta habita siue consueta in tam amplis modo et forma prout nos aut Domina Elizabetha nuper Regina Anglie siue iidem Balliuus et Jurati habuimus percepimus seu gauisi sumus habuit percepit siue gauisus fuit aut habuerunt percepuerunt vel gauisi fuerunt

Habendum tenendum et gaudendum predicta ponderacione et mensuracione ac proficuis comoditatibus et emolumentis inde prefatis Balliuo et Juratis et successoribus suis imperpetuum ad solum et proprium opus et usum eorundem Balliui et successorum suorum imperpetuum

[16] Reddendo inde anuatim nobis heredibus et successoribus nostris annualem redditum siue anualem summam viginti solidorum legalis monete Anglie per annum ad manus Receptoris Revencionum nostrarum heredum et successorum nostrorum dicte Insule de Garneszey ad festum Sancti Michaelis Archangeli solvendis imperpetuum

[17] Et vlterius de ampliori gracia nostra et ex certa sciencia et mero motu nostris dedimus et successoribus nostris quantum in nobis est damus concedimus et confirmamus prefatis Balliuo Juratis et ceteris Incolis et habitatoribus Insularum et locorum maritimorum predictorum Necnon Mercatoribus et aliis eo confluentibus tot tanta talia huiusmodi et consimilia jura ordinaciones jurisdicciones immunitates impunitates indempnitates exampciones libertates franchesias et priuilegia quecunque quot quanta qualia et que

prefatis Ballivo et Jurat et ceteri Incole et habitatores Insular et locor mariti-
mor predict quot quanta qualia et que prefat Balliuis et Jurat et ceteri Incole
et habitator mercator et al aut eor aliquis antehac legitmie et rite usi freti seu
gauisi fuerunt usus fretus seu gauisus fuit ac omnia et singula quecunque alia
in aliquibus Cartis aut literis patentibus nostris seu progenitorum siue prede-
cessorum nostrorum quondam Regum Anglie seu Ducium Normandie aut
aliorum eis seu predecessoribus antehac data concessa vel confirmata preantea
usa et non revocata seu abolita quocunque nomine aut quibuscunque nomini-
bus iidem Ballivus Jurati aut ceteri Incole et habitatores ear insularum et
locorum maritimorum predictorum aut eorum predecessores seu aliquibus
censeantur nominentur aut vocitentur seu censeri nominari aut vocitari de-
buerunt seu soliti fuerunt ac ea omnia et singula licet in presentibus minime
expressa prefatis Ballivo et Juratis ac ceteris Incolis et Inhabitatoribus Insu-
larum et locorum maritimorum predictorum necnon mercatoribus et aliis eo
confluentibus indigenis et alienigenis per presentes confirmamus et consolida-
mus et de integro ratificamus adeo plene libere et integre prout ea omnia et
singula in eisdem litteris patentibus contenta modo perticulariter verbatim et
expresse in presentibus recitata et declarata fuissent

Salua semper atque illabefacta suprema regia potestate dominacione atque
Imperio Corone nostre Anglie tam quoad ligeanciam subieccionem et obedien-
ciam Insularum predictarum et aliorum quorumcunque infra Insulas et loca
predicta commorancium siue degencium quam quoad regalitatem priuilegia res
redditus vectigalia ac cetera iura proficua commoditates et emolumenta
quecunque infra Insulas et loca predicta nobis heredibus et successoribus
nostrorum per prerogativam Corone nostre Anglie siue Ducatus Normanie
seu aliter ex antiquo debita et Consueta. Salvis eciam appellacionibus et
provocacionibus quibuscunque insulanorum predictorum ac aliorum ibidem
commorancium siue degencium in omnibus eiusmodi casibus et non aliis que
legibus et consuetudinibus Insularum et locorum predictorum regali nostre
cognicioni atque examinacioni reservantur aliqua sentencia clausa re aut
materia quacunque superius in presentibus expressa siue specificata in con-
trarium inde in aliquo non obstante

[18] *Et ulterius de uberiori gracia nostra speciali ac ex certa sciencia et mero*
motu nostris dedimus concessimus et confirmavimus ac per presentes pro nobis
heredibus et successibus nostris quantum in nobis est damus concedimus et
confirmamus prefatis Ballivo et Juratis et Inhabitantibus Insule predicte et
successoribus suis omnia et singula terras tenementa redditus revenciones et

125

hereditamenta quecunque aliquibus Ecclesiis Hospitalibus et Scholis infra Insulam predictam aut aliquam inde partem vel parcellam spectantem vel pertinentem aut pro reparacione predictarum ecclesiarum hospitalium siue Scholarum aut manutencione Rectorum siue Ministrorum in eisdem Ecclesiis aut pauperum et aliorum in eisdem Hospitalibus aut ludimagistrorum et scholarum in scholis predictis aut pro aliis piis et publicis usibus infra Insulam predictam antehac data concessa legata vel appunctuata Habendum tenendum et gaudendum predicta terras tenementa redditus revenciones et hereditamenta cum eorum pertinenciis prefatis Ballivus et Juratis et Inhabitantibus predictis et Successoribus suis solumodo disponenda ad usus et intenciones ad quas respectiue data legata siue appunctuata fuerunt per seperales Donatores eorundem et ad nullos alios usus aut intenciones quascunque absque aliquo redditu siue Computo aut aliquo alio inde nobis heredibus vel successoribus nostris quoquomodo reddendo solvendo vel faciendo

[19] Dedimus eciam et concessiumus ac per presentes pro nobis heredibus et successoribus nostris damus et concedimus dictis Ballivo Juratis et Inhabitantibus Insularum predictarum et Successoribus suis plenam potestatem et authoritatem habendi capiendi recipiendi et possidendi sibi et successoribus suis imperpetuum omnia et quecunque terras tenementa redditus revenciones et hereditamenta infra insulam predictam aut aliquam inde partem que de tempore in tempus et ad omnia tempora imposterum per aliquam personam vel aliquas personas personas data legata concessa siue appunctuata erint alicui Ecclesie Capelle Hospitali siue Schole infra Insulam predictam aut ad et versus seperacionem supportacionem alicuius Ecclesie siue Capelle aut alicuius Hospitalis siue Schole infra Insulam predictam aut manutencionem supportacionem et sustentacionem Rectoris aut Minstris in dictis Ecclesia siue Capelle aut Magistro Custodi siue Pauperi in huiusmodi Hospitalibus aut manutencionem sustentacionem vel educacionem ludimagistri ac Iuuenum et Scholarium in huiusmodi scholis aut ad alios pios aut publicos usus infra Insulam predictam quoscunque absque aliquo redditur sive Computo proinde nobis heredibus vel successoribus nostris reddendo solvendo vel faciendo Aliquo Statuto Actu ordinacione proclamacione vel consuetudine huius Regni nostri Anglie facto edito ordinato siue prouiso aut aliqua alia re causa uel materia quacunque in contrarium in aliquo non obstante Nihilominus intencio nostra est et per presentes statuimus et ordinamus pro nobis heredibus et successoribus nostris quod predicta terre tenementa redditus revenciones et hereditamenta ac proficua eorundem de tempore in tempus solumodo conver-

126

tantur et disponentur ad usus et intenciones ad quas respectiue data legata concessa siue appunctuata erint per seperales Donatores earundem vt prefertur et ad nullos alios usus aut intenciones quascunque

[20] *Cumque Inhabitantes predicte Insule de Garnezey virtute licenciarum et litterarum patencium diversorum progenitorum et predecessorum nostrorum Regum et Reginarum Anglie super consideracione necessitatis dictorum Inhabitancium habita a tempore cuius contrarii memoria hominum non existit eskippare onerare exportare et abcariare annuatim usi sunt ad unum tempus siue diversa tempora in anno a diversis portubus infra hoc Regnum nostrum Anglie in eisdem licenciis et literis patentibus perticulariter mencionatis ad predictam Insulam de Garnezey seperales proporciones victualia et alia necessaria inferius mencionata videlicet pro Castro de Cornett infra dictam Insulam in Ceruisia anglice Beere Centum Dolia, aut pro quolibet dolio Ceruisie ad dictum numerum duo quarteria brasii anglice malte et lupulos anglice hopps pertinentum duodecem Boves sexcenta lez flitches lardi anglice Bacon mille et ducentum libra butiri viginti pondera Casei anglice twenty weigh of Cheese tria millia Salparum anglice stockfish, trescentum libris Cebi anglice Tallowe viginti lez Dickers Corii et in ligno Carbone et aliis necessariis pro eodem Castris quantum raconabiliter requiretur Et pro predicta Insula de Guernesey in Ceruisia quingenta Dolia Centum et quinquaginta lez Dickers Corii ac viginti et quinque lez dozens pellium vitularum anglice Calueskinnes ac in ligno et Carbone cum omibus aliis necessariis pro eadem Insula quantum racionabilitier requiretur absque solucione alicuius Custume parue Custume toluet siue alio debito quocunque Necnon informamur quod virtute licenciarum predictarum et sub generalibus verbis predictis dicti Inhabitantes Insule predicte pro eorum maximo et necessario usu annuatim eskippauerunt et exportauerunt in Insulam predictam a portubus predictis quigenta lez Toddes lane [a tod of Wool = 28 lbs] inter cetera, ac superinde iidem Inhabitantes licencias predictas confirmari et explanari authoritate et potestate nostre [sic] regali nobis humilime supplicauerunt cum augmentacione addicione et supplemento quarundem aliarum rerum pro subvencione et augmentacione status Insule predicte et suppeditacione necessitate Insulanorum et Inhabitancium eiusdem prout nobis melius fieri et fore videretur*

[21] *Nos obsequia et servicia predictorum Insulanorum nobis et progenitoribus nostris maxima cum fidelitate et cura antehac prestitis ac aliter serio*

perpendentes necnon sua grauia onera et expense in tuicione Insule predicte ac predicti portus siue le peere ac diversorum Castrorum et locorum in defensione eiusdem assidue exposite ac eorum paupertatem et indigenciam ad hoc prestandum absque potestatis regie adiuuamente considerantes ac eorum curam et diligenciam in rebus gerendis et vite modum precipue ad merca-turium et commerciam devotum ac Corone Anglie constanciam intuentes de gracia nostra speciali ac ex certa sciencia et mero motu nostris dedimus conces-simus approbavimus et confirmavimus ac per presentes pro nobis heredibus et successoribus nostris damus concedimus approbamus et confirmamus prefatis Inhabitantibus Insule predicte et successoribus suis licenciam et plenam potes-tatem et authoritatem eskippandi imbarcandi onerandi exportandi et abcariandi anuatim ad unum tempus vel diuersa tempora in anno a portubus nostris de London Southampton Weymouth Poole Lyme et Plymouth aut eorum aliquibus vel aliquo in Regno nostro Anglie ad predictam Insulam de Guernesey pro predicto Castro de Cornett et pro necessario usu et sus-tentacione Inhabitantium dicte Insule tam predicta quingenta lez Toddes lane quam predictas seperales quantitates et numeros Ceruisie vel brasii et lupulos pertinentes bovium lardi Casei Salparum ligni Carbonis Coriorum Pellium vitularum cum omnibus huiusmodi aliis necessariis pro Castro et Insula predicta quolibet de tempore in tempus recionabiliter [sic] requirentur absque aliqua custuma magna vel parva aut aliquo tolueto aut alia re nobis heredibus vel successoribus nostris aut ffirmariis siue Officiariis nostris heredum vel successorum nostrorum proinde reddendo solvendo vel faciendo

[22] Et ulterius pro consideracione predicta damus et concedimus prefatis Inhabitantibus Insule de Guernesey predicte et successoribus suis per presentes plenam et absolutam licenciam libertatem et authoritatem durante beneplacito nostro ad vel apud predictos portus nostros de London Southampton Wey-mouth Poole Lyme et Plymouth aut eorum aliquem vel aliquos eskippandi imbarcandi et onerandi et ab eisdem aut eorum aliquibus vel aliquo expor-tandi abcariandi et transportandi in Insula predicta pro necessario usu et sustentacione Insulanorum et Inhabitancium ibidem annuatim ad vnum tempus vel diversa tempora in annum tot et tanta alia quantitate et numbero omnium et omnimodo bonorum mercimoniorum et merchandizarum muni-cone tanto modo excepta vltra predictas seperales proporciones superius preconcessa aut concedi mencionata qualiter eis magis opportunum et necessa-rium fore videbitur et non excedentes in toto in aliquo vno anno in Custuma annualem summam Centum et quinquaginta librarum secundum ratas per

eos antehac solutas penitus liberati et acquietati de et ab omni Custuma magna vel parva imposicione et alia solucione vel re qua cunque nobis heredibus et successoribus nostris aut ffirmariis siue Officiariis nostris heredum vel successorum nostrorum proinde reddenda vel facienda Et quod hec licencia nostra ultima mencionata ad suam et cetera predicta iis continuabitur durante beneplacito nostro tantum et non aliter

[23] Quare volumus ac per presentes pro nobis heredibus et successoribus nostris firmiter iniungendo precipimus omnibus et singulis Custumariis Comptrorotulatoribus Supervisoribus Scrutatoribus et aliis Officiariis et Ministris nostris portum predictorum quod ipsi et eorum quilibet pacifice libere et quiete permittant predictas provisiones et necessaria bona mercimonia et merchandizas annuatim ad vnum tempus siue diversa tempora in anno apud portum predictum vel Crecam earundem eskippari et onerari et ab eisdem exportari et transportari ad predictum Castrum et Insulam absque solucione alicuius Custume magne vel parve aut alicuius imposicionis toluete siue alii debiti pro eisdem aut eorum aliquibus secundum veram intencionem presencium adeo plene libere et integre ad omnia intenciones et proposita prout aliqua genera victualium aut aliarum provisionum extra aliquos portus huius Regni nostri Anglie ville Calic' aut marchiis eiusdem pro relauamine subditorum ibidem antehac comorantium siue inhabitantium exire usi et permissi fuerunt et absque aliqua molestacione siue impedimento marinariorum vasorum aut aliarum rerum predictorum subditorum nostrorum predicti Castri aut Insule pro provisione necessariis bonis merchandiziis et mercimoniis predictis ad portus predictos venientium virtute siue colore alicuius Commissionis restriccionis proclamacionis siue Mandati antehac facti siue imposterum per nos aut priuatum Concilium nostrum dirigendi nisi predicta Commissio proclamacio siue Mandatum continebit plenam restriccionem et annihilacionem huius presentis Concessionis nostre aut alicuius inde partis vel parcelle

[24] Prouiso semper quod dicti subditi nostri [de] Guernesey aut eorum aliquis vel aliqui ad predictum portum aut aliquam crecam eordem veniendo afferent secum scriptum siue billam aut scriptum siue billam manibus propriis Capitanei Castri et Insule predicte vel Deputati sui aut Balliui et Iuratorum eiusdem Insule pro tempore existenti perticulariter mencionandam proporciones et quantitates predictas victualium et aliorum necessariorum aut

bonorum mercium et mechandizarum quas ipsi [sic, for ipse?] vel ipsi ad portus et crecas predictas veniendo exinde transportare assignabitur

[25] Volentes et per presentes mandantes predictos Custumarios Officiarios et Ministros in portibus et Crecis predictis quod ipsi aut eorum aliquis de tempore in tempus capient aut capiet obligaciones de personis Insule predicte aut aliis qui eskippabunt aut onerabunt aliquam partem proporcionem vel quantitatem predictam aut predictum lignum Carboni boni mercimoniorum aut merchandizarum in forma predicta Quod dicte persone eadem sic eskippantes et onerantes tantumodo ad et in Castrum et Insulam predictam transportabunt et deliberabunt ibidem occupandam et ad nullum alium locum quemcunque. Ac eciam quod dicti Officiarii in libris suis de tempore in tempus intrabunt et fidele computum annatim retinebunt de omnibus rebus ad portum vel crecam predictam virtute presencium eskippandis et onerandis ea intencione quod certiores fiant de vera execucione premissorum absque aliquo incremento proporcione vel quantitate predicta Et he litere nostre patentes vel Irrotulamentum earundem erunt dictis Custumariis Contrarotulatoribus Superuisoribus Scrutatoribus et aliis Officiariis et minstris predictis sufficiens warrantum et exoneracio in hac parte

[26] Eo quod expressa mencio de vero valore annuo aut de certitudine premissorum vel eorum alicuius aut de aliis donis siue concessionibus per nos seu per aliquem progenitorum siue predecessorum nostrorum prefatis Balliuo et Juratis de Guernesey predictis ante hec tempora factis in presentibus minime facta existit Aut aliquo statuto Actu Ordinacione Prouisione Proclamacione siue restriccione antehac habito facto edito ordinato siue prouiso aut aliqua alia re causa vel materia quacunque in contrarium inde in aliquo non obstante

In cuius rei testimonium literas literas nostras fieri fecimus patentes

Teste me ipso apud Westmonasterium vicesimo primo die Maii Anno Regni nostri Tercio

per breue de priuato Sigillo

Wolseley

~ ~ ~

Charles, by the grace of God, king of England, Scotland, France, and Ireland, Defender of the Faith, etc.

[1] To all to whom these present letters shall come, greeting. Whereas our beloved and faithful lieges and subjects, the bailiff and the jurats of our Island of Guernsey, and the other sojourners in and inhabitants of both the same island and our islands of Aureneye, alias Alderney, and Sark, within our duchy of Normandy, and their predecessors, have from time beyond what the memory of men can reach, by virtue of several charters, grants, confirmations, and most ample writs, of our illustrious progenitors and ancestors, both kings of England and dukes of Normandy, and others, used, enjoyed, and been in possession of very many rights, jurisdictions, privileges, immunities, liberties, and franchises, freely, quietly, and without any infringement of the same, both within the kingdom of England, and elsewhere within our dominions, and other places under our subjection on this side of, or beyond, the seas; by the aid and benefit of which grants, the aforesaid islands and the maritime places have stood out and continued constantly, faithfully, and unblameably in our faith, obedience, and service, and have enjoyed and gone on in their commerce and trade with merchants, both natives and aliens, as well in time of peace, as in time of war, and exercised and executed their duties in giving their decrees, and taking cognisance of all and every cause, quarrel, action, both civil and criminal, and capital pleas; and the right of jurisdiction they were vested with, to take into their consideration, to take order, decide, discuss, hear, and determine, and to proceed in the premises, and keep records of their proceedings according to the laws and customs practised of old, and approved in the said islands and other places aforesaid; except in certain cases reserved from time to time to our royal cognisance:

[2] And we considering of how great advantage and moment all and singular the premises are, and have been, toward the safe-keeping and conservation of the said islands and other maritime places in their fidelity and allegiance to our crown of England; and being always mindful (as is just) how courageously and loyally the said islanders and inhabitants have behaved themselves in our own and in our progenitors' service. And considering what great detriments, losses and dangers they have sustained and do daily sustain, both for the constant safeguarding of the said islands and places, and for the recovery and defence of our Castle of Mont Orgueil, in our island of Jersey; to the end, not only to show some distinguished testimony and certain marks of our favour, affection, and royal beneficence towards the inhabitants aforesaid, but also to encourage them, and their posterity for ever, to persevere and continue inviolably in their accustomed

131

and due obedience towards us, and our heirs and successors; we have thought proper to grant to them these our royal letters patent, confirmed under the great seal of England, in form following.

[3] Know ye therefore, that we, of our special favour, certain knowledge, and mere motion, have given and granted, and for ourselves, our heirs and successors, we do by these present letters give and grant, to the said bailiff and jurats of our island of Guernsey aforesaid, and to the other sojourners and inhabitants, both of the same island, and of our other islands aforesaid, of Aureney, alias Alderney, and Sark; that they themselves and every one of them (though not herein stated or declared by their particular names) shall, for the time to come, be for ever free, exempted, and acquitted, in all our cities, boroughs, markets, and trading towns, fairs, mart-towns, and other places and ports, within our kingdom of England, and within all our provinces, dominions, territories, and other places under our subjection, this side of, or beyond, the seas, from and of all tributes, tolls, customs, subsidies, hidage, taylage, pontage, panage, murage, fossage, works, and warlike expeditions (except in case our body, or that of our heirs and successors, should be held in prison (which God avert)), and of and from all other contributions and exactions from their persons, money, goods and other duties whatsoever, that may be due from, to be rendered by, or be payable by, and claimed from, the said islanders, or any of them, to us, our heirs and successors, ever in any manner, by virtue of any charters, grants, confirmations, and writs of our said progenitors, formerly kings of England and dukes of Normandy, or others, or by virtue or reason of any reasonable and legal usage, prescriptions, or customs.

[4] And whereas some other privileges, jurisdictions, immunities, liberties, and franchises have been graciously given, granted, and confirmed by our progenitors and predecessors, formerly kings of England and dukes of Normandy, and others, to the aforesaid islanders, and have been used and observed constantly in the said islands and other maritime places, from the time whereof the memory of men reaches not to the contrary; one of which is, that in time of war merchants of all nations and others, both aliens and denizen, both enemies and friends, could and might freely, lawfully, without danger or punishment, come to, resort to, go to and fro, and frequent the said islands, and other aforesaid maritime places, with their ships, merchandise, and goods; both to avoid storms, and to conduct their other lawful business there, and to exercise there free commerce, business and trade, and securely, and without danger, remain there, and depart from thence, and return to the same, as often as they think fit, without any harm, molestation, or hostility whatsoever, in their goods, merchandise, or

persons; and this not only within the said islands and maritime places, and all around the same, but likewise at such spaces and distances from the islands as the sight of man goes to, that is as far as the eye of man can reach: We, by virtue of our royal authority, do, for ourselves, our heirs and successors, indulge and enlarge, and renew, reiterate, and confirm, by these present letters, as far as in us lies, the same immunities, impunities, liberties, and privileges, and all the other premisses last mentioned, finding them to be reasonable and seasonable, to the said bailiff and jurats, and the other sojourners, inhabitants and merchants, and others, whether enemies or friends, and to each of them, in as ample form and manner as heretofore they have used and enjoyed the same. In order therefore to prevent any violation or infraction of this our grant, concession, and confirmation, or any thing therein contained, in any manner whatsoever, we declare and give this warning by these present letters to all our officers and subjects in all parts of our kingdom of England, and throughout all our lordships and places under our obedience, wheresoever they lie, or are situated. And if any one of our said officers and subjects shall be so rash as to presume or attempt to transgress these our strict orders and commands, we order and decree (as far as in us lies), that he shall not only restore what has been taken or seized, but shall also be compelled to make a fuller restitution and satisfaction of all costs, interests, and damages, by whatever legal remedy, and he shall be severely punished for his audacious contempt of our royal power, and of our laws.

[5] Further, we, of our more gracious favour, do, by these present letters, ratify, approve, establish, and confirm, all and every one of the laws, ordinances, constitutions, records, inquisitions, and customs which have been duly and legally from ancient times used, received, found, had, and approved within the aforesaid islands and maritime places; giving and granting to the aforesaid bailiff and jurats, and all other magistrates and officers of justice, and others who are appointed for performing the functions and executing the duties of any office, full and absolute authority, power, and faculty to have the cognisance, jurisdiction, and judgment concerning and touching all and all sorts of pleas, processes, law-suits, actions, quarrels, and causes arising within the islands and maritime places aforesaid; both those actions which are real, personal, and mixed, and those which are criminal and capital, and to proceed in the said islands, and not elsewhere, in hearing the parties in their pleadings, and prosecutions of their processes, in their defence; and to hear, examine, and supersede the same, making decrees, determining, absolving, condemning, and putting their sentences in execution, according to the laws and customs previously practised and

approved in the islands and maritime places aforesaid; without admitting any challenge or appeal, except in such cases as are reserved to our royal cognisance by the ancient customs of the islands and places aforesaid. Which authority, power, and faculty (except in the cases reserved to us), we commit, give, grant, and confirm, for ourselves and our heirs and successors aforesaid, to the said bailiffs and jurats, and to the others, by these present letters, as freely, fully, and entirely, as the said bailiff and jurats, or others or any of them, heretofore have rightfully and lawfully used, practised, and enjoyed, or might legally have used and enjoyed.

[6] Moreover, our will and pleasure is, and we grant, for ourselves, our heirs, and successors by these present letters, to the said bailiff and jurats, and the other inhabitants and sojourners in the islands and maritime places aforesaid, that for the time to come, none of them be cited, or summoned, or drawn into any lawsuit, or forced in any manner by any writs or process, issued from any of our courts of the kingdom of England, to appear and answer before any judges, courts, or other officers of justice, out of any of the islands and maritime places aforesaid, touching or concerning any thing, dispute, causes, or matters in controversy whatsoever, arising in the aforesaid islands, but that the aforesaid islanders, and each of them, may lawfully, notwithstanding the said writs and processes, remain, reside quietly, and abide in the aforesaid islands, waiting for justice there; without incurring any punishment, corporal or pecuniary, by way of fine, mulct, ransom, or forfeiture, by reason of any offence, contempt, or contumacy, committed towards us, our heirs and successors, for which they might be sued, arraigned, or condemned; except only in the cases, and not others, which by the laws and customs of the islands and places aforesaid are reserved to our royal cognisance and determination.

[7] And whereas we are informed that the jurats and bailiffs of the aforesaid island of Guernsey, and the other sojourners and inhabitants both of the same island of Guernsey and of our aforesaid islands of Alderney and Sark have previously been free and quit of and from the toll called 'petite custum' and of and from all other tallages, tolls, cariage services, customs and similar asponsages, and all their wreck, emption and redemption, and of our rightful prize, viz. of one tun of wine *ante mallum* and another *post mallum*

[8] Know that we, of our special favour, certain knowledge, and mere motion, have given and confirmed, ratified and approved, and by these present letters for ourselves, our heirs and successors, we give and confirm, ratify and approve, to the aforesaid bailiff and jurats of our Island of Guern-

sey aforesaid, and to the other sojourners and inhabitants, as well of the said Island, as of our aforesaid islands of Aureney, alias Alderney, and Sark, and to their successors, exemptions and acquittances from and of the payment of toll otherwise called 'petite Custome', and of and from all other taylage, tolls, carriage services, customs, and similar asponsages, and all their wreck, emption and redemption and of our rightful prise, viz. of one tun of wine *ante mallum* and another *post mallum*.

[9] And also the like, and as great, and as ample liberties, franchises, privileges, immunities, discharges, and acquittances whatsoever, as the same bailiff and jurats of the aforesaid island of Guernsey and the other sojourners and inhabitants both of the same island of Guernsey and of the aforesaid islands of Aureney alias Alderney and Sark, by whatever name of incorporation or names of incorporations, or any of them, previously legitimately had, held or used or enjoyed, or ought to have had, held, used or enjoyed, of an hereditary state, by reason of, or on the grounds of, any charters or letters patent given, granted or confirmed by us or by any of our progenitors or predecessors formerly kings or queens of England to them or their predecessors by whatsoever name, incorporation or by whatsoever names or incorporations before this or by reason or on the grounds of any prescription, use or custom in the same island of Guernsey and in the aforesaid islands of Alderney and Sark or in any of them before this had, used or accustomed, or by any other legal manner, right or title whatsoever, to be had and held to them and their successors for ever, of us, our heirs and successors, by such, similar, equivalent and equal rent and service as they were previously held of us or of our most dearly beloved father, Lord James of blessed memory, or of Lady Elizabeth formerly queen of England, and not otherwise.

[10] And further, of our fuller and special favour, certain knowledge and mere motion, we have granted and by these present letters for us, our heirs and successors, we grant to the aforesaid bailiff and jurats of our island of Guernsey and to the other sojourners and inhabitants, as of the same isle as of our aforesaid isles of Alderney and Sark and their successors, that for the time to come they themselves and their successors should perpetually henceforth be free and quit of and from the payment of any custom, subsidy, tonnage or poundage whatsoever kind owed or payable to us, our heirs or successors of or for any goods or merchandise of any kind growing, coming forth, made or produced within the aforesaid islands of Guernsey, Alderney and Sark and which were transported, conveyed, or brought by the aforesaid bailiff and jurats of the island of Guernsey or other sojourners and inhabitants, both of the same island and of our islands of Alderney and

Sark aforesaid at any time in the past in this our realm of England or any port or creek of the same realm, by the present letters, for such transport.

[11] And, moreover, our will and pleasure is, and, by these present letters, for ourselves, our heirs and successors, of our special favour, certain knowledge, and mere motion, we grant to the rector of the parish church of St Peter in our aforesaid island of Guernsey and his successors annually for ever to and towards the maintenance, sustenance and relief of the same rector and his successors for the time being, sixty quarters of our wheat, the same sixty quarters of wheat to be had, taken and received annually from the rents, revenues and other profits issuing, owed or payable to us, our heirs and successors, from the parish of St. Saviour in the same island of Guernsey by reason of the fraternities, obits, masses and other similar things, dissolved by strength of certain acts of parliament in this realm of England ordained and provided for such a case, or by any other title or right whatsoever, in manner and form and at the same days and times as the aforesaid rector or his predecessor has been accustomed to have, take and receive the same.

[12] And whereas we are credibly informed that the inhabitants of our said island of Guernsey have taken on to build, construct and erect, at their great charges, burdens and expenses, a certain harbour or the 'peere' in the sea beside the aforesaid island of Guernsey, the which harbour or 'peere' is now almost completed and finished, to the great security and prosperity of all the merchants and others coming to those parts to buy, sell and do business.

[13] And whereas, furthermore, we are similarly informed that the bailiff and jurats of the said island of Guernsey and their predecessors, in the time of the reign of the Lady Elizabeth formerly queen of England, levied and took, and were accustomed to levy and take, for and towards the fabric and structure of the harbour or 'peere', a certain duty or custom, commonly called 'pettie Custome', of certain merchandise, goods, ships, and other things, both those brought or imported into the same island of Guernsey from time to time and those growing or made, in the same island.

[14] Know that we, for the perpetual repair, maintenance, and improvement of the aforesaid port or 'le Peere', and also for the support and maintaining of other public expenses and works of the same island, of our special favour, certain knowledge and mere motion, we have granted and conceded, and by these present letters, for ourselves, our heirs and successors, we grant and concede full, free, and lawful power, right and authority

to the aforesaid bailiff and jurats and their successors, that they themselves and their successors forever henceforth can and may freely, lawfully and without danger or punishment, take, have and receive the like, and as great, and as ample sums of money, by the name of the small custom, in English 'pettie Custume', as they were accustomed to take, have or receive in the time of the reign of said former Queen Elizabeth, towards the full and perfect construction and building of the aforesaid port or 'le Peere' and towards the repair, maintenance and improvement of the same for ever, and also towards the support and maintaining of other public expenses and works of the same island, both of and for all and singular merchandise, goods, ships and other things brought or imported, or to be brought or imported, into the same island from time to time, and of all and singular merchandise and other things growing or made in the same island, or to grow or be made, of as many, as large, similar and like sums of money, by the name of the small custom, called in English 'pettie Custume' as in the time of the reign of the said former Queen Elizabeth they were accustomed legitimately to take, have or receive

[15] And moreover, of our more gracious special favour, certain knowledge, and mere motion, we have granted and conceded, and by these present letters, for our heirs and successors, we grant and concede, to the aforesaid bailiff and jurats and their successors for ever the weighing and measuring of all of this kind of merchandise and of whatever other things, which were accustomed to be weighed or measured at the 'common Beame and measures', in French 'poids et mesures du Roy', of the aforesaid island, and all profits, commodities and emoluments whatsoever usually taken, had or accustomed for this weighing and measuring, in as ample manner and form as we or Lady Elizabeth formerly queen of England or the same bailiff and jurats either had, received or enjoyed, or have had, received or enjoyed. To have, hold, and enjoy the aforesaid weighing and measuring, and the profits, commodities and emoluments therefore, to the aforesaid bailiff and jurats and their successors for ever, and to the sole and exclusive benefit and use of the same bailiff and jurats and their successors for ever.

[16] Rendering thence annually to us, our heirs and successors an annual rent or annual sum of twenty shillings of English legal tender, to be paid into the hands of the receiver of our revenues, and those of our heirs and successors of the said island of Guernsey at the feast of St Michael the Archangel each year in perpetuity.

[17] And moreover, of our more gracious favour, certain knowledge, and mere motion, we have given, granted, and confirmed, and by our present letters, for ourselves, our heirs and successors (as far as in us lies), we do give, grant, and confirm to the aforesaid bailiff and jurats, and other sojourners in, and inhabitants of, the aforesaid islands and maritime places; as also to merchants and others meeting there, the like, and as great, and as ample rights, ordinances, jurisdictions, immunities, impunities, indemnities, exemptions, liberties, franchises, and privileges whatsoever, as the aforesaid bailiff and jurats, and other sojourners and inhabitants, and merchants and others, or any of them, have heretofore rightfully and legally used, practised, and enjoyed; and all and singular other things whatsoever that has been heretofore given, granted, and confirmed to them or to their predecessors, in any charters or letters patent, of us or our progenitors, formerly kings of England, or dukes of Normandy, or others, and not revoked or abolished, by whatsoever name or names the same bailiff and jurats, and other sojourners in, or inhabitants of, the same islands and maritime places aforesaid, or their predecessors, or any of them, may be supposed to have been comprised, called, or named, or ought to have been called or named, in the said letters patent, and all and singular which things, though not herein expressly mentioned, we do by these present letters confirm, consolidate, and ratify anew to the aforesaid bailiff and jurats, and other sojourners, and inhabitants, of the islands and maritime places aforesaid, and also merchants and others coming together there, those born there, and those born elsewhere, as fully, freely, and entirely, as if all and singular the things particularly mentioned and declared in the same letters patent were particularly and expressly recited and declared in these our present letters patent. Saving always entire and without detriment the regal and sovereign power, dominion, and empire of our crown of England, as to what may concern the allegiance, subjection, and obedience of the aforesaid islanders, and others, whoever they may be, dwelling for a shorter or longer time in the same island; and also as to what may concern the regality, privileges, incomes, revenues, tributes, and other rights, profits, commodities, and emoluments whatsoever, anciently due and accustomed to be paid to us, our heirs and successors, according to our royal prerogative as kings of England, or the prerogative of the duchy of Normandy, in the islands and places aforesaid; saving also to the aforesaid islanders, and others dwelling or being in the said islands, a right to appeal in all cases reserved to our cognisance and consideration by the laws and customs of the said island; but in no other case: Notwithstanding any sentence, clause, thing, or matter whatsoever expressed above, or specially contained to the contrary in these present letters.

[18] And further of our more gracious special favour, certain knowledge and mere motion, we have given, granted, and confirmed and by these present letters patent, for ourselves, our heirs and successors, as far as in us lies, we give, grant, and confirm to the aforesaid bailiff and jurats and to the inhabitants of the aforesaid island and their successors all and singular the lands, tenements, rents, revenues and inheritances whatsoever before this granted, bequeathed and appointed to any churches, hospitals and schools within the aforesaid island, or any part or parcel belonging or pertaining to them, or for the repair of the aforesaid churches, hospitals or schools, or the maintenance of the rectors or ministers in the same churches, or of the poor or others in the same hospitals, or of the masters and scholars in the aforesaid schools, or for other pious and public uses within the aforesaid island; to have, hold, and enjoy the aforesaid lands, tenements, rents, revenues and inheritances with their appurtenances to the aforesaid bailiff and jurats and inhabitants and their successors, only to be disposed of for the uses and intentions to which they had been respectively given, bequeathed or appointed by their separate donors, and to no other uses or purposes whatsoever without any rent or account, or anything else thence to be rendered, paid or made to us our heirs or successors in any manner

[19] Furthermore, we have given and granted and by these present letters for ourselves, our heirs, and successors we give and grant to the aforesaid bailiff and jurats and to the inhabitants of the aforesaid island and their successors full power and authority of having, receiving and occupying, to themselves and their successors for ever, all and whatsoever lands, tenements, rents, revenues, and inheritances within the island aforesaid or any part of them, from time to time and at all times hereafter, given, left, granted, or appointed by any person or any persons to any churches, hospitals, and schools within the aforesaid island, or to or towards separate support of any church or chapel, or of any hospital or school, in the aforesaid island, or the maintenance, support and sustenance of the rectors or ministers in the said churches or chapels, or of the master, warden or poor folk in hospitals of this kind, or the maintenance, sustenance or education of the masters and young people and scholars in schools of this kind, or for other pious and public uses within the aforesaid island whatsoever, without any render or account thence to us, our heirs or successors to be rendered, paid or made; any statute, act, ordinance, proclamation or custom of this our kingdom of England made, proclaimed, ordained, or provided, or any other thing, cause or matter whatsoever to the contrary in anything notwithstanding. Nevertheless, our intention is, and by these present letters we establish and ordain, for us, our heirs and successors, that the aforesaid

lands, tenements, rents, revenues, and inheritances, and the profits of the same, from time to time, should only be converted and spent towards the uses and purposes to which they were respectively given, bequeathed, granted or appointed, by their separate donors, as aforesaid, and towards no other uses or purposes whatsoever

[20] And whereas the inhabitants of the aforesaid island of Guernsey, by virtue of the licences and letters patent of diverse of our ancestors and predecessors, kings and queens of England, on consideration of the need of the aforesaid inhabitants, accustomed from a time beyond what the memory of men can reach to ship, load, export and carry away annually, at one time or on diverse occasions in the year, from diverse ports in this our realm of England specifically mentioned in the same licences and letters patent, to the aforesaid islands of Guernsey, individual proportions of victuals and other necessaries mentioned below: viz., for Castle Cornet in the said island 100 tuns of 'Beere', or for each tun of beer to the said number two quarters of 'malte' and 'hopps', twelve bulls, 600 flitches of 'Bacon', 1,200lb of butter, 'twenty weigh of Cheese', 3,000 'stockfish', 300lb of 'Tallowe', 20 dickers [dicker = measure of 10 hides] of leather and however much wood, coal and other necessaries are reasonably required for the same castle. And for the aforesaid island of Guernsey, 500 tuns of beer, 150 dickers of leather, and 25 dozen 'Calueskinnes', and however much wood, coal and other necessaries are reasonably required for the same island, without payment of any custom, small custom, toll or other due whatsoever. And we are also informed that by virtue of the aforesaid licences, and under the aforesaid general words, the said inhabitants of the aforesaid island, for their own very great and necessary use annually ship and export into the aforesaid island from the aforesaid ports 500 'Toddes' of wool [a tod of Wool = 28 lbs] amongst other things, and over and above this the same inhabitants have made most humble suit to us for the confirmation and explanation of the aforesaid licences by our royal authority and power, with the augmentation, addition, and supplement of certain other things to contribute to and augment the status of the aforesaid island, and for the support of the needs of the same islanders and inhabitants, according as may seem to us to be better.

[21] We, carefully thinking on the obedience and services of the aforesaid islanders shown to us and to our ancestors with the greatest faithfulness and care before this time and otherwise, and also considering their grievous burdens and expenses in the protection of the aforesaid island, and the aforesaid port or 'le peere', and in the vigorous defence of the different castles and places, which have been shown to us, and their poverty and

indigence pledged to this, without the help of the royal power, and with a view to their care and diligence in doing things and their way of life, especially their devotion to trade and commerce, and constancy to the crown of England, of our special favour, certain knowledge, and mere motion, have given, granted, approved, and confirmed, and by these present letters, for ourself, our heirs and successors, we give, grant, approve, and confirm to the aforesaid inhabitants of the aforesaid island, and to their successors, licence and full power and authority to ship, embark, load, export, and carry away each year at one time or at different times in the year, from our ports of London, Southampton, Weymouth, Poole, Lyme, and Plymouth, or any of them, or anywhere in our realm of England, to the aforesaid island of Guernsey, for the aforesaid Castle Cornet, and for the needs, use and support of the inhabitants of the said island, both the aforesaid five-hundred 'Toddes' of wool and the aforesaid individual quantities and numbers of beer or associated malt and hops, bulls, bacon, cheese, stockfish, wood, coal, leather, calfskins, with all other necessaries of this kind for the aforesaid castle and island as shall be reasonably required from time to time, without any custom great or small, or any toll, or anything to be rendered, paid, or made to us, our heirs or successors, or our farmers or officials or those of our heirs or successors.

[22] And further, for the aforesaid consideration, we give and grant by these present letters to the aforesaid inhabitants of the aforesaid island of Guernsey, and to their successors, full and absolute licence, liberty, and authority, during our pleasure, to or at our aforesaid ports of London, Southampton, Weymouth, Poole, Lyme, and Plymouth, or any one or more of them, of shipping, embarking, and loading, and of exporting, carrying away, and transporting into the aforesaid island, from one or more of the same, for the needs, use, and support of the islanders and inhabitants there annually, at one or many times in the year, as many and as much, in quantity and number, of all and all sorts of goods, items, and merchandise, munitions only excepted, beyond the aforesaid separate proportions granted above or mentioned as conceded, as will seem to be more appropriate and necessary for them, and not exceeding in total in any one year the sum of £150 in annual customs according to the rates paid for them before this time only, freed and quit of and from the imposition of all customs, great or small, and from other payment or thing whatsoever to be rendered or made thence to us, our heirs and successors, or the farmers of officials of ourself, our heirs and successors. And that this our licence last mentioned to him and the rest aforesaid will continue for them during our pleasure only, and not otherwise.

[23] Wherefore we will and by these present letters for ourself, our heirs and successors, we firmly instruct and order all and singular our customs officers, controllers, supervisors, inspectors and other officials and ministers of the ports aforesaid that they themselves and every of them should allow the aforesaid provisions and needful goods, items and merchandise annually at one time or at different times in the year to be shipped and loaded peaceably, freely and without restriction at the aforesaid port or creek, and from the same to be exported and transported to the aforesaid castle and island without the payment of any custom, great or small, or of any imposition, toll or other due for the same, or any of the same, according to the true intention of the present letters, as fully, freely, and entirely to all the intentions and purposes, just as other types of victuals, or of other provisions, were used and permitted to leave any ports of this our realm of England to the town of Calais, or its marches, for the relief of our subjects hitherto staying or living there, and from any interference or restriction of ships, vessels, or other things of our aforesaid subjects, for the provision of the castle and island aforesaid, with necessary things, goods, items and merchandise aforesaid, coming to the port aforesaid, by virtue or colour of any commission, restriction, proclamation or order made in the past, or in time to come by us or by our privy council directed, except in the case that the aforesaid commission, proclamation or mandate will contain a full restriction and cancellation of this our present grant or of any part of parcel of it.

[24] Provided always that our said subjects of Guernsey or any of them, coming to the aforesaid port or any creek of the same should carry with them a writing or bill in the personal hand of the captain of the castle and island aforesaid, or his deputy, or the bailiff and jurats of the same island for the time being, mentioning the aforesaid proportions and quantities of victuals and other necessary items, or other good, items and merchandise which he or they themselves have assigned to be transported thence coming to the port or creek aforesaid

[25] Willing and by these present letters ordering the aforesaid customs officers, officials and ministers in the aforesaid ports and creeks that they themselves, or any of them, from time to time, should take bonds from the people of the aforesaid isle or others, who ship or load any aforesaid part, proportion or quantity, or the aforesaid wood, coal, trade goods or merchandise, in the form aforesaid; that the same said persons thus shipping and loading only to and in the castle and island aforesaid will transport and deliver there and to no other place whatsoever. And furthermore that the said officials will enter in their books from time to time and will keep a

true account annually of all things to be shipped and loaded to the aforesaid port or creek, by virtue of the present letters, with the intention that they should be more certain of the true execution of the premises without any increase, proportion or quantity aforesaid. And these our letters patent, or the enrolment of the same, will be sufficient warrant and discharge to the said customs officials, controllers, supervisors, inspectors and other officials and officers aforesaid.

[26] And that although express mention of the true annual value, or of the certainty of the premises, or any of them, or of the other gifts or grants by us or any of our predecessors to the aforesaid bailiff and jurats of Guernsey, made before this time, is not mentioned in these present letters, or any statute, act, ordinance, proviso, proclamation or restriction to the contrary thereof, made, published, ordained, or provided, or any other thing, cause, or matter whatsoever to the contrary notwithstanding.

In testimony whereof, we have caused these our letters to be made patent. Witness myself, at Westminster, the twenty-first day of May, in the third year of our reign.

By writ of privy seal.

Wolseley

Charles II

Commentary

The Channel Islands had experienced the civil wars of the 1640s and 1650s in a particularly dramatic way. While Guernsey, with the exception of Castle Cornet, had been true to the parliamentarian cause, Jersey had been a refuge for Charles, prince of Wales, in 1646, and again in 1649. Jersey had finally succumbed in 1651, Castle Cornet shortly after in the same year, on 19 December.[114]

On the Restoration of Charles as king the local regime was displaced, and Amias Andros was installed as bailiff, in May 1661.[115] The Stuart regime went about imposing Anglican conformity, too.[116] But, in 1668, the king confirmed the charter of his father, Charles I, and he did so without any reductions in the island's rights and privileges.

CHARLES II 1668[117]

Carolus Secundus Dei gratia Anglie Scocie ffrancie et hibernie Rex fidei defensor &c.

Omnibus ad quos presentes Literae pervenerint salutem Cum Dilecti et fideles subditi nostri Ballivus et Jurati Insule nostre de Garnsey ac ceteri Incole et Inhabitantes tam ipsius Insule quam Insularum nostrarum de Aureney alias Alderney et Sarke infra Ducatum nostrum Normaniae et Predecessores eorum a tempore cuius contrarii memoria hominum non existit Chartas et Concessiones Confirmaciones et amplissima Diplomata illustrium Progenitorum et Antecessorum nostrorum tam Regum Anglie quam Ducum Normanie ac aliorum quamplurima Jura Jurisdicciones Privilegia Immunitates Libertates exempciones et ffranchesias libere et quiete inviolabiliter vsi freti et gavisi fuerunt tam infra Regnum nostrum Anglie quam alibi infra

---

[114] Marr, *Guernsey*, pp. 147-50; S. Elliott Hoskins, *Charles the Second in the Channel Islands: A Contribution to his Biography and to the History of his Age* (2 vols., London: R. Bentley, 1854).
[115] Marr, *Guernsey*, p. 91.
[116] Marr, *Guernsey*, p. 20.
[117] Greffe.

Dominia et loca ditioni nostre subiecta vltra citraque Mare Quorum opi et Beneficio predicte Insule et loca Maritimia predicta et in fide et obedientia et Servitio tam nostri quam eorundem Progenitorum nostrorum constanter fideliter inculpate prestiterunt ac perseverarunt liberaque Comercia cum Mercatoribus et aliis Indigenis tam pacis quam Belli tempore habuerunt et exercuerunt iudicia etiam et Cogniciones omnium et omnimodo Causarum querelarum Accionum et Placitorum tam Civilium quam Criminalium et Capitalem ac Judicialem potestatem ea omnia tractandi ordinandi decidendi discutiendi audiendi et terminandi atque in eisdem procedendi et in Acta redigendi secundum Leges et Consuetudines Insule et locorum predictorum ex antiquo receptas et approbatas preterquam in ceteris Casibus Cognitioni nostre Regali reservatis de tempore in tempus exercuerunt executi sunt et peregerunt

[2] Que omnia et singula cuius et quanti momenti sunt et fuerunt ad tutelam et conservacionem Insularum et locorum Maritimicorum predictorum in fide et obedientia Corone nostre Anglie Nos vt equum est perpendentes neque non immemores quam fortiter et fideliter Insulani predicti ac ceteri Incole et habitatores ibidem nobis et Progenitoribus nostris inservierunt quantaque detrimenta dampna et pericula tam pro assidua tuitione earundem Insularum et locorum quam pro recuperacione et defensione Castri nostri de Mount Orgueil infra Insulam nostram de Jersey sustinuerunt Indiesque sustinent non solum vt regia nostra Benevolentia favor et effectus erga prefatam Insulam illustri aliquo nostre Benevolentie testimonio ac certis Indicibus comprobetur verum etiam vt ipsi et eorum posteri deinceps imperpetuum prout antea solitam et debitam obedientiam erga nos heredes et Successores nostros teneant & inviolabiliter observent has Literas nostras Patentes magno Sigillo Anglie roboratas in forma qua sequitur illis dignati sumus

[3] Sciatis igitur quod nos de gratia nosta speciali ac ex certa scientia et mero motu nostris Dedimus concessimus et confirmavimus ac per presentes pro nobis heredibus et Successoribus nostris Damus Concedimus et confirmamus prefatis Ballivo et Juratis Insule nostre predicte de Gernsey et ceteris Incolis Inhabitatoribus tam ipsius Insule quam predictarum Insularum nostrarum de Aureney alias Alderney et Sarke et Successoribus suis quod ipsi et eorum quilibet et eorum Successores licet in presentibus non recitati aut cogniti per Seperalia nomina sint semper in futuro ita liberi quieti et immunes in omnibus Civitatibus Burgis Emporiis Nundinis Mercatis Villis Mercatoriis et aliis

locis et Portubus infra Regnum nostrum Anglie ac infra omnes Provincias Dominia Territoria et loca ditioni nostre subiecta tam infra quam vltra Mare de et ab omnibus Vectigalibus Theoloniis Custumis Subsidiis hidagiis tollagiis pontagiis Pannagiis muragiis fossagiis operibus Expedicionibus Bellicis nisi in casu vbi Corpus nostrum heredum vel Successorum nostrorum (quod absit) in Prisona detineatur et de omnibus aliis Contribucionibus et exaccionibus in personis monetis rebus et aliis deueriis quibuscunque nobis heredibus vel Successoribus nostris quovismodo debitis reddendis seu solvendis provt prefati Insulani seu eorum aliquis virtute aliquarum Cartarum Concessionum Confirmationum sive Diplomatum per predictos Progenitores sive Antecessores nostros quondam Reges Anglie et Duces Normanie sive alios sive virtute et vigore alicuius racionabilis et legalis vsus prescriptionis vel Consuetudinis vnquam aliquando fuerunt aut esse debuerunt vel potuerunt debuit vel potuit quovismodo

[4] Cumque nonnvlla alia Privilegia iurisdictiones Immunitates Libertates et ffranchesias per predictos Progenitores et Predecessores nostros quondam Reges Anglie et duces Normanie ac alia prefatis Insulanis indulta donata concessa et confirmata fuerunt ac a tempore cuius contrarii memoria hominum non existit infra Insulam et loca Maritimia predicta inviolabiliter vsitata et observata fuerunt de quibus vnum est quod tempore Belli omnium Nacionum Mercatores et alii tam Alienigeni quam Indigeni tam hostes quam amici libere licite et impune queant et possint dictas Insulas et loca maritimia cum Navibus Mercibus et Bonis suis tam pro evitandis tempestatibus quam pro aliis licitis suis negotiis inibi peragendis adire accedere et commeare et frequentare ac libera Commercia negotiones et rem mercatoriam ibidem exercere ac tuto secure commorare indeque remeare et redire toties quoties absque dampno molestia seu Hostilitate quacunque in rebus mercibus bonis et Corporibus suis Idque non solum infra Insulas et loca maritima predicta ac precincta earundem verum etiam infra spatia vndique ab eisdem distantia vsque ad visum hominis id est quatenus visus oculi possit assequi Nos eadem immunitate impunitate libertate privilegia ac cetera omnia premissa vltimo recitata rata grataque habentes Ea pro nobis heredibus et Successoribus nostris quantum in nobis est prefatis Ballivo et Juratis ac ceteris Incolis Inhabitantibus Mercatoribus et aliis tam hostibus quam amicis et eorum cuilibet per presentes indulgemus et elargemur authoritateque nostra Regia renovamus reiteramus et Confirmamus in tam amplis modo et forma prout predicti Incole et Habitatores Insularum predictarum ac predicti Alienigene et Indigene preantea vsi et

gavisi fuerunt vniversis igiter [sic] et singulis Ministris et Subditis nostris per vniversum Regnum nostrum Anglie ac cetera Dominia et loca ditioni nostre subiecta vbilicet constituta per presentes denunciamus et firmiter injungendo precipimus ne hanc nostram donationem Concessionem et Confirmationem seu aliqua in eisdem expressa et contenta temerarie infringere seu quovismodo violare presumant Et si quis ausu temerario contrafecerit sue attemptaverit Volumus et determinavimus quantum in nobis est quod restituat non solum ablata et exerpta sed quod etiam pro dampno interesse et expensis ad plenariam recompencionem et satisfaccionem compellatur per quecunque Juris nostri remedia severeque puniatur vt regie nostre placitis ac Legum nostrarum Contemptor temerarius

[5] Preterea ex vberiori gratia nostra per presentes ratificamus approbamus stabilimus et confirmamus omnes et singulas Leges Ordinaciones Constituciones Recorda Inquisiciones et Consuetudines infra Insulas et loca Maritima predicta rite et legittime vsitatas compertas habitas et ex antiquo receptas et approbatas Dantes et tribuentes prefatis Ballivo et Juratis ac omnibus aliis Magistratibus Ministris et ceteris quibuscunque ibidem in Officio ffunctione aliqua constitutis plenam integram ac absolutam Authoritatem Potestatem et facultatem ordinandi Cognoscendi jurisdicendi et judicandi de et super omnibus et omnimodis placitis Processibus Libertatibus Actionibus Querelis et Causis Quibuscunque infra Insulas et loca predicta emergentibus tam realibus personalibus et Mixtis quam Criminalibus et Capitalibus Eaque omnia et singula ibidem et non alibi placitandi et peragendi prosequendi et defendendi atque in eisdem vel prosequendi examinandi audiendi terminandi absolvendi Condemnandi decidendi atque Executioni mandandi secundum leges et Consuetudines Insularum et locorum maritimorum predictorum preantea vsitatas et approbatas absque provocatione seu appellatione quacunque preterquam in Casibus que Congnitioni nostre regali ex vetustis consuetudinibus Insularum et locorum predictorum reservantur Quamquidem authoritatem Potestem et facultatem preterquam in eisdem casibus reservatis Nos pro nobis heredibus et successoribus nostris prefatis Ballivo et juratis ac aliis damus committimus concedimus et confirmamus per presentes adeo plene libere et integre provt prefati Ballivus et Jurati ac alii vel eorum aliquis vnquam ante hac eisdem rite et legitime vsi functi et gavisi sunt vel vti fungi aut gaudere debuerunt aut licite debuerunt potuerunt aut potuit

147

[6] Volumus preterea ac pro Nobis heredibus et Successoribus nostris per presentes Concedimus prefatis Ballivo et Juratis ac aliis Incolis et Habitatoribus infra Insulas et loca maritima predicta quod nullus eorum de cetero per aliqua Brevia seu processus ex aliquibus Curiis nostris infra Regnum nostrum Anglie emergentibus sive earum aliqua citetur evocetur in placito trahetur seu quovismodo aliter respondere cogatur extra Insulas et loca maritima predicta coram quibuscunque Iudicibus Justiciariis Magistratibus aut Ministris nostris de aut super aliqua re lite materia seu causa quocunque infra Insulas predictas emanen sed quod Insulani predicti et eorum quilibet huiusmodi Brevibus et processibus non obstantibus impune valeant et possint valeat et possit infra Insulas et loca Maritima predictae residere commorari quiescere et Iusticiam ibidem expectare absque aliqua pena Corporali sive pecuniaria sive Redempcione aut mulcta proinde incurrenda seu forisfacienda Necnon absque aliqua offensione vel causa contemptus seu contumacione per Nos heredes aut Successores nostros illis seu eorum alicui aut aliquibus proinde infligendi irrogandi vel aliter adiudicandi Exceptis tantumodo huiusmodi Casibus et non aliis qui per Leges aut consuetudines Insularum et locorum predictorum legali nostre Cognicioni atque examini reservantur

[7] Cumque informamur quod Jurati et Ballivi Insule de Garnsey predicte ac ceteri Incole et Inhabitantes tam ipsius Insule de Garnsey quam predicte Insule nostre de Aureney alias Alderney et Sarke antehac exonerati et acquietati fuerunt de et ab solucione Tolueti alias vocati Petit Custum Ac de et ab omnibus tollagiis toluetis Carriagiis Consuetudinibus et Consimilibus asponsagiis et omni Wrecc' achato et rechato suo ac de recta prisa nostra (vizt) de vno dolio vini ante mallum et alio post mallum

[8] Sciatis quod nos de gratia nostra speciali et ex certa scientia et mero motu nostris Concessimus et confirmavimus ratificavimus et approbavimus Ac per presentes pro Nobis heredibus et Successoribus nostris Concedimus Confirmamus ratificamus et approbamus prefato Ballivo et Juratis Insule de Garnsey predictis ac ceteris Incolis et Inhabitantibus tam ipsius Insule de Garnsey quam predictarum Insularum nostrarum de Aureney alias Alderney et Sarke predictarum et Successoribus suis predictis exoneraciones vel acquietancias de et ab solucione Tolueti alias vocati Petit Custum ac de et ab omnibus aliis Tallagiis Tolnetis Carriagiis Consuetudinibus et consimilibus asponsagiis et omni wrecc' achato et rechato suo ac de recta prisa nostra (vizt) de vno dolio vini ante mallum et alio post mallum

148

*[9] Necnon tot tanta talia huiusmodi et consimilia alia libertates ffranchesie
privilegia Immunitates exoneraciones ac acquietancias quecunque quot quanta
qualia et que iis Ballivis et Juratis Insule de Garnsey predicte ac ceteri Incole
et Inhabitantes tam ipsius Insule de Garnsey quam predictarum Insularum
de Aureney et Sarke predictarum per quodcunque nomen Incorporacionis sive
per quecunque nomina incorporationum antehac legittime habuerunt tenuerunt aut vsi vel gavisi fuerunt aut habere tenere vti vel gaudere debuerunt de
Statu hereditario aut eorum aliquis antehac legittime habuit tenuit vsus vel
gavisus fuit aut habere tenere vti vel gaudere debuit de Statu hereditario
racione vel pretextu aliquarum Cartarum vel Literarum Patentium per nos
aut per aliquem Progenitorum sive Antecessorum nostrorum nuper Regum vel
Reginarum Anglie eis aut Predecessoribus suis per quodcunque nomen Incorporacionis sive per quecunque nomina Incorporacionum antehac datarum
concessarum seu confirmatarum aut racione aut pretextu alicuius prescripcionis
vsus seu Consuetudinis in eadem Insula de Garnsey aut in predictis Insulis
de Alderney et Sarke aut in earum aliqua antehac habitarum vsitatum sive
consuetarum aut aliquo alio legali modo iure seu titulo quocunque Habendum eis et successoribus suis imperpetuum Tenendum de Nobis heredibus et
Successoribus nostris per talia eadem huiusmodi et consimilia Redditus et
Servicia per qualia et provt antehac de Nobis aut precharissimo nuper Patre
nostro Domino Carolo beate memorie aut precharissimo nuper Avo nostro
Domino Jacobo beate memorie aut Domina Elizabetha nuper Regina Anglie
tenebantur et non per alia*

*[10] Et vlterius de abundantiori gratia nostra speciali ac ex certa scientia et
mero motu nostris Concessimus ac per presentes pro nobis heredibus et Successoribus nostris Concedimus prefatis Ballivo et Juratis Insule nostre de
Garnsey ac ceteris Insulis et Inhabitantibus tam ipsius Insule quam Insularum nostrarum de Alderney et Sarke predictarum et Successoribus suis
Quod ipsi et Successores sui de cetero imperpetuum exonerati et acquietati
sint et erunt de et ab solucione alicuius Custume Subsidii Tonnagii sive
Poundagii cujuscunque nobis heredibus vel Successoribus nostris debiti sive
solubili de aut pro aliquibus mercibus sive merchandizis quibuscunque infra
predictas Insulas de Garnsey Alderney et Sarke crescentibus provenientibus
factis sive operatis et que per prefatum Ballivum et Juratos Insule de Gernsey
aut ceteri Incoles [sic] et Inhabitantes tam ipsius Insule quam Insularum
nostrarum de Alderney et Sarke predictarum aliquo tempore imposterum in*

hoc Regno nostro Anglie aut aliquem Portum sive Crecam eiusdem Regni transportata conveiata sive adducta pro tali transportacione

[11] Et vlterius volumus Ac per presentes pro nobis heredibus et Successoribus nostris de gratia nostra speciali ac ex certa scientia et mero motu nostris Concedimus Rectori Ecclesie parochialis Sancti Petri infra predictam Insulam nostram de Garnsey et Successoribus suis annatim imperpetuum ad et versus manutencionem sustentacionem et relevamencionem eiusdem Rectoris et Successorum suorum pro tempore Sexaginta quarteria frumenti nostri percipiendi accipiendi et recipiendi eadem sexaginta quarteria frumenti annatim de Redditibus Revencionibus et aliis proficuis nobis heredibus et successoribus nostris annatim provenientibus debitis sive solubilis in Parochia Sancti Salvatoris infra eandem Insulam de Garnsey racione ffraternitatis obitum missarum et alii huiusmodi vigore aliquorum Actorum Parliamenti infra hoc Regnum Anglie in eo casu editorum et provisiorum dissolutorum aut aliquo alio Titulo sive iure quocunque eisdem modo ac eisdem diebus et temporibus provt predictus Rector aut eius Predecessor eadem antehac percipere capere et recipere consueverit

[12] Cumque nos credibiliter informamur quod Inhabitantes dicte Insule de Garnsey magnis oneribus Sumptibus et expensis suis edificarunt construerunt et erecti sunt quendam portum sive Le Peere in Mare prope Insulam de Garnsey predictam Quiquidem Portus sive Le Peere pene perfectus et consummatus fuit ad magnam securitatem et Emolumentum omnium Mercatorum et aliorum in partes illas merchandizandi et negotiandi causa confluentium

[13] Cumque etiam Nos similiter informamur quod Ballivus et Jurati dicte Insule de Garnsey et Predecessores sui tempore regni Domine Elizabethe nuper Regine Anglie levaverunt et receperunt et levare et percipere consueverunt ad et versus fabricam et Structuram Portus sive Le Peere quandam Consuetudinem sive Custumam vulgariter vocatam Petty Custume de quibusdam merchandizis mercibus et aliis rebus tam in eandem Insulam de Garnsey a tempore in tempus adductis sive Importatis quam in eandem Insulam crescentibus sive operatis

[14] Sciatis quod nos pro perpetua reparacione sustentacione et emendacione eiusdem Portus sive Le Peere Necnon pro supportacione et manutencione aliorum publicorum expensuum et onerum eiusdem Insule De gratia nostra

speciali ac ex certa scientia et mero motu nostris Dedimus et Concessimus ac per presentes pro Nobis heredibus et Successoribus nostris Damus et concedimus plenam liberam et licitam potestatem facultatem et authoritatem prefato Ballivo et Juratis et Successoribus suis quod ipsi et Successores sui de cetero imperpetuum libere licite et impune capere recipere possint et valeant ad perpetuam sustentacionem et emendacionem predicti Portus sive Le Peere Necnon ad Supportacionem et manutencionem aliorum publicorum expensuum et onerum eiusdem Insule tam de et pro omnibus et singulis merchandizis mercibus Navibus at aliis rebus in eandem Insulam de tempore in tempus adductis sive importatis adducendis sive importandis quam de omnibus et singulis merchandizis ac aliis rebus in eadem insula crescentibus sive operatis crescendis sive operandis tot tanta talia et huiusmodi denaria summas nomine parve Custum Anglice Petty Custome quot quanta qualia et que tempore Regni dicte nuper Regine Elizabethe capere percipere sive recipere legittime consueverunt

[15] Et ulterius de vberiori gratia nostra speciali et ex certa scientia et mero motu nostris Dedimus et concessimus Ac per presentes pro Nobis heredibus et Successoribus nostris Damus et Concedimus prefato Ballivo et Juratis et Successoribus suis imperpetuum ponderacionem et mensuram omnium et huiusmodi Merchandizarum et aliarum rerum quarumcunque que antehac ponderari seu mensurari solebant apud Le Common Beame and Measure Gallice poids et mensures du Roy Insule predicte Ac omnia proficua Commoditates et Emolumenta quecunque pro huiusmodi ponderacione et mensuracione antehac vsualiter percepta habita sive consueta in tam amplis modo et forma provt dictus Pater noster aut Domina Elizabetha nuper Regina Anglie sive iidem Ballivus et Jurati habuimus percepimus sive gavisi fuimus habuit percepit sive gavisus fuit aut habuerunt perceperunt vel gavisi fuerunt Habendum tenendum et gaudendum predicta ponderacione et mensuracione ac proficuis Commoditatibus et Emolumentis inde prefato Ballivo et Juratis et Successoribus suis imperpetuum ad solum et proprium opus et vsum eorundem Ballivi et Juratorum et Successorum suorum imperpetuum

[16] Reddendo inde annatim Nobis heredibus et Successoribus nostris annualem redditum sive annualem summam viginti solidis legalis monete Anglie per annum ad manus Receptoris Revencionum nostrorum heredum et Successorum nostrorum dicte Insule de Garnsey ad ffestam Sancti Michaelis Archangeli solvendis imperpetuum

[17] Et vlterius de ampliori gratia nostra speciali ac ex certa Scientia et mero motu nostris Dedimus Concessimus et confirmavimus Ac per presentes pro Nobis heredibus et Successoribus nostris quantum in nobis est Damus concedimus et Confirmamus prefato Ballivo Juratis et ceteris Incolis et habitatoribus Insularum et locorum maritimorum predictorum Necnon Mercatoribus et aliis eo confluentibus tot tanta talia huiusmodi et consimilia iura Ordinaciones Jurisdicciones Immunitates impunitates indempnitates exempciones Libertates ffranchesias et privilegias quecunque quot qualia quanta et que prefatus Ballivus et ceteri Incole et habitatores Mercatores et alii aut eorum aliquis antehac legittime et rite vsi freti seu gavisi fuerunt vsus fretus seu gavisus fuit in omnia et singula quecunque alia in aliquibus Chartis aut Literis Patentibus nostris seu Progenitorum sive Predecessorum nostrorum quondam Regum Anglie seu Ducum Normanie aut aliorum eis seu eorum Predecessoribus antehac data concessa vel confirmata preantea vsus et non revocatus seu abolitus quocunque nomine aut quibuscunque nominibus iidem Ballivus Jurati et ceteri Incole et habitatores earundem Insularum et locorum maritimorum predictorum aut eorum Predecessorum seu eorum aliquis vel aliqui in eisdem Literis Patentibus seu eorum aliquibus censeantur nominentur aut vocitentur seu censeri nominari aut vocitari debuerunt seu soliti fuerunt ac ea omnia et singula licet in presentibus minime expressa prefato Ballivo et Juratis ac ceteris Incolis et Inhabitatoribus Insularum et locorum maritimorum predictorum Necnon Mercatorum et aliis eo confluentibus indigenis et Alienigenis per presentes Confirmamus et Consolidamus et de integro ratificamus adeo plene libere et integre provt ea omnia et singula in eisdem Literis Patentibus contenta modo perticulariter verbatim et expresse in presentibus recitata declarata fuissent Salva semper atque illa bifacta Suprema regia potestate dominacione atque Imperio Corone nostre Anglie tam quoad Ligeantiam subjeccionem et obedientiam Insularum predictarum et aliorum quorumcunque [sic] infra Insulas et loca predicta comorancium sive degencium quam quoad Regalitates privilegia res vel redditus vectigalia et cetera iura proficua Comoditates et Emolumenta quecunque infra Insulas et loca predicta nobis heredibus et Successoribus nostris per Prerogativam Corone nostre Anglie sive Ducatus Normanie seu aliter ex antiquo debita et consueta Salvis etiam appellacionibus et provocacionibus quibuscunque Insularum predictarum ac aliorum ibidem commorantium sive degencium in omnibus eiusmodi Casibus et non aliis que Legibus et Consuetudinibus Insule et locorum predictorum regali nostre Cognicioni atque examinationi reservatur Aliqua

152

Sententia Clausa re aut materia quacunque Superius in presentibus expressa sive specificata in contrarium inde in aliquo non obstante

[18] Et vlterius gratia nostra speciali Ac ex certa scientia et mero motu nostris Dedimus concessimus et confirmavimus ac per presentes pro Nobis heredibus et Successoribus nostris quantum in nobis est Damus concedimus et confirmamus prefato Ballivo Juratis et Inhabitantibus Insule predicte et Successoribus suis omnia et Singula terras Tenementa redditus Revenciones et hereditamenta quecunque aliquibus Ecclesiis Hospitalibus et Scholis infra Insulam predictam aut aliquam inde partem vel parcellam spectantem vel pertinentem aut pro reparacione predictarum Ecclesiarum Hospitalium sive Scholarum aut manutencione Rectorum sive Minstrorum in eisdem Ecclesiis aut pauperum aut aliorum in eisdem Hospitalibus ac Ludimagistrorum et Scholarum in scholis predictis aut pro aliis piis et publicis vsibus infra Insulam predictam antehac data concessa legata vel appunctuata Habendum gaudendum et tenendum predictas Terras tenementa Redditus Revencionibus et hereditamentis cum eorum pertinentiis prefato Ballivo et Juratis ac Inhabitantibus et Successoribus suis solumodo disponenda ad vsus et intenciones ad quas respective data legata sive appunctuata fuerunt per seperales donatores eorundem et ad nullos alios vsus et intenciones quascunque absque aliquo redditu sive Computo aut aliquo alio inde nobis heredibus vel Successoribus nostris quoquomodo reddendo solvendo vel faciendo

[19] Dedimus etiam et Concessimus ac pro Nobis heredibus et succesoribus nostris Damus et Concedimus Dilectis Ballivo et Jurat et Inhabitantibus Insule predicte et Successoribus suis plenam potestatem et authoritatem habendi capiendi et possidendi sibi et Successoribus suis imperpetuum omnia et quecunque terras tenementa Redditus Revenciones et hereditamenta infra Insulam predictam aut aliquam inde partem que de tempore in tempus et ad omnia tempora imposterum per aliquam personam vel aliquas personas data legata et concessa sive appunctuata erint alicui Ecclesie sive Capelle Hospitali sive Schole infra Insulam predictam aut ad et versus reparaciones aut Supportacionem alicuius Ecclesie sive Capelle aut alicuius Hospitalis sive Schole infra Insulam predictam aut manutencionem supportacionem et sustentacionem Rectoris aut Ministris in dicta Ecclesia sive Cappella aut Magistro Custodi sive pauperi in huiusmodi Hospitalibus aut manutencionem sustentacionem vel educacionem Ludimagistri ac Iuvenum et Scholarum in huiusmodi Schola aut ad alios pios aut publicos vsus infra

Insulam predictam quoscunque absque aliquo redditus sive Computo proinde Nobis heredibus vel Successoribus nostris reddendo solvendo vel faciendo aliquo Statuto Actu Ordinacione Proclamacione vel Consuetudine huius Regni nostri Anglie facto edito ordinato sive proviso aut aliqua alia re causa vel materia quacunque in contrarium in aliquo non obstante. Nihilominus Intencio nostra est et per presentes statuimus et ordinamus pro Nobis heredibus et Successoribus nostris quod predicta terrae tenementa redditus revenciones et hereditamenta ac proficua earundem de tempore in tempus solumodo convertantur et disponentur ad vsus et intenciones ad quas respective data legata concessa sive appunctuata erint per seperales Donatores earundem vt prefertur et ad nullos alios vsus et intenciones quascunque

[20] Cumque Inhabitantes predicte Insule de Garnsey virtute licentiarum et Literarum Patentium diversorum Progenitorum et Predecessorum nostrorum Regum et Reginarum Anglie super consideracione necessitatis dictorum Inhabitantium habita a tempore cuius contrarium memoria hominum non existit eskippare onerare exportare et abcarriare annatim vsi sunt ad vnum tempus sive diversa tempora in anno diversis Portubus infra hoc Regum [sic] nostrum Anglie in eisdem licentiis et Literis Patentibus perticulariter mencionatis ad predictam Insulam de Garnsey seperales proporciones victualia et alia necessaria inferius mencionata vizt pro Castro de Corett [sic] infra dictam Insulam in Cervitia Anglice Beere Centum dolie aut pro qualibet dolio Cervisie ad dictum numerum duo quarter brasii Anglice Mault et Lupulos Anglice Hoppes pertinentum duodecim Boves sexcentum Les fflicthes lardi Anglice Bacon mille et ducentum libra butiri viginti pondera Casei Anglice Twenty weight of Cheese tria millia Salparum Anglice Stockfish Trescentum libris coli Anglice Tallow viginti lez dickers Corii et in ligno Carbone et aliis necessariis pro eodem Castro quantum racionabiliter requiretur Et quod predicta Insula de Garnsey in Cervicia quingenta dolia Centum et quinquaginta les dickers Corii ac viginti et quinque Les dozens pellium vitularum anglice Calve Skinnes ac in Ligno et Carbone cum omnibus aliis necessaris pro eadem Insula quantum racionabiliter requiretur absque solucione alicuius Custume parve Custume toluet sive alia debito quocunque Necnon informamus [sic] quod virtute Licentiarum predictarum et sub generalibus verbis predictis dicti Inhabitantes Insule predicte pro eorum maximo et necessario vsu annatim eskippaverunt et exportaverunt in Insulas predictas a Portubus predictis quingenta les Todds Lane inter cetera et Superinde iidem Inhabitantes licencias predictas confirmare et explanari Authoritate et potes-

tate nostra regali Nobis humilime supplicaverunt cum augmentacione addicione et Supplemento quarundam aliarum rerum pro subvencione et augmentacione Status Insule predicte et suppeditacione necessitate Insulanarum Inhabitantium eiusdem provt Nobis melius fieri aut fore videbitur

[21] Nos obsequio et Servicia predictorum Insulanorum Nobis et Progenitoribus nostris maxime cum fidelitate et cura antehac prestitit ac aliter serio perpondentes Necnon sua gravia onera et expensus in tuicione Insulae predictae ac predicti Portus sive Le Peere ac diversorum Castrorum et locorum in defensione eiusdem assidue expositos eorum paupertatem et Indigentiam ad hoc prestandum absque potestate regia adiumente considerantes ac eorum curam et diligentiam in rebus gerendis et vite modum precipue ad Mercatorum et Comerciam deuottum ac Corone Anglie constantiam intuentes De gratia nostra speciali ac ex certa scientia et mero motu nostris Dedimus Concessimus approbavimus et Confirmavimus ac per presentes pro Nobis heredibus et Successoribus nostris Damus concedimus approbamus et confirmamus prefatis Inhabitantibus Insule predicte et Successoribus suis predictam licentiam et plenam potestatem et authoritatem eskippandi imbarcandi onerandi exportandi et abcariandi annatim ad vnum tempus vel diversa tempora in anno a Portubus nostris de London Southampton Weymouth Poole Lyme et Plimouth aut eorum aliquibus vel aliquo in Regno nostro Anglie ad predictam Insulam de Garnsey pro predicto Castro de Cornett et pro necessaris vsu et sustentacione Inhabitantium dicte Insule tam predicta quingenta les Toddes lane quam predictas seperales quantitates et numeros Cervisie vel Brasii et Lupulos pertinentes Bovium lardi Casei Salparum ligni Carbonis Coriorum Pellium vitularum cum omnibus huiusmodi aliis necessariis pro Castro et Insula predicta quolibet de tempore in tempus racionabiliter requirentur absque aliqua Custuma magna vel parva aut aliquo Tolueto aut alia re nobis heredibus vel Successoribus nostris aut ffirmariis sive Officiariis nostris heredum vel Successorum nostrorum proinde reddendo solvendo vel faciendo

[22] Et vlterius pro Consideracione predicta Damus et Concedimus prefatis Inhabitantibus Insule de Garnsey predicte et Successoribus suis per presentes plenam et absolutam licentiam libertatem et authoritatem durante beneplacito nostro ad vel apud predictos Portus nostros de London Southampton Weymouth Poole Lyme et Plimouth aut eorum aliquem vel aliquos eskippendi imbarcandi et onerandi et ab eisdem aut eorum aliquibus vel aliquo exportandi abcarriandi et transportandi in Insula predicta pro necessario vsu et

155

sustentacione Insularum et Inhabitantium ibidem annuatim ad vnum tempus vel diversa tempora in anno tot et tanta alia quantitate et numero omnium et omnimodo bonorum mercimoniorum et merchandizarum municione tantummodo excepta vltra predictas separales proporciones superius preconcessa aut concedi mencionata qualiter eis magis opportunum et necessarium fore videbitur et non excedentes in toto in aliquo vno anno in Custuma annualem summam Centum et quinquaginta librarum secundum ratas per eos ante hac solutas penitus libertati et acquietati de et ab omni Custum magna vel parva Imposicione et alia solutione vel re quacunque Nobis heredibus et Successoribus nostris aut ffirmariis sive Officiariis nostris heredum vel Successorum nostrorum proinde reddenda vel facienda Et quod hec licentia nostra vltima mencionata ad suam et cetera predicta iis continuabitur durante beneplacito nostro tantum et non aliter

[23] Quare volumus ac per presentes pro Nobis heredibus et Successoribus nostris firmiter injungendo precipimus omnibus et singulis Custumariis Contrarotulatoribus Supervisoribus Scrutatoribus et aliis Officiariis et Ministris nostris Portum predictorum quod ipsi et eorum quilibet pacifice libere et quiete permittant predictas provisiones et necessaria bona Mercimonia et Merchandizas annuatim ad vnum tempus sive plura tempora in anno apud Portum predictum vel Crecam earundem eskippari et onerari et ab eisdem exportari et transportari ad predictum Castrum et Insulam absque solucione alicujus Custume magne vel parve aut alicuius Imposicionis Toluete sive alii debiti pro eisdem aut eorum aliquibus secundum veram Intencionem presentium adeo plene libere et integre ad omnia Intenciones et proposita provt aliqua genere victualium aut aliarum provisionum extra aliquas Portus hujus Regni nostri Anglie ville Callic' aut Marchiis eiusdem pro relevamine Subditorum ibidem antehac Commorantium sive Inhabitantium exire vsi et permissi fuerunt et absque molestacione sive Impedimento aliquorum Marinarum vasearum aut aliarum rerum predictorum Subditorum nostrorum predicti Castri aut Insule pro provisione necessariis bonis Merchandiziis et mercimoniis predictis ad Portus predictos venientium virtute sive colore alicuius Commissionis Restriccionis Proclamationis sive Mandati ante hac facti sive imposterum per Nos aut Privatum Concilium nostrum dirigendi nisi predicta Commissio Proclamacio sive Mandatum continebit plenam Restriccionem et Annihilacionem huius presentis Concessionis nostre aut alicujus inde partis sive Parcelle

[24] Proviso semper quod dicti Subditi nostri de Garnsey aut eorum aliquis vel aliqui ad predictum Portum vel aliquam Crecam earundem veniendo afferent secum Scriptum sive Billam aut Scriptas sive Billas manibus propriis Capitanei Castri et Insule predicte vel Deputati sui aut Ballivi et Juratorum eiusdem Insule pro tempore existente [sic] perticulariter mentionandes proporciones et quantitates predictas Victualium at aliorum necessariorum aut bonorum Mercium aut Merchandizarum quas ipse vel ipsi ad Portum et Crecam predictam veniendo exinde transportare assignabitur vel assignabuntur

[25] Volentes ac per presentes mandantes predictos Custumarios et Officiarios et Ministros in Portibus et Crecis predictis quod ipsi et eorum aliquis de tempore in tempus capiet aut capiet [sic] Obligaciones de personis Insule predicte aut aliis qui eskippabunt aut onerabunt aliquam partem Proporcionem vel quantitatem predictam aut predictum Lignum Carboni Boni Mercimoniorum aut Merchandizarum in forma predicta Quod dicte persone eadem eskippantes et onerantes tantumodo ad et in Castrum et Insulam predictam transportabunt et deliberabunt Ibidem occupandam et ad nullum alium locum quemcunque Ac etiam quod dicti Officiarii in Libris suis de tempore in tempus intrabunt et fidele Computum annuatim retinebunt de omnibus rebus ad Portum vel crecam predictam virtute presentium eskippandis et onerandis Ea intencione quod certiores fiant de vera Execucione premissorum absque aliquo Incremento proporcione vel quantitate predicta Et he Litere nostre Patentes vel Irrotulamentum earundem erunt dictis Custumariis Contrarotulatoribus Supervisoribus Scrutatoribus et aliis Officiariis et Ministris predictis sufficiens Warrantum et exoneracio in hac parte

[26] Eo quod Expressa mencio de vero valore annuo vel de certitudine premissorum sive eorum alicujus aut de aliis donis sive Concessionibus per Nos seu per aliquem Progenitorum sive Predecessorum nostrorum prefatis Ballivo et Juratis Insule de Garnsey ac ceteris Incolis et Inhabitantibus tam ipsius Insule de Garnsey quam predictarum Insularum nostrarum de Aureney alias Alderney et Sarke predictarum antehac tempora facta in presentibus minime facta existit aut aliquo Statuto Actu Ordinacione Provisione Proclamacione sive Restriccione in contrarium inde antehac habito facto edito ordinato sive provisum aut aliqua alia re causa vel materia quacunque in aliquo non obstante In Cujus rei Testimonium has Literas nostras fieri

fecimus Patentes Teste me ipso apud Westmonasterium vndecimo die ffebruarii Anno regni nostri vicesimo

Per breve de Privato Sigillo Pigott

~ ~ ~

Charles the second, by the grace of God, king of England, Scotland, France, and Ireland, Defender of the Faith, etc.

[1] To all to whom these present letters shall come, greeting. Whereas our beloved and faithful lieges and subjects, the bailiff and the jurats of our Island of Guernsey, and the other sojourners in and inhabitants of both the same island and our islands of Aureneye, alias Alderney, and Sark, within our duchy of Normandy, and their predecessors, have from time beyond what the memory of men can reach, by virtue of several charters, grants, confirmations, and most ample writs, of our illustrious progenitors and ancestors, both kings of England and dukes of Normandy, and others, used, enjoyed, and been in possession of very many rights, jurisdictions, privileges, immunities, liberties, and franchises, freely, quietly, and without any infringement of the same, both within the kingdom of England, and elsewhere within our dominions, and other places under our subjection on this side of, or beyond, the seas; by the aid and benefit of which grants, the aforesaid islands and the maritime places have stood out and continued constantly, faithfully, and unblameably in our faith, obedience, and service, and have enjoyed and gone on in their commerce and trade with merchants, both natives and aliens, as well in time of peace, as in time of war, and exercised and executed their duties in giving their decrees, and taking cognisance of all and every cause, quarrel, action, both civil and criminal, and capital pleas; and the right of jurisdiction they were vested with, to take into their consideration, to take order, decide, discuss, hear, and determine, and to proceed in the premises, and keep records of their proceedings according to the laws and customs practised of old, and approved in the said islands and other places aforesaid; except in other cases reserved from time to time to our royal cognisance:

[2] And we considering of how great advantage and moment all and singular the premises are, and have been, toward the safe-keeping and conservation of the said islands and other maritime places in their fidelity and allegiance to our crown of England; and being always mindful (as is just) how courageously and loyally the said islanders and inhabitants have behaved themselves in our own and in our progenitors' service. And considering what great detriments, losses and dangers they have sustained and

158

do daily sustain, both for the constant safeguarding of the said islands and places, and for the recovery and defence of our Castle of Mont Orgueil, in our island of Jersey; to the end, not only to show some distinguished testimony and certain marks of our favour, affection, and royal beneficence towards the inhabitants aforesaid, but also to encourage them, and their posterity for ever, to persevere and continue inviolably in their accustomed and due obedience towards us, and our heirs and successors; we have thought proper to grant to them these our royal letters patent, confirmed under the great seal of England, in form following.

[3] Know ye therefore, that we, of our special favour, certain knowledge, and mere motion, have given and granted, and for ourselves, our heirs and successors, we do by these present letters give and grant, to the said bailiff and jurats of our island of Guernsey aforesaid, and to the other sojourners and inhabitants, both of the same island, and of our other islands aforesaid, of Aureney, alias Alderney, and Sark; that they themselves and every one of them (though not herein stated or declared by their particular names) shall, for the time to come, be for ever free, exempted, and acquitted, in all our cities, boroughs, markets, and trading towns, fairs, mart-towns, and other places and ports, within our kingdom of England, and within all our provinces, dominions, territories, and other places under our subjection, this side of, or beyond, the seas, from and of all tributes, tolls, customs, subsidies, hidage, taylage, pontage, panage, murage, fossage, works, and warlike expeditions (except in case our body, or that of our heirs and successors, should be held in prison (which God avert)), and of and from all other contributions and exactions from their persons, money, goods and other duties whatsoever, that may be due from, to be rendered by, or be payable by, and claimed from, the said islanders, or any of them, to us, our heirs and successors, ever in any manner, by virtue of any charters, grants, confirmations, and writs of our said progenitors, formerly kings of England and dukes of Normandy, or others, or by virtue or reason of any reasonable and legal usage, prescriptions, or customs.

[4] And whereas some other privileges, jurisdictions, immunities, liberties, and franchises have been graciously given, granted, and confirmed by our progenitors and predecessors, formerly kings of England and dukes of Normandy, and others, to the aforesaid islanders, and have been used and observed constantly in the said island and other maritime places, from the time whereof the memory of men reaches not to the contrary; one of which is, that in time of war merchants of all nations and others, both aliens and denizen, both enemies and friends, could and might freely, lawfully, without danger or punishment, come to, resort to, go to and fro,

and frequent the said islands, and other aforesaid maritime places, with their ships, merchandise, and goods; both to avoid storms, and to conduct their other lawful business there, and to exercise there free commerce, business and trade, and securely, and without danger, remain there, and depart from thence, and return to the same, as often as they think fit, without any harm, molestation, or hostility whatsoever, in their goods, merchandise, or persons; and this not only within the said islands and maritime places, and all around the same, but likewise at such spaces and distances from the islands as the sight of man goes to, that is as far as the eye of man can reach: We, by virtue of our royal authority, do, for ourselves, our heirs and successors, indulge and enlarge, and renew, reiterate, and confirm, by these present letters, as far as in us lies, the same immunities, impunities, liberties, and privileges, and all the other premisses last mentioned, finding them to be reasonable and seasonable, to the said bailiff and jurats, and the other sojourners, inhabitants and merchants, and others, whether enemies or friends, and to each of them, in as ample form and manner as heretofore they have used and enjoyed the same. In order therefore to prevent any violation or infraction of this our grant, concession, and confirmation, or any thing therein contained, in any manner whatsoever, we declare and give this warning by these present letters to all our officers and subjects in all parts of our kingdom of England, and throughout all our lordships and places under our obedience, wheresoever they lie, or are situated. And if any one of our said officers and subjects shall be so rash as to presume or attempt to transgress these our strict orders and commands, we order and decree (as far as in us lies), that he shall not only restore what has been taken or seized, but shall also be compelled to make a fuller restitution and satisfaction of all costs, interests, and damages, by whatever legal remedy, and he shall be severely punished for his audacious contempt of our royal power, and of our laws.

[5] Further, we, of our more gracious favour, do, by these present letters, ratify, approve, establish, and confirm, all and every one of the laws, ordinances, constitutions, records, inquisitions, and customs which have been duly and legally from ancient times used, received, found, had, and approved within the aforesaid islands and maritime places; giving and granting to the aforesaid bailiff and jurats, and all other magistrates and officers of justice, and others who are appointed for performing the functions and executing the duties of any office, full and absolute authority, power, and faculty to have the cognisance, jurisdiction, and judgment concerning and touching all and all sorts of pleas, processes, law-suits, actions, quarrels, and causes arising within the islands and maritime places aforesaid; both those

actions which are real, personal, and mixed, and those which are criminal and capital, and to proceed in the said islands, and not elsewhere, in hearing the parties in their pleadings, and prosecutions of their processes, in their defence; and to hear, and examine the same, making decrees, determining, absolving, condemning, and putting their sentences in execution, according to the laws and customs previously practised and approved in the islands and maritime places aforesaid; without admitting any challenge or appeal, except in such cases as are reserved to our royal cognisance by the ancient customs of the islands and places aforesaid. Which authority, power, and faculty (except in the cases reserved to us), we commit, give, grant, and confirm, for ourselves and our heirs and successors aforesaid, to the said bailiffs and jurats, and to the others, by these present letters, as freely, fully, and entirely, as the said bailiff and jurats, or others or any of them, heretofore have rightfully and lawfully used, practised, and enjoyed, or might legally have used and enjoyed.

[6] Moreover, our will and pleasure is, and we grant, for ourselves, our heirs, and successors by these present letters, to the said bailiff and jurats, and the other inhabitants and sojourners in the islands and maritime places aforesaid, that for the time to come, none of them be cited, or summoned, or drawn into any lawsuit, or forced in any manner by any writs or process, issued from any of our courts of the kingdom of England, to appear and answer before any judges, courts, or other officers of justice, out of any of the islands and maritime places aforesaid, touching or concerning any thing, dispute, causes, or matters in controversy whatsoever, arising in the aforesaid islands, but that the aforesaid islanders, and each of them, may lawfully, notwithstanding the said writs and processes, remain, reside quietly, and abide in the aforesaid islands, waiting for justice there; without incurring any punishment, corporal or pecuniary, by way of fine, mulct, ransom, or forfeiture, by reason of any offence, contempt, or contumacy, committed towards us, our heirs and successors, for which they might be sued, arraigned, or condemned; except only in the cases, and not others, which by the laws and customs of the islands and places aforesaid are reserved to our royal cognisance and determination.

[7] And whereas we are informed that the jurats and bailiffs of the aforesaid island of Guernsey, and the other sojourners and inhabitants both of the same island of Guernsey and of our aforesaid islands of Alderney and Sark have previously been free and quit of and from the toll called 'petite custum' and of and from all tallages, tolls, cariage services, customs and similar asponsages, and all their wreck, emption and redemption, and of our rightful prize, viz. of one tun of wine *ante mallum* and another *post mallum*

[8] Know that we, of our special favour, certain knowledge, and mere motion, have given and confirmed, ratified and approved, and by these present letters for ourselves, our heirs and successors, we give and confirm, ratify and approve, to the aforesaid bailiff and jurats of our Island of Guernsey aforesaid, and to the other sojourners and inhabitants, as well of the said Island, as of our aforesaid islands of Aureney, alias Alderney, and Sark, and to their successors, exemptions and acquittances from and of the payment of toll otherwise called 'petite Custome', and of and from all other taylage, tolls, carriage services, customs, and similar asponsages, and all their wreck, emption and redemption and of our rightful prise, viz. of one tun of wine *ante mallum* and another *post mallum.*

[9] And also the like, and as great, and as ample liberties, franchises, privileges, immunities, discharges, and acquittances whatsoever, as the same bailiff and jurats of the aforesaid island of Guernsey and the other sojourners and inhabitants both of the same island of Guernsey and of the aforesaid islands of Aureney alias Alderney and Sark, by whatever name of incorporation or names of incorporations, or any of them, previously legitimately had, held or used or enjoyed, or ought to have had, held, used or enjoyed, of an hereditary state, by reason of, or on the grounds of, any charters or letters patent given, granted or confirmed by us or by any of our progenitors or predecessors formerly kings or queens of England to them or their predecessors by whatsoever name, incorporation or by whatsoever names or incorporations before this or by reason or on the grounds of any prescription, use or custom in the same island of Guernsey and in the aforesaid islands of Alderney and Sark or in any of them before this had, used or accustomed, or by any other legal manner, right or title whatsoever, to be had and held to them and their successors for ever, of us, our heirs and successors, by such, similar, equivalent and equal rent and service as they were previously held of us or of our most dearly beloved late father, Lord Charles, of blessed memory, or of our most dearly beloved late grandfather, Lord James of blessed memory, or of Lady Elizabeth formerly queen of England, and not otherwise.

[10] And further, of our fuller and special favour, certain knowledge and mere motion, we have granted and by these present letters for us, our heirs and successors, we grant to the aforesaid bailiff and jurats of our island of Guernsey and to the other sojourners and inhabitants, as of the same isle as of our aforesaid isles of Alderney and Sark and their successors, that for the time to come they themselves and their successors should perpetually henceforth be free and quit of and from the payment of any custom, subsidy, tonnage or poundage whatsoever kind owed or payable to us, our

heirs or successors of or for any goods or merchandise of any kind growing, coming forth, made or produced within the aforesaid islands of Guernsey, Alderney and Sark and which were transported, conveyed, or brought by the aforesaid bailiff and jurats of the island of Guernsey or other sojourners and inhabitants, both of the same island and of our islands of Alderney and Sark aforesaid at any time in the past in this our realm of England or any port or creek of the same realm, by the present letters, for such transport.

[11] And, moreover, our will and pleasure is, and, by these present letters, for ourselves, our heirs and successors, of our special favour, certain knowledge, and mere motion, we grant to the rector of the parish church of St Peter in our aforesaid island of Guernsey and his successors annually for ever to and towards the maintenance, sustenance and relief of the same rector and his successors for the time being, sixty quarters of our wheat, the same sixty quarters of wheat to be had, taken and received annually from the rents, revenues and other profits issuing, owed or payable to us, our heirs and successors, from the parish of St. Saviour in the same island of Guernsey by reason of the fraternities, obits, masses and other similar things, dissolved by strength of certain acts of parliament in this realm of England ordained and provided for such a case, or by any other title or right whatsoever, in manner and form and at the same days and times as the aforesaid rector or his predecessor has been accustomed to have, take and receive the same.

[12] And whereas we are credibly informed that the inhabitants of our said island of Guernsey have taken on to build, construct and erect, at their great charges, burdens and expenses, a certain harbour or the 'peere' in the sea beside the aforesaid island of Guernsey, the which harbour or 'peere' is now almost completed and finished, to the great security and prosperity of all the merchants and others coming to those parts to buy, sell and do business.

[13] And whereas, furthermore, we are similarly informed that the bailiff and jurats of the said island of Guernsey and their predecessors, in the time of the reign of the Lady Elizabeth formerly queen of England, levied and took, and were accustomed to levy and take, for and towards the fabric and structure of the harbour or 'peere', a certain duty or custom, commonly called 'pettie Custome', of certain merchandise, goods, ships, and other things, both those brought or imported into the same island of Guernsey from time to time and those growing or made, in the same island.

[14] Know that we, for the perpetual repair, maintenance, and improvement of the aforesaid port or 'le Peere', and also for the support and maintaining of other public expenses and works of the same island, of our special favour, certain knowledge and mere motion, we have granted and conceded, and by these present letters, for ourselves, our heirs and successors, we grant and concede full, free, and lawful power, right and authority to the aforesaid bailiff and jurats and their successors, that they themselves and their successors forever henceforth can and may freely, lawfully and without danger or punishment, take and receive the like, and as great, and as ample sums of money, by the name of the small custom, in English 'pettie Custume', as they were accustomed to take, have or receive in the time of the reign of said former Queen Elizabeth, towards the full and perfect construction and building of the aforesaid port or 'le Peere' and towards the repair, maintenance and improvement of the same for ever, and also towards the support and maintaining of other public expenses and works of the same island, both of and for all and singular merchandise, goods, ships and other things brought or imported, or to be brought or imported, into the same island from time to time, and of all and singular merchandise and other things growing or made in the same island, or to grow or be made, of as many, as large, similar and like sums of money, by the name of the small custom, called in English 'pettie Custume' as in the time of the reign of the said former Queen Elizabeth they were accustomed legitimately to take, have or receive

[15] And moreover, of our more gracious special favour, certain knowledge, and mere motion, we have granted and conceded, and by these present letters, for our heirs and successors, we grant and concede, to the aforesaid bailiff and jurats and their successors for ever the weighing and measuring of all of this kind of merchandise and of whatever other things, which were accustomed to be weighed or measured at the 'common Beame and measures', in French 'poids et mesures du Roy', of the aforesaid island, and all profits, commodities and emoluments whatsoever usually taken, had or accustomed for this weighing and measuring, in as ample manner and form as we or Lady Elizabeth formerly queen of England or the same bailiff and jurats either had, received or enjoyed, or have had, received or enjoyed. To have, hold, and enjoy the aforesaid weighing and measuring, and the profits, commodities and emoluments therefore, to the aforesaid bailiff and jurats and their successors for ever, and to the sole and exclusive benefit and use of the same bailiff and jurats and their successors for ever.

[16] Rendering thence annually to us, our heirs and successors an annual rent or annual sum of twenty shillings of English legal tender, to be paid into the hands of the receiver of our revenues, and those of our heirs and successors of the said island of Guernsey at the feast of St Michael the Archangel each year in perpetuity.

[17] And moreover, of our more gracious favour, certain knowledge, and mere motion, we have given, granted, and confirmed, and by our present letters, for ourselves, our heirs and successors (as far as in us lies), we do give, grant, and confirm to the aforesaid bailiff and jurats, and other sojourners in, and inhabitants of, the aforesaid islands and maritime places; as also to merchants and others meeting there, the like, and as great, and as ample rights, ordinances, jurisdictions, immunities, impunities, indemnities, exemptions, liberties, franchises, and privileges whatsoever, as the aforesaid bailiff and jurats, and other sojourners and inhabitants, and merchants and others, or any of them, have heretofore rightfully and legally used, practised, and enjoyed; and all and singular other things whatsoever that has been heretofore given, granted, and confirmed to them or to their predecessors, in any charters or letters patent, of us or our progenitors, formerly kings of England, or dukes of Normandy, or others, and not revoked or abolished, by whatsoever name or names the same bailiff and jurats, and other sojourners in, or inhabitants of, the same islands and maritime places aforesaid, or their predecessors, or any of them, may be supposed to have been comprised, called, or named, or ought to have been called or named, in the said letters patent, and all and singular which things, though not herein expressly mentioned, we do by these present letters confirm, consolidate, and ratify anew to the aforesaid bailiff and jurats, and other sojourners, and inhabitants, of the islands and maritime places aforesaid, and also merchants and others coming together there, those born there, and those born elsewhere, as fully, freely, and entirely, as if all and singular the things particularly mentioned and declared in the same letters patent were particularly and expressly recited and declared in these our present letters patent. Saving always entire and without detriment the regal and sovereign power, dominion, and empire of our crown of England, as to what may concern the allegiance, subjection, and obedience of the aforesaid islanders, and others, whoever they may be, dwelling for a shorter or longer time in the same island; and also as to what may concern the regality, privileges, incomes, revenues, tributes, and other rights, profits, commodities, and emoluments whatsoever, anciently due and accustomed to be paid to us, our heirs and successors, according to our royal prerogative as kings of England, or the prerogative of the duchy of Normandy, in the islands and

places aforesaid; saving also to the aforesaid islanders, and others dwelling or being in the said islands, a right to appeal in all cases reserved to our cognisance and consideration by the laws and customs of the said island; but in no other case: Notwithstanding any sentence, clause, thing, or matter whatsoever expressed above, or specially contained to the contrary in these present letters.

[18] And further of our more gracious special favour, certain knowledge and mere motion, we have given, granted, and confirmed and by these present letters patent, for ourselves, our heirs and successors, as far as in us lies, we give, grant, and confirm to the aforesaid bailiff and jurats and to the inhabitants of the aforesaid island and their successors all and singular the lands, tenements, rents, revenues and inheritances whatsoever before this granted, bequeathed and appointed to any churches, hospitals and schools within the aforesaid island, or any part or parcel belonging or pertaining to them, or for the repair of the aforesaid churches, hospitals or schools, or the maintenance of the rectors or ministers in the same churches, or of the poor or others in the same hospitals, or of the masters and scholars in the aforesaid schools, or for other pious and public uses within the aforesaid island; to have, hold, and enjoy the aforesaid lands, tenements, rents, revenues and inheritances with their appurtenances to the aforesaid bailiff and jurats and inhabitants and their successors, only to be disposed of for the uses and intentions to which they had been respectively given, bequeathed or appointed by their separate donors, and to no other uses or purposes whatsoever without any rent or account, or anything else thence to be rendered, paid or made to us our heirs or successors in any manner

[19] Furthermore, we have given and granted and by these present letters for ourselves, our heirs, and successors we give and grant to the aforesaid bailiff and jurats and to the inhabitants of the aforesaid island and their successors full power and authority of having, receiving and occupying, to themselves and their successors for ever, all and whatsoever lands, tenements, rents, revenues, and inheritances within the island aforesaid or any part of them, from time to time and at all times hereafter, given, left, granted, or appointed by any person or any persons to any churches, hospitals, and schools within the aforesaid island, or to or towards separate support of any church or chapel, or of any hospital or school, in the aforesaid island, or the maintenance, support and sustenance of the rectors or ministers in the said churches or chapels, or of the master, warden or poor folk in hospitals of this kind, or the maintenance, sustenance or education of the masters and young people and scholars in schools of this kind, or for other pious and public uses within the aforesaid island whatsoever, without

any render or account thence to us, our heirs or successors to be rendered, paid or made; any statute, act, ordinance, proclamation or custom of this our kingdom of England made, proclaimed, ordained, or provided, or any other thing, cause or matter whatsoever to the contrary in anything notwithstanding. Nevertheless, our intention is, and by these present letters we establish and ordain, for us, our heirs and successors, that the aforesaid lands, tenements, rents, revenues, and inheritances, and the profits of the same, from time to time, should only be converted and spent towards the uses and purposes to which they were respectively given, bequeathed, granted or appointed, by their separate donors, as aforesaid, and towards no other uses or purposes whatsoever

[20] And whereas the inhabitants of the aforesaid island of Guernsey, by virtue of the licences and letters patent of diverse of our ancestors and predecessors, kings and queens of England, on consideration of the need of the aforesaid inhabitants, accustomed from a time beyond what the memory of men can reach to ship, load, export and carry away annually, at one time or on diverse occasions in the year, from diverse ports in this our realm of England specifically mentioned in the same licences and letters patent, to the aforesaid islands of Guernsey, individual proportions of victuals and other necessaries mentioned below: viz., for Castle Cornet in the said island 100 tuns of 'Beere', or for each tun of beer to the said number two quarters of 'malte' and 'hopps', twelve bulls, 600 flitches of 'Bacon', 1,200lb of butter, 'twenty weigh of Cheese', 3,000 'Stockfish', 300lb of 'Tallow', 20 dickers [dicker = measure of 10 hides] of leather and however much wood, coal and other necessaries are reasonably required for the same castle. And for the aforesaid island of Guernsey, 500 tuns of beer, 150 dickers of leather, and 25 dozen 'Calve Skinnes', and however much wood, coal and other necessaries are reasonably required for the same island, without payment of any custom, small custom, toll or other due whatsoever. And we are also informed that by virtue of the aforesaid licences, and under the aforesaid general words, the said inhabitants of the aforesaid island, for their own very great and necessary use annually ship and export into the aforesaid island from the aforesaid ports 500 'Toddes' of wool [a tod of Wool = 28 lbs] amongst other things, and over and above this the same inhabitants have made most humble suit to us for the confirmation and explanation of the aforesaid licences by our royal authority and power, with the augmentation, addition, and supplement of certain other things to contribute to and augment the status of the aforesaid island, and for the support of the needs of the same islanders and inhabitants, according as may seem to us to be better.

[21] We, carefully thinking on the obedience and services of the aforesaid islanders shown to us and to our ancestors with the greatest faithfulness and care before this time and otherwise, and also considering their grievous burdens and expenses in the protection of the aforesaid island, and the aforesaid port or 'le peere', and in the vigorous defence of the different castles and places, which have been shown to us, and their poverty and indigence pledged to this, without the help of the royal power, and with a view to their care and diligence in doing things and their way of life, especially their devotion to trade and commerce, and constancy to the crown of England, of our special favour, certain knowledge, and mere motion, have given, granted, approved, and confirmed, and by these present letters, for ourself, our heirs and successors, we give, grant, approve, and confirm to the aforesaid inhabitants of the aforesaid island, and to their successors, licence and full power and authority to ship, embark, load, export, and carry away each year at one time or at different times in the year, from our ports of London, Southampton, Weymouth, Poole, Lyme, and Plymouth, or any of them, or anywhere in our realm of England, to the aforesaid island of Guernsey, for the aforesaid Castle Cornet, and for the needs, use and support of the inhabitants of the said island, both the aforesaid five-hundred 'Toddes' of wool and the aforesaid individual quantities and numbers of beer or associated malt and hops, bulls, bacon, cheese, stockfish, wood, coal, leather, calfskins, with all other necessaries of this kind for the aforesaid castle and island as shall be reasonably required from time to time, without any custom great or small, or any toll, or anything to be rendered, paid, or made to us, our heirs or successors, or our farmers or officials or those of our heirs or successors.

[22] And further, for the aforesaid consideration, we give and grant by these present letters to the aforesaid inhabitants of the aforesaid island of Guernsey, and to their successors, full and absolute licence, liberty, and authority, during our pleasure, to or at our aforesaid ports of London, Southampton, Weymouth, Poole, Lyme, and Plymouth, or any one or more of them, of shipping, embarking, and loading, and of exporting, carrying away, and transporting into the aforesaid island, from one or more of the same, for the needs, use, and support of the islanders and inhabitants there annually, at one or many times in the year, as many and as much, in quantity and number, of all and all sorts of goods, items, and merchandise, munitions only excepted, beyond the aforesaid separate proportions granted above or mentioned as conceded, as will seem to be more appropriate and necessary for them, and not exceeding in total in any one year the sum of £150 in annual customs according to the rates paid for them before this

time only, freed and quit of and from the imposition of all customs, great or small, and from other payment or thing whatsoever to be rendered or made thence to us, our heirs and successors, or the farmers of officials of ourself, our heirs and successors. And that this our licence last mentioned to him and the rest aforesaid will continue for them during our pleasure only, and not otherwise.

[23] Wherefore we will and by these present letters for ourself, our heirs and successors, we firmly instruct and order all and singular our customs officers, controllers, supervisors, inspectors and other officials and ministers of the ports aforesaid that they themselves and every of them should allow the aforesaid provisions and needful goods, items and merchandise annually at one time or at different times in the year to be shipped and loaded peaceably, freely and without restriction at the aforesaid port or creek, and from the same to be exported and transported to the aforesaid castle and island without the payment of any custom, great or small, or of any imposition, toll or other due for the same, or any of the same, according to the true intention of the present letters, as fully, freely, and entirely to all the intentions and purposes, just as other types of victuals, or of other provisions, were used and permitted to leave any ports of this our realm of England to the town of Calais, or its marches, for the relief of our subjects hitherto staying or living there, and from any interference or restriction of ships, vessels, or other things of our aforesaid subjects, for the provision of the castle and island aforesaid, with necessary things, goods, items and merchandise aforesaid, coming to the port aforesaid, by virtue or colour of any commission, restriction, proclamation or order made in the past, or in time to come by us or by our privy council directed, except in the case that the aforesaid commission, proclamation or mandate will contain a full restriction and cancellation of this our present grant or of any part of parcel of it.

[24] Provided always that our said subjects of Guernsey or any of them, coming to the aforesaid port or any creek of the same should carry with them a writing or bill in the personal hand of the captain of the castle and island aforesaid, or his deputy, or the bailiff and jurats of the same island for the time being, mentioning the aforesaid proportions and quantities of victuals and other necessary items, or other good, items and merchandise which he or they themselves have assigned to be transported thence coming to the port or creek aforesaid

[25] Willing and by these present letters ordering the aforesaid customs officers, officials and ministers in the aforesaid ports and creeks that they

themselves, or any of them, from time to time, should take bonds from the people of the aforesaid isle or others, who ship or load any aforesaid part, proportion or quantity, or the aforesaid wood, coal, trade goods or merchandise, in the form aforesaid; that the same said persons thus shipping and loading only to and in the castle and island aforesaid will transport and deliver there and to no other place whatsoever. And furthermore that the said officials will enter in their books from time to time and will keep a true account annually of all things to be shipped and loaded to the aforesaid port or creek, by virtue of the present letters, with the intention that they should be more certain of the true execution of the premises without any increase, proportion or quantity aforesaid. And these our letters patent, or the enrolment of the same, will be sufficient warrant and discharge to the said customs officials, controllers, supervisors, inspectors and other officials and officers aforesaid.

[26] And that although express mention of the true annual value, or of the certainty of the premises, or any of them, or of the other gifts or grants by us or any of our predecessors to the aforesaid bailiff and jurats of Guernsey, made before this time, is not mentioned in these present letters, or any statute, act, ordinance, proviso, proclamation or restriction to the contrary thereof, made, published, ordained, or provided, or any other thing, cause, or matter whatsoever to the contrary notwithstanding.

In testimony whereof, we have caused these our letters to be made patent. Witness myself, at Westminster, the eleventh day of February, in the twentieth year of our reign.

By writ of privy seal.

Pigott

Conclusion

With the Charles II charter of 1668, the sequence of charters ends. James II's reign, characterised in the remainder of his dominions by repeated challenges to and rewritings of the charters of towns and other corporations, saw no reconfirmation of the privileges of the past, and so the picture remained unchanged until the Revolution of 1688/9. Then, an Order in Council ended the 'neutrality' of the islands in time of war,[118] but, otherwise, the confirmation of charters included in the Bill of Rights provided some confidence that the rights of the islanders had achieved some permanence. Future struggles were played out in terms of arguments over the meaning and validity of past charters, not new versions of the old.

The documents presented here, a sequence of nineteen charters issued from 1341 to 1668, grant and confirm rights and privileges centring on the islanders' customs and laws, and various commercial and fiscal dispensations. More than any other documents they define the crucial relationship between Guernsey and the crown, and set out the basis on which the island's people conducted their lives. In many ways, therefore, they are the central documents in the history of Guernsey from the fourteenth century to the seventeenth, and indeed beyond. Yet precisely what they tell us about the experience of Guernsey and its communities during that period is neither clear nor uncontroversial.

At first sight, indeed, they may seem hugely unrewarding documents: densely written, full of legal formulae and references to obscure tolls and duties – and inherently repetitious as one monarch confirmed the grants of her or his predecessors. Perhaps unsurprisingly therefore this is the first attempt at a detailed account of the full sequence of documents, and what discussion of them there has been in the past has been has somewhat perfunctory. Many interpretations have been cavalier to say the least. There is still a tendency

---

[118] Marr, *Guernsey*, pp. 91-2.

amongst many British historians to see the island's rights as being the over-indulgent whim of some past regime, eccentrically allowed to live on, largely through some oversight. The documents, at first sight, might support this view, in the sense that they are grants from the crown.

On the other hand, much closer to the truth is the position advanced by John le Patourel in his talk to the Guernsey Society in 1944.[119] He was at pains to stress that the charters simply recognised customs and rights which belonged to the people of Guernsey. He was particularly interested in a body of custom which long predated the first of the grants set out here.

We have, then, two diametrically opposed positions – one seeing the charters as the whim of the crown, the other as simply recognitions, in the face of likely crown hostility, of inherent island privileges. It is, perhaps, in the light of the foregoing discussion, more realistic to see in the charters a more complex and more interesting phenomenon, a representation of the interplay of forces which, in the aftermath of 1204, came to make Guernsey different.

---

[119] John le Patourel, 'The Charters and Privileges, Laws and Customs of the Island of Guernsey', *Guernsey Society Bulletin*, 2:1 (1946), 3-8.